AENEAS, SICILY, AND ROME

PRINCETON MONOGRAPHS
IN ART AND ARCHAEOLOGY
XL
DEPARTMENT OF ART AND ARCHAEOLOGY
PRINCETON UNIVERSITY

AENEAS, SICILY, AND ROME

BY G. KARL GALINSKY

PRINCETON UNIVERSITY PRESS

PRINCETON, NEW JERSEY

1969

Second Printing, 1971

Printed in the United States of America
by Princeton University Press, Princeton, New Jersey

This book has been composed in Linotype Times Roman

Illustrations printed by the Meriden Gravure Company
Meriden, Connecticut

To Ann and Arthur Hanson

PREFACE

THIS BOOK is a series of studies about the Trojan legend of Rome and its background. The Roman belief in Trojan descent, which found its best-known expression in Vergil's *Aeneid*, was so Roman a phenomenon that it would be difficult to find a good modern analogy. The example of the Mayflower society is sometimes cited as a parallel, but her voyage all too quickly ended in the social pages of the newspapers and now even is on the verge of disappearing from there. The ramifications of Rome's Trojan legend were infinitely vaster and more varied. This creed had many manifestations—literary, artistic, political, historiographical, and religious—which are closely interrelated, and any study of the subject must take into account this total framework of aspects. To do equal justice to all would require a monumental study. In this book the emphasis is on the archaeological and art historical aspect, partly because it has often been neglected, at times with unfortunate results,[1] and partly because recent archaeological discoveries and finds of relevant artifacts have advanced our knowledge of the subject considerably, even though some of the excavations discussed here are only at the beginning.

To this general emphasis Chapter IV perhaps is an exception. Its topic, the adoption of the legend by Rome, requires a somewhat more detailed discussion of the historical and literary sources and the political and religious factors. This discussion also puts into their proper perspective the artistic monuments described in other chapters, notably Chapters I, V, and the Appendix.

The other chapters of the book have different emphases.

---

[1] E.g., the Etruscan statuettes of Aeneas and Anchises from the fifth century were discovered at the very time Jean Perret, with more than 600 pages of *Quellenkritik*, tried to prove that the Trojan legend of Rome originated with Pyrrhus.

The reader of the *Aeneid* often is led to believe that Vergil merely gave the most splendid expression to a virtually crystallized tradition, especially as regards the portrayal of Aeneas. As a result, both the variety of the earlier Aeneas legend and Vergil's creative achievement are easily underestimated. Chapter I, therefore, is an attempt to correlate the literary testimonia with the artistic representations of Aeneas. Chapter II is a description of the archaeological and conceptual background of the Trojan legend in Sicily, which was to become especially important in Roman times, and Chapter III is a discussion of the tradition of Aeneas in Etruria. An earlier version of Chapter V appeared under the same title in *AJA* 70 (1966). In many respects, this article was a trial balloon. The chapter has been thoroughly revised to suit the present volume and numerous improvements and changes have been made in both text and documentation. I am indebted to many friends and colleagues for their constructive criticisms on it.

The choice of the topic has led by necessity to a selection and limitation of the material presented in each chapter. To some readers the perspective may be unfamiliar. My Sicilian friends expected a fuller discussion of Sicilian archaeology and prehistory, and another reader urged me to write a complete discussion of the Lavinian cults. Several studies, which relate to the topic but would swell this volume unduly, meanwhile have appeared or been accepted as separate publications by scholarly journals. The book has not been written specifically for the needs of the undergraduate or classical scholar, but rather for the use of anyone who is interested in Roman civilization, and for the readers of Vergil in particular.

The foundation for this study was laid in a seminar on Sicilian archaeology conducted by Professor Erik Sjöqvist at Princeton University in the spring of 1964. He was so kind as to recommend to me further inquiry into this topic. Since then he has patiently supervised and encouraged the various transmutations and development of this study. To his synoptic approach to all things classical this book owes much. Thanks are also due to Professors George E. Duckworth and John Arthur Hanson of Princeton University for reading and criticizing earlier drafts of the manuscript. I am also grateful to Professor Agnes K. Michels for her constructive criticisms on the first part of Chapter IV, and to Professor David R. Coffin for kindly advising me on Ligorio and his circle. Besides Professor Sjöqvist and one other reader, who wishes to remain anonymous, Professor Andrew Alföldi was kind enough to read the entire manuscript. I have benefited greatly from his criticisms and, as is evident, from his many contributions especially to the study of early Rome. All this does not imply the readers' approval of the views expressed in these chapters whose topics do not easily breed unanimity of opinion.

It is a most pleasant task to thank the Italian and American scholars who greatly helped me during my brief but enjoyable stay in Rome and Sicily in the summer of 1967. I am especially grateful to Professor Vincenzo Tusa, Soprintendente alle Antichità in Palermo, for giving me generously of his time for discussions, and for making unpublished material available to me. Further thanks are due to Drs. P. Sommella and C. Giuliani for patiently answering my queries at Lavinium. I also acknowledge with gratitude the hospitality of the American Academy in Rome in the summer of 1967 and the fall of 1968, when this book went into production.

The number of museums and persons that helped me in securing the illustrations is large, and their aid is acknowledged here. Several pictures were taken especially for this book, and I should like to thank in particular J. Balty, A. Blyth, R. A. G. Carson, M. Chuzeville, P. Devambez, A. Economides, K. Einaudi, L. Elam, N. Elswing, K. Erim, J. Fitz, U. Gehrig, H. Giroux, H. Groppengiesser, L. Lonborg, E. Nash, A. Parker, R. Noll, G. Ristow, H. S. Roberts, †K. F. C. Rose, M. R. Scherer, E. Simon, M. Torelli, J. M.

Trafford, and V. Tusa. The assistance of Dr. Hellmut Sichter-
mann of the German Archaeological Institute in Rome has
been invaluable. The Ashmolean Museum in Oxford provided
me with many of the coin photographs and casts through the
kind efforts of my former student Curtis L. Clay, III, and also
Drs. Colin Kraay and C. V. H. Sutherland.

Thanks are also due to the Research Institute of the University of Texas for its very generous support of my work, and
to the National Endowment for the Humanities for awarding
me a summer fellowship in 1967. I also wish to thank the Fine
Arts Editor of Princeton University Press, Harriet Anderson,
for her patient help and advice.

The unfailing support and patience of my wife have been a
constant source of encouragement and cheer. My debt to Ann
and Art Hanson for years of *xenia* can be adequately stated
only on another page of this book.

Austin, September 1968

CONTENTS

LIST OF ILLUSTRATIONS

ABBREVIATIONS

THE abbreviations used for the periodicals are mostly those employed by J. Marouzeau, *L'Année Philologique*. The full titles of the books that are cited in abbreviated form are found in the Selected Bibliography.

AA: Archäologischer Anzeiger
ABSA: Annals of the British School at Athens
AC: L'Antiquité Classique
AJA: American Journal of Archaeology
AJP: American Journal of Philology
ArchClass: Archeologia Classica
ARW: Archiv für Religionswissenschaft
BA: Bollettino d'Arte
BCAR: Bullettino della Commissione Archeologica Comunale di Roma
BCH: Bulletin de Correspondance Héllénique
BJ: Bonner Jahrbücher
BMC Coins: British Museum Catalogue of Coins
BMIR: Bullettino del Museo dell'Impero Romano
BVAB: Bulletin van de Vereeniging tot Bevordering der Kennis van de Antike Beschaving
CAH: Cambridge Ancient History
CIL: Corpus Inscriptionum Latinarum
CJ: Classical Journal
CP: Classical Philology
CQ: Classical Quarterly
CR: Classical Review
CW: Classical World
Dessau: H. Dessau, *Inscriptiones Latinae Selectae*
EFH: Entretiens de la Fondation Hardt
FGH: F. Jacoby, *Die Fragmente der griechischen Historiker*
HZ: Historische Zeitschrift
IG: Inscriptiones Graecae

JDAI: Jahrbuch des Deutschen Archäologischen Instituts
JHS: Journal of Hellenic Studies
JOAI: Jahreshefte des Oesterreichischen Archäologischen Instituts
JPh: Journal of Philology
JRS: Journal of Roman Studies
JWI: Journal of the Warburg and Courtauld Institute, London
LEC: Les Etudes Classiques
MAAR: Memoirs of the American Academy in Rome
MAL: Monumenti Antichi, R. Accademia Nazionale dei Lincei
MDAI(A): Mitteilungen des Deutschen Archäologischen Instituts, Athenische Abteilung
MDAI(R): Mitteilungen des Deutschen Archäologischen Instituts, Römische Abteilung
MdI: Mitteilungen des Deutschen Archäologischen Instituts, Berlin
MEFR: Mélanges d'Archéologie et d'Histoire de l'Ecole Française de Rome
MH: Museum Helveticum
MMAI: Monuments et Mémoires publiés par l'Académie des Inscriptions et Belles Lettres, Fondation Piot
Mn: Mnemosyne
MNIR: Mededelingen van het Nederlandsch historisch Institut te Rome
NC: Numismatic Chronicle
NJA: Neue Jahrbücher für das klassische Altertum
NSA: Notizie degli Scavi di Antichità

ABBREVIATIONS

NZ: Numismatische Zeitschrift

PBA: Proceedings of the British Academy

PBSR: Papers of the British School at Rome

PP: La Parola del Passato

RA: Revue Archéologique

RAAN: Rendiconti dell'Accademia di Archeologia, Lettere e Belle Arti di Napoli

RAL: Rendiconti della Classe di Scienze morali, storiche e filologiche dell'Accademia dei Lincei

RE: Pauly-Wissowa, Real-Encyclopädie der classischen Altertumswissenschaft

REA: Revue des Etudes Anciennes

RhM: Rheinisches Museum für Philologie

RHR: Revue de l'Histoire des Religions

RPAA: Rendiconti della Pontificia Accademia di Archeologia

RPh: Revue Philologique

RSI: Rivista Storica Italiana

SBAW: Sitzungsberichte der Bayerischen Akademie der Wissenschaften, Philos.-Hist. Klasse, München

SE: Studi Etruschi

SHAW: Sitzungsberichte der Heidelberger Akademie der Wissenschaften, Philos.-Hist. Klasse

SIFC: Studi Italiani di Filologia Classica

SIG: Sylloge Inscriptionum Graecarum

SMSR: Studi e Materiali di Storia delle Religioni

TAPA: Transactions of the American Philological Association

ZfN: Zeitschrift für Numismatik

AENEAS, SICILY,
AND ROME

. . . nos, qui sequimur probabilia, neque ultra id, quod veri simile occurrerit, progredi possumus, et refellere sine pertinacia et refelli sine iracundia parati sumus.

Cic., *Tusc.* 2.2.5.

CHAPTER I

PIUS AENEAS

THE LEGEND of Aeneas is not synonymous with the legend of Trojan migrations. This important distinction has to be observed especially in a study of the Trojan legend in Sicily where, as we shall see, the legend of a Trojan landing had been in existence long before it was fused with the Aeneas legend. But in later times, especially after the *Aeneid* had been written, the Trojan legend and the legend of Aeneas became virtually indistinguishable. Aeneas had, of course, always been the most prominent of the Trojan refugees, and it was the characteristic method of the ancient mythographers, poets, and even historians to have a single human prototype stand for the often varied and complex experience of a larger group of people.[1] Certainly by the time of Augustus, the experience and fate of Aeneas were identified with those of the Trojans in general.

It seems inevitable that this fact should have obscured differences and distinctions which were considered quite important by the earlier tradition and which are indispensable for arriving at a balanced picture of the subject which we are about to consider. What applies to the distinction, or lack of it, between Aeneas and the Trojans, to an even greater degree holds good for the portrayal of Aeneas himself. After the publication of the *Aeneid*, the hero, for times to come, was

[1] T. Dohrn, "Des Romulus' Gründung Roms," *MDAI(R)* 71 (1964) 18, sums this up well in his conclusion: "One of the essential categories of ancient thinking is to make all events take on human form. Developments of long duration are telescoped as it were into one human lifetime and transferred to one single human being." The lack of distinction between the Aeneas legend and the Trojan legend is prevailing in virtually all scholarly studies pertaining to this subject, with the exception of G. Columba, *Atti Accademia di Palermo* n.s. 17 (1932) 232-233, and E. Manni, *Sicilia pagana* (Palermo 1963) 83.

cast as the pious, dutiful son of Anchises and Venus. Although some later authors disagreed sharply with this characterization of the hero, his *pietas* was that quality for which he was known best and which came to overshadow all his other traits. This is clearly reflected in St. Augustine's reference to the Trojan in the introduction to his *De civitate Dei* (1.3): *Aeneas ipse, pius totiens appellatus.* Vergil, of course, had introduced his hero programmatically as *insignem pietate virum (Aeneid* 1.10), and in over twenty places in the *Aeneid* the Trojan is characterized by this epithet *pius.* Aside from Vergil, however, the list of references to Aeneas' *pietas* is not overly long.[2] While acknowledging the popularity of this "image" of the hero, many writers appear to have been less than enthusiastic about joining in the praises of this characterization, and some even were sarcastic. St. Augustine's remark is deprecating and it reflects an attitude that was not restricted to Christian writers.[3] But while the *literati* might have stood aside and were reluctant to eulogize *pius* Aeneas, there is every indication that the people eagerly accepted this portrayal of the Trojan ancestor. The evidence comes from the artistic monuments of the first and second centuries A.D., which testify to the unprecedented popularity of the Aeneas *pius* theme during that period.[4] At the same time, this evidence clearly suggests that the emperors were most eager to propagate this notion. As is so often the case, this propagandistic intent is most conspicuous on the coin issues.

A good example is a sestertius issued during the reign of

[2] Pease, *Liber Quartus* 333-334, has compiled most of the relevant passages.

[3] See, e.g., Porph., *ad Hor., C.S.* 41; Seneca, *Ben.* 6.36.1; *quis pium dicit Aenean, si patriam capi voluerit ut captivitati patrem eripiat?* Cf. Tertullian, *Ad Nat.* 2.9: *pius Aeneas ob unicum puerum et decrepitum senem Priamo et Astyanacte destitutis.* For details see H. Georgii, *Die antike Äneiskritik* (Stuttgart 1891) esp. 564-565, and V. Ussani, *SIFC* n.s. 22 (1947) 108-123.

[4] A very comprehensive listing of these artifacts is given by Giglioli, *BMIR* 12 (1941) 3-16, and Schauenburg, *Gymnasium* 67 (1960) 184-185 with notes 81 to 88. Sadurska, *Les tables iliaques* 99-100, has some additions.

4

Antoninus Pius (Fig. 1).[5] Its reverse shows Aeneas carrying
Anchises who, *capite velato*, holds the *cista sacra* with the
Penates in his lap. With his right hand, Aeneas leads the little
Ascanius, and the Trojan provenance of the group is emphasized by Ascanius' Phrygian cap. The contrast of this representation with the earliest appearance of this motif on a Roman
coin is striking. That was the famous denarius issued by Julius
Caesar in 48 B.C. (Fig. 2a).[6] Although Aeneas wears no
armor on that coin, he is portrayed in a much more vigorous
and warlike manner than on the Antonine sestertius. The
representation of Aeneas as a nude warrior follows the Greek
tradition and is a further instance of Caesar's preference for
Greek models—a preference that is known especially from the
architecture commissioned by him.[7] Brimming with strength
and striding ahead, Aeneas does not lead his son but instead
carries the Palladium, which is a more martial emblem of
Troy's survival than the sacred chest with the peaceful household gods. Like all the Julii, Caesar claimed to have descended
from Aeneas and Venus, and a reference to this Trojan descent
is likely to have been the primary purpose of the coin, especially since the head of Venus appears on the obverse (Fig.
2b). It is noteworthy, however, that Caesar, who was a man
of considerable military ambition and had just defeated Pom-
pey at Pharsalus, chose to give the Trojan as bellicose an
appearance as this particular motif permitted. Nor is it a
coincidence that the Emperor Trajan, whose aggressive military policy led to the greatest expansion the Roman empire

[5] *BMC Coins Emp.* 4.207 no. 1292, pl. 30.5.

[6] *BMC Coins Rep.* 2.469 nos. 31-35, pl. 110.20; Sydenham no. 1012. In
42 B.C. Octavian issued an aureus with Aeneas and Anchises to announce
his dynastic claims: *BMC Coins Rep.* 1.579 nos. 4257 and 4258, pls. 57.8-9;
Sydenham nos. 1104, 1104a (our Fig. 40b); cf. T. S. Duncan, "The Aeneas
Legend on Coins," *CJ* 44 (1948-1949) 15.

[7] See, e.g., E. Sjöqvist, "Kaisareion. A Study in Architectural Iconography," *Opusc. Rom.* 1 (1954) 86-108. On the nudity of the body see V.
Poulsen's discussion of a statue of Caesar in the Ny Carlsberg Glyptotek
(no. 576) in *BVAB* 29 (1954) 48-49.

had ever known, decided to reissue this Caesarean denarius (Fig. 3).[8]

Whereas Aeneas' *pietas* was not emphasized on the Caesarean coin, the sestertius of Antoninus leaves little doubt that this was one of the issuer's intentions. A portrait of the emperor with the legend PIUS is on the obverse and complements the representation of Aeneas. For Antoninus such a coin was particularly appropriate. The senate had honored him with the surname Pius primarily because of his *clementia*, and "because he was conspicuous for the reverence he paid to the divine."[9] By the time of the second century A.D., the Trojan genealogy had ceased being the prerogative of the imperial family and had become the common property of the entire Roman people. Antoninus therefore placed the emphasis on his spiritual inheritance from Aeneas, and Aeneas was presented as the legendary model of the emperor. Aeneas' *pietas*, however, is distinctly secondary to that of the *pius* emperor for it serves only as a means to ennoble the latter. Even so it follows that the notion of Aeneas' *pietas* was greatly emphasized and promulgated among the people.

The connection between the *pietas* of Aeneas and the *pietas* of the emperor is made equally explicit on a sestertius of Galba (Fig. 4).[10] A portrait of the emperor, with a laurel crown and an aegis, is shown on the obverse. On the reverse is the repre-

[8] *BMC Coins Emp.* 3.141 no. 31, pl. 23.4.

[9] Paus. 8.43.5; cf. Dio Cass. *Epit.* 70.2. A comprehensive discussion of the literary and numismatic evidence relating to the surname of the emperor has been published by C. H. Dodd, *NC* 4th ser. 11 (1911) 5-41. Dodd demonstrates convincingly that Antoninus was not given this cognomen by virtue of his filial piety because he allegedly assisted his father-in-law Annius Verus in the Senate. This explanation was already discounted by the author of *Hist. Aug., Ant.* 2.3-7, and also applies to the interpretation of the Aeneas-Anchises "*pietas*" groups: *quod quidem non satis magnae pietatis est argumentum, cum impius sit magis qui ista non faciat quam pius qui debitum reddat.*

[10] *BMC Coins Emp.* l.ccxvii and 358; H. Cohen, *Description historique des monnaies frappées sous l'empire romain* 1 (Paris 1880) 329 no. 160. The coin is discussed in detail by J. Liegle, *ZfN* 42 (1932-1935) 60-66.

6

sentation of a female figure. Her head is veiled, and she lifts her right hand in the direction of an altar. The relief on the altar represents the group of Aeneas, Anchises, and Ascanius. The legend again indicates that it is not primarily the *pietas* of Aeneas that is extolled here; the program of the coin is the PIETAS AUGUSTI. Galba's *pietas* was set in relief so as to contrast with the frivolousness of his predecessor Nero. Again the representation of Aeneas was chosen as a means to an end, although in this instance it does not even serve as the mythological model of the emperor's *pietas*. Rather, it is used as an allusion to the cult of Divus Augustus and thus expresses Galba's desire to legitimize his reign.

Aside from the coins, such menial everyday utensils as lamps perhaps testify best to the widespread popularization of the concept of Aeneas' *pietas*. Like the coins, the lamps with the motif of Aeneas' escape from Troy were found in many parts of the Roman empire. Of particular interest is a specimen which today is in the Kestner Museum in Hanover (Fig. 5). It was found in Rome, although the landscape on it suggests that it was to be exported to Africa. The inscription on it reads as follows: AENEAS ANCHISES ASCANIUS REX PIE (*CIL* 15. 6236). It is not merely Aeneas who is singled out for his *pietas*, nor does any particular action seem to be associated with this concept. Rather, this characteristic is applied to all known Trojan ancestors of the Romans, and Trojan descent *per se* is equated with *pietas*. The appellative *rex* suggests that this concept was propagated not entirely independently of the ruling house. The emperors themselves of course avoided this title,[11] but in the *Aeneid* we find Aeneas, who is identified

[11] The title, however, was not quite as odious as is often assumed. As early as 68 B.C. Julius Caesar repeatedly emphasized this term in the funeral oration on his aunt Julia (Suet., *Iul.* 6.1). Augustus, even if only in jest, could write about Horace: *veniet ergo ab ista parasitica mensa ad hanc regiam* (Suet., *Vita Horati*, p. 45.11 Reiff.). In *Pont.* 1.8.21 Ovid addresses Augustus as *rex*. Cf. the remarks by F. Bömer, *P. Ovidius Naso. Die Fasten* 2, p. 391. (I am grateful to the Kestner Museum for providing the picture of the lamp and the pertinent information.)

with Augustus throughout the epic, being introduced at the African court of Dido as such a *pius rex* *(Aeneid* 1.544-545):

> rex erat Aeneas nobis, quo iustior alter
> nec pietate fuit.

It is very likely that the representation and inscription on this small artifact were ultimately inspired by the *Aeneid*.

The interest the emperor's family took in displaying Aeneas as their ancestor is well known. Except for certain minor variations, the representations of the Aeneas group on lamps and coins, in statuary, relief sculpture, and in painting resemble each other to a very considerable extent. In trying to account for this similarity, the Italian scholar Camaggio made the observation, which has generally been accepted since, that most of these representations were inspired by a common prototype.[12] This was a group of the Trojans which was set up in the Forum of Augustus in Rome. From Ovid's reference to it in the *Fasti* (5.563-564) it is apparent that its purpose was to extol the lineage of the Julian family:

> hinc videt Aenean oneratum pondere sacro
> et tot Iuliae nobilitatis avos.

This original has not been preserved, but copies of it were erected in cities throughout Italy and the Empire. A terracotta replica of the statuary group in the Pompeian forum gives us a good idea of the composition of the original (Fig. 6).[13] The bearded Aeneas is shown bearing Anchises and the *cista* on his left shoulder and leading Ascanius with his right hand. Although Aeneas wears armor, no effort is made to give him a warlike appearance. What is emphasized is the swiftness and

---

[12] M. Camaggio, *Atti Acc. Pontaniana* 58 (1928) 125-147.

[13] Naples, Museo Nazionale, nos. 110338, 110342, 20597. See A. Levi, *Le terrecotte figurate del Musco Nazionale di Napoli* (Naples 1926) 193 no. 842, fig. 143; H. von Rohden, *Die Terrakotten von Pompeji* (Berlin 1880) 49, pl. 37.1 and fig. 26; S. Aurigemma in Spinazzola, *Pompei* 152 and fig. 187.

care with which he engages in his task. He strides forth, his fluttering mantle shielding Ascanius, thus making the union between Ascanius and Aeneas as close as that between Aeneas and Anchises. Aeneas' face reveals the strain of the flight; he seems to be almost out of breath, yet he diligently holds his father whose passive and unmoved mien contrasts with Aeneas' vivid features and energetic stride.

This group reappears, for instance, in a relief of the Altar of the Gens Augusta in Carthage (Fig. 7).[14] As the denarius of Trajan signaled the revival of Caesarean themes, so the subject matter of the altar reliefs and its dedication to the Gens Augusta suggest an Augustan revival at the time of Hadrian. As on the coin of Galba, the Aeneas legend again is seized upon as a particularly Augustan theme. Aside from alluding to the Trojan legend, the reliefs represent Roma and 'Apollo, as well as a sacrifice to the *Genius Augusti*. Although the cult of the Genius of the emperor was popular especially in Italy and Rome, it was also known in some of the provinces. It has rightly been observed that any participation in this cult was an acknowledgment, on the part of the people, of a political reality rather than an expression of a religious creed.[15] There can be little doubt, however, that the allusion to the ancestor Aeneas, Venus' son, serves to underscore the divinity of the emperor much more effectively than did the ancient Roman concept of the *genius* of the *pater familias*. This is why Aeneas cannot be missing from the Augustan Altar of Peace and other Augustan-inspired altars in Italy and the provinces. Aeneas is represented not primarily because of his *pietas*, but

[14] The most detailed discussion of the altar is L. Poinssot, *Notes et Documents* 10 (Paris 1929) 5-38, pls. 1-16, with the earlier bibliography. Important discussions since are J. Sieveking, *Gnomon* 7 (1931) 20-21; B. M. Maj, *RPAA* 12 (1935) 157-168; and Ryberg, *Rites* 89-90, whose conclusions about the date I have accepted. Similarly, the composite Aphrodite from Aphrodisias (Fig. 160) most probably dates from the Hadrianic period and recalls the Venus on the Ara Pacis Augustae; see Chapter V.

[15] So Latte, *RRG* 308. For the Roman concept of the Genius Augusti and its worship in Italy and the provinces see Taylor, *Divinity of the Roman Emperor*, passim.

his presence serves to underline the emperor's special association with the gods.

Moreover, even when Aeneas' *pietas* is singled out in official
imperial sculpture it exalts, above all, the *pietas* of the emperor himself. In this respect the Ara Pacis Augustae is the
forerunner of the Antonine coin. In one of the relief slabs of
this altar Aeneas is shown performing a sacrifice (Fig. 8).
The relief decorations of that altar, which will be discussed in
more detail in Chapter V, center around the sacrifice of
Augustus. The emperor's sacrifice to Pax is the theme which
unites the reliefs, and the sacrifice made by Aeneas after his
arrival in Italy is purposely related to it. The sacrifice brought
by Aeneas *pro reditu suo* is the loftiest precedent for Augustus'
sacrifice. We will see shortly that there is little certainty that
the motif of Aeneas' carrying Anchises out of Troy has to be
taken inherently for an expression of the hero's *pietas*. In the
relief of the Augustan altar, however, he is indisputably represented as *pius*: with veiled head, *capite velato*, he participates
in a sacred action. As on the Antonine sestertius, Aeneas is
not meant to be the center of our attention. His *pietas* is
subordinated to that of the emperor, which it helps to underscore.

These select but representative examples clearly suggest that
the theme of *pius* Aeneas in art owed much of its popularity
to the deliberate encouragement of the imperial house. The
same holds true for the *pius Aeneas* theme in literature, and
this was fully recognized by the ancients.[16]

The relatively late emphasis on the *pietas* of Aeneas has
led to the neglect and misinterpretation of the earlier literary
and artistic evidence about the Trojan, and it has even become
the basis of some quite influential theories. L. R. Farnell, for
instance, in his important study of the Greek cults, based his
hypothesis that the wanderings of Aeneas were the legendary

---

[16] See the remarks of Claudius Donatus, p. 51, below.

record of the diffusion of the cult of Aphrodite Aineias, on the assumption that the Aineadae were the priests of this cult in the Troad. To support this assumption, Farnell speaks of the "peculiar, sacred, and mysterious character of Aeneas in Homer," and then goes on to say that Aeneas in the *Iliad* appears as the "emanation of a divinity."[17] More recently, the German scholar Franz Bömer, who postulates an Etruscan origin for the Roman Aeneas legend, has advanced the argument that the Romans in the early fifth century, long before Vergil and Augustus, saw in Aeneas a reflection of their own *pietas*. They therefore decided to adopt him as their ancestor over Odysseus, because the latter lacked the aura of sacredness and had a reputation for calculating shrewdness instead.[18]

The character of Aeneas, however, was far more contradictory. In that part of the Greek literary tradition, which can safely be said to be exclusive of Roman influences or reflections, Aeneas' *pietas* is a trait that is virtually nonexistent. It is other qualities of the hero that are given conspicuous prominence.

The hero's valor in battle is one of these. In the *Iliad* no aura of religious mystery surrounds Aeneas. Rather, he is consistently portrayed as one of the bravest and most spirited Trojan warriors. He is second in this respect only to Hector, with whom he is often mentioned in the same breath (*Iliad* 5.467-468; 6.75; 11.57-58; 16.536; 17.513, 534, 754). After Aeneas has distinguished himself in battle against Diomedes (*Iliad* 5.239-310), Homer characterizes Aeneas and Hector through the words of Helenus, "best by far of the seers" (*Iliad* 6.77-79):

[17] *The Cults of the Greek States* 2 (Oxford 1896) 638-640; cf. A. Sainte-Beuve, *Etude sur Virgile* (Paris 1891) 113: "Une sorte de prestige et de mystère religieux l' [i.e. Aeneas] environne." For the cult of Aphrodite Aineias see Chapter II, pp. 65-70.

[18] *Rom und Troia* 39-40, 47-49; cf. Momigliano, *JRS* 35 (1945) 104: "It is remarkable that precisely Aeneas, φίλος ἀθανάτοισι θεοῖσιν, was chosen to be patron of pious Rome."

Aeneas and Hector, for both Trojans and Lycians
the toil of battle is always yours. On every occasion,
whether for council or war, you are the best and
the bravest.

Homer of course faced a certain dilemma in portraying
Aeneas. He knew that Aeneas was one of the few Trojans who
would escape. As a result, the poet had to protect his hero
from becoming so involved in battle that the outcome would
be fatal for him. The role which therefore accrued to Aeneas
is that of the second most valiant Trojan warrior after Hector,
who also is the most prominent of the dead in the epic. There
is a recurrent emphasis on Aeneas' prowess in battle. "Greatly
eager for battle" ($\mu\acute{\epsilon}\gamma\alpha$ $\pi\tau o\lambda\acute{\epsilon}\mu o\iota o$ $\mu\epsilon\mu\eta\lambda\acute{\omega}\varsigma$), he sets out against
Idomeneus after his anger has been stirred (13.468-469; cf.
16.616). His physical attributes, such as his speed, make him
a formidable opponent (13.482; cf. 5.571), and Idomeneus,
who a moment earlier was not perturbed by fear, now is suddenly overcome with fright, and openly admits it to his men
(13.481-484):

Help me, my friends! Support me! I stand alone
and Aeneas rushes upon me. I dread his assault
for he is mighty in battle and in the slaying of warriors.
He is in the full flower of his youth, and the strongest of all.

Later in the epic, Aeneas, one of the *aristoi* of the Trojans,
rescues Hector (14.424-432) and fights in the front line of
the Trojans who rout the Greeks in Book 15 (332). Recog-
nizing the stature of Aeneas, Hector then calls on him to
capture Achilles' horses (17.485-490), and despite their lack
of success, their Greek enemies compliment the two Trojan
heroes on being "the best of the Trojans" ($T\rho\acute{\omega}\omega\nu$ $\check{\alpha}\rho\iota\sigma\tau o\iota$
17.513). And although Aeneas and Hector at first have to
retreat, the book ends on the note of their routing the opposition (17.755-761):

And, as a cloud of starlings or daws, with shrieking and
  clamor
fly for their lives, when they see the hawk come pouncing
  upon them,
(deadly foe of each smaller bird, who dreads and avoids
  him),
so fled the sons of Achaea before Aeneas and Hector.
Shrieking they fled, in clamorous rout; their prowess
  forgotten.
In and around the trench were heaped up the spoils and
  the armor,
costly and rich, of the fleeing Greeks; yet the battle
  went on.

The portrayal of Aeneas as a fighting man is rounded out
in Book 20. Achilles has returned to battle, Hector is doomed
and with him, the house of Priam. This is the moment the poet
has chosen "to give prominence to the hero, who is reserved
for the future, if not by the splendor of an illustrious victory—
for that would be contrary to all likelihood—at least by the
glory of a noble attempt."[19]

Achilles' encounter with Aeneas is designed to foreshadow
and, at the same time, to contrast with Achilles' encounter
with Hector. The close connection with the two Trojan heroes,
which has been emphasized throughout the epic, now receives
its final meaning and interpretation.[20] Like Hector later (22.
98-130), Aeneas initially does not want to battle Achilles
(οὐκ ἐθέλοντα 20.87) but he eventually responds to Achilles'

---

[19] J. A. Hild, "La légende d'Enée avant Virgile," *RHR* 6 (1882) 48:
". . . pour recommander le héros réservé à l'avenir si non par l'éclat d'une
illustre victoire (la vraisemblance ne le permettrait pas) du moins par la
gloire d'une généreuse tentative."

[20] The opinion that the passage in Book 20 is a later addition by the
court poet of the Aeneadae has been voiced most recently by E. Heitsch,
Aphroditehymnos, Aeneas und Homer (Göttingen 1965). *Contra*, e.g., H.
Erbse, *RhM* 110 (1967) 1-25. The skillful manner in which this episode is
integrated into the epic at least shows that this "interpolation" is no ill-
fitting appendage.

alleged boasts (ἀπειλαί 20.83), which have not been mentioned up to this point. The kind of taunt involved here is
rather general (cf. 13.219-220; 8.229-234). A tenuous pretext
is thus established to goad an unwilling hero into the fight.
Driven by the god, Aeneas goes into battle and consequently,
he also has to be rescued through divine interference. Yet in
bravery he is Achilles' equal: both men are singled out as
being "by far the best men" (ἔξοχ᾽ ἄριστοι 20.158). From the
outset, however, there can be no doubt as to who will prevail:
the lion metaphor, which heralded Aeneas' first appearance in
a battle scene in the epic (5.299), now recurs in a more
elaborate form and is applied to Achilles (20.164-173).[21]
Concerned about the turn of events, Poseidon then issues the
famous prophecy (20.306-308) that Aeneas will rule over the
Trojans, and thereupon rescues the hero. Fittingly enough,
the portrayal of Aeneas in the *Iliad* concludes with Poseidon's
prediction that after the death of Achilles, Aeneas, as a warrior, will be the inferior of no other hero, neither Greek nor
Trojan (20.337-339):

> But when Achilles himself shall be slain, and meet his fate,
> then be bold, and advance once more to the front of the
>   battle:
> for no other Greek shall in fight overcome and despoil you.

This characterization of Aeneas as a valiant warrior left its
mark on Greek art. At Olympia a statuary group of Aeneas
fighting against Diomedes could still be seen at the time of
Pausanias (5.22.2). It was set up there as a votive gift together
with a group representing the combat of Achilles and Memnon.
Aeneas' clash with Diomedes is a subject which also is found
on several vases. A fine example is a cup by the Kleophrades
Painter (Fig. 9), which was found at Kameiros and now is in

---

[21] For this intentional repetition of similes compare *Iliad* 15.263-270,
where Homer clearly interprets the limitations of Hector by re-using the
entire metaphor applied to Paris in 6.506-514. See W. S. Anderson, *TAPA*
88 (1957) 28 n. 16.

London.[22] Of all the ancient poets, Homer alone treated the combat between Aeneas and Diomedes, and the painting agrees in all major details with the description in the fifth Book of the *Iliad*. The only addition to the Homeric account is the goddess Athena, who protects Diomedes just as Aphrodite protects Aeneas. Perhaps, as has been suggested,[23] this addition can be accounted for by the necessity of an exact balance in the composition. But there are exceptions to this rule in Greek vase painting, and the addition of this goddess serves to make even more explicit what is already shown in the *Iliad*: Aeneas is in no way particularly privileged by the interference of a goddess in his behalf. The Kleophrades Painter chose the moment which sums up the combat best. Diomedes emerges victoriously and from the left to the right, as victors generally do on Greek vases, he moves in on Aeneas. The Trojan has sunk on his knee, his spear is broken, and blood is streaming from his side. But his fighting spirit has not deserted him: with his right hand he still is struggling feebly to raise his sword.

A similar representation appears on a votive tablet from Corinth dated to about 560 B.C. (Fig. 10).[24] On the right Diomedes, who again is moving from the left to right, is shown fighting with Aeneas over the body of Pandarus; only the . . . *ros* of the latter's name has been preserved. Although only a half of this painting remains and the part with the figure of Aeneas has been lost, it is worth noting that the artistic representation differs from the poem in that the figure of Athena again is added to that of Diomedes. She already is standing in the chariot, whereas in *Iliad* 5 she does not mount it until

[22] London E 73. The fullest description is by Percy Gardner, *JPh* 7 (1877) 215-226 with pl. B. See also Johansen, *Iliad* 206 with figs. 84-85; K. Bulas, *Les illustrations antiques de l'Iliade* (Lwow 1929) 34 with fig. 19; Beazley, *ARV²* 192 no. 106.

[23] By Gardner, *JPh* 7 (1877) 223.

[24] Published by Payne, *Necrocorinthia* 135 no. 10; Johansen, *Iliad* 57-63 with figs. 9-10; Schefold, *Myth and Legend* 88-89 with fig. 37. See also *Antike Denkmäler* 1, pl. 7.15.

15

later. As Schefold has aptly observed: "The painter translates the poet's intentions into the language of visual art and thus shows how Athene is the constant support of the hero."[25] This further confirms our interpretation of the Kleophrades cup.

The combat between Diomedes and Aeneas is also found on the fragment of a black-figure vase in the Acropolis Museum in Athens (Fig. 11).[26] The composition follows the principles of the two earlier representations of the same subject matter. Aeneas appears as a mighty warrior with a towering plume. He fiercely plunges into battle and both he and Diomedes are encouraged by their patron goddesses.

Aeneas' role in the battle over the body of Patroclus in *Iliad* 17 is another episode from the epic which attracted the artists' attention. On an early Corinthian bowl a representation of this combat is coupled with the duel of Achilles and Hector (Fig. 12).[27] There is no reason for quarreling with the artist's judgment that these are two of the most important battles in the epic, which can fittingly be represented together. Here, as in Book 17 of the *Iliad*, Aeneas is not defeated but holds his ground against the two Ajaxes. Since Aeneas already is represented as one of the protagonists in one battle, it is not surprising that Sarpedon, and not Aeneas, was chosen as Hector's companion in his fight against Achilles. This solution is somewhat awkward, for Sarpedon, the mightiest of the Trojan heroes next to Hector and Aeneas, had of course fallen in Book 16. Whether these scenes really indicate the artist's lack

[25] *Myth and Legend* 89.

[26] B. Graef, *Die antiken Vasen von der Akropolis zu Athen* 1 (Berlin 1925) 78 no. 646a and b, pl. 42; Beazley and Caskey, *Attic Vase Paintings in the Museum of Fine Arts Boston* 2.19. Other representations of the same combat occur on a fragment of a large vase by the Syleus Painter (Beazley, *ARV*² 253 no. 54) and of a Chian chalice from Naucratis (*JHS* 44 [1924] pl. 6.6). Three other vases with the same motif were found in Etruria and are listed in Chapter III (Figs. 102, 104, 105).

[27] Published by E. Pottier, *MMAI* 16 (1908) 107-113 and pl. 13; Johansen, *Iliad* 70-75 with fig. 15; D. Feytmans, *Les vases grecs de la Bibliothèque Royale de Belgique* (Brussels 1948) 20-27 and pl. 4; E. Buschor, *Griechische Vasenmalerei* (Munich 1913) 58 with fig. 39.

of any deep understanding of the poem of Achilles' wrath is open to question.[28] For the artist's decision not to group the four most outstanding Greek and Trojan heroes together, but depict them in two mutually complementary combats may actually be rather meaningful. The most valiant and the second most valiant warriors of both sides are carefully paired with each other. It is more than coincidental, I believe, that Aeneas in his painting is shown holding the very position Achilles holds in his; the two heroes are meant to correspond to each other. This is not only an allusion to their combat in Book 20, which in turn anticipates the duel between Hector and Achilles in 22, but also serves to indicate that the prestige of Aeneas, the only survivor of the Trojan race, is in fact matched only by that of Achilles.

The east frieze of the Siphnian Treasury at Delphi also reflects the conception that Aeneas could not be absent from any representation which aimed to typify the *Iliad*. Around the middle of the sixth century B.C. the Siphnians, through the timely discovery of silver mines, had become *nouveaux riches* and gladly took the opportunity to demonstrate that they too shared in the heritage of Greek epic and mythology. Of the friezes in the Treasury, the reliefs on the east side may be said to be the most important ones, as they faced the Sacred Way that led to the sanctuary of Apollo. Thus they were bound to capture the attention even of the most casual onlooker. The frieze is divided into two scenes: an assembly of the gods on the left and a battle scene on the right (Fig. 13).[29]

---

[28] Among others, Bulas (note 22, above) 54, and Schefold, *Myth and Legend* 88, have expressed doubt that the painter knew the Homeric epic well enough. However, as the example of the Siphnian frieze (see next note) shows, it was not uncommon for an artist to adapt Homeric material creatively for his own purposes without being ignorant of some of the epic's details. A similar method was followed by the sculptor of the Belvedere Altar with regard to the *Aeneid*; see below, pp. 24-25. For a somewhat different argument from mine, see Johansen, *loc.cit.*

[29] I follow the interpretation of C. Picard and P. de la Coste-Messelière, *Fouilles de Delphes* 4.2 (Paris 1928) passim and esp. 102 and 108-111.

The battle proper is flanked by two teams of horses with their charioteers, while the center of the composition is held by four warriors struggling over the fallen body of another. The inscriptions make it clear that the scenes were interpreted as episodes from the *Iliad*, and the leftmost warrior was designated as Aeneas. The other Trojan fighter doubtless is Hector; as in the epic, Aeneas is second only to him. The Greek opponents appear to be Menelaos and perhaps Ajax, while the body of the fallen Trojan has been identified with that of Sarpedon.

These representations do not exactly correspond to specific Iliadic episodes. Rather, they are meant to form a kind of synthesis of the epic: a typical assembly of gods is shown, and the most typical Greek and Trojan heroes are grouped together. In the words of Charles Picard: "The combat is completely 'theoretical': the two Trojan warriors, in the order of their importance, are Hector and Aeneas, the men who defend their city most effectively throughout the entire poem; if Menelaos is the first of the Greeks, it is because the war takes place for the sake of his own quarrel; if Automedon guards the horses, it is because he, throughout the *Iliad*, is the 'perfect' charioteer."[30]

Another episode with which Aeneas was associated in vase painting is Achilles' ambush of Troilus. Of the human heroes who try to rescue Troilus, Aeneas and Hector are represented most frequently. A cup by Oltos in the Louvre (Fig. 14) is a good example.[31] Troilus has dropped on one knee, and Aeneas,

[30] *Fouilles de Delphes* 4.2.111: "Et de même, le combat est tout 'théorique': les deux guerriers troyens sont, par ordre d'importance, Hector et Enée, ceux qui défendent le plus efficacement leur ville, à travers tout le poème; si Ménélas est le premier des Achéens, c'est que la guerre se livre pour sa propre 'querelle'; si Automedon garde les chevaux, c'est qu'il est bien, dans l'*Iliade*, l'écuyer 'parfait.' " Even if the inscriptions are not contemporary with the creation of the frieze, but were added somewhat later, they reflect the prevailing interpretation the figures were given.

[31] Louvre G 18; *CVA* France fasc. 17 (Louvre fasc. 10) III 1b, pl. 4.4; Beazley, *ARV*² 63 no. 68; J. C. Hoppin, *A Handbook of Attic Red-figure Vases* 2 (Cambridge, Mass. 1919) 260 no. 41.

whose spear point protrudes beyond Troilus' head, tries to protect him against the onrushing Achilles. The frequent appearance of Aeneas in this scene doubtless stems from the desire to juxtapose him with the only Greek hero who was truly superior to him. As in the Homeric epic, Aeneas is portrayed as a mighty warrior whose loyalty to Priam's family makes him risk even his life.

An important example of the popularity of the Troilus episode in Corinthian vase painting is a fragment from a column-krater in the Louvre, which dates from the first quarter of the sixth century B.C. (Fig. 15).[32] Achilles is on the left and has snatched the body of Troilus from the altar of Apollo. A group of Trojan warriors try to come to Troilus' rescue. Hector and Aeneas are the pendant to Achilles on the far right. The two most outstanding Trojan warriors are again paired. As on the Siphnian frieze, Hector appears on the first plane, whereas Aeneas is pictured on the second, but this is the only difference between the two: on both the frieze and the vase their posture and movements are exactly parallel. Aeneas is as good a fighter as Hector, although he is, of course, not quite as important as the son of Priam. The emphasis on the brutal aspects of Achilles' character antedates his more human portrayal in the *Iliad*. The conception that Aeneas is one of the two chief protagonists of the Trojans can therefore be traced to an early time.

Further representations of the Troilus episode with Aeneas were found in Etruria. We shall see later that this fact is not without significance.[33]

The prestige which Aeneas enjoyed among the Trojans and which also reflects his importance as a warrior is illustrated by a Boeotian relief pithos in the Boston Museum of Fine Arts

[32] Louvre E 638 (bis); Payne, *Necrocorinthia* 318 no. 1196; Pottier, *MMAI* 16 (1908) 113-119 with pl. 14; M. Heidenreich, *MdI* 4 (1951) 115 no. 4. Lists of the representations of Troilus have been compiled by Miss Heidenreich 114-119, and F. Brommer, *Vasenlisten*[2] 264-269.
[33] See Chapter III.

(Fig. 19).[34] It dates from the middle of the seventh century
B.C. On the upper part of the body of the vase, four oxen are
seen walking to the right. Beneath them, a warrior wearing a
helmet and shield and carrying what appears to be a goad is
driving three oxen to the right. Turned to the right also, a
helmeted warrior, with spears in both hands and a shield at
his side, crouches in front of the oxen and is ready to pounce
on the four approaching warriors. The only interpretation
which gives all these representations a coherent unity is Achilles' theft of the cattle of Aeneas, to which reference is made
in the *Iliad* (20.89-93). Since he was unable straightway to
take the city of Priam, Achilles attacked the holdings of the
second most important Trojan, Aeneas, on Mount Ida. He
stole Aeneas' cattle, which amounts to some importance in an
agricultural society, and went on to sack the city of Lyrnessos.
Aeneas had taken refuge there but was able to escape its
destruction. This episode curiously anticipates the later hap-
penings at Troy. The crouching warrior in the relief is Achilles.
He is preparing to ambush, as he did Troilus, the four men
who are trying to retrieve the cattle. Aeneas may be one of
these warriors.

That his excellence as a warrior was indeed one of the outstanding traits of Aeneas was fully recognized by Vergil.
Although the Augustan poet created the truly *pius* Aeneas,
the Trojan's martial prowess is singled out as that quality
which is second only to his *pietas*. This is evident from Book

[34] Boston Museum of Fine Arts 528. Described by A. Fairbanks, *A
Catalogue of Greek and Etruscan Vases* 1 (Cambridge, Mass. 1928) 180-
181 with pl. 52; R. Hampe, *Frühe griechische Sagenbilder in Böotien*
(Athens 1936) 71-73 with pl. 39; J. Schäfer, *Studien zu den griechischen
Reliefpithoi des 8. bis 6. Jahrhunderts v. Chr. aus Kreta, Tenos und
Boiotien* (Kallmünz 1957) 75-76; Schefold, *Myth and Legend* 44 with pl.
25b. I follow the interpretation of Hampe 72: "Considering the great role
which the Trojan themes played especially in the art of the middle of the
seventh century, it is more than merely probable that the interpretation of
the theft of the Trojan cattle must be preferred to all others." Cf. P.
Zancani-Montuoro and U. Zanotti Bianco, *Heraion alla Foce del Sele* 2
(Rome 1954) 226-227.

Two where Venus succeeds only with the greatest exertion in taming the hero's desire for battle by reminding him of the greater responsibility to his family and the survival of the Trojan race. Throughout the book Aeneas fights valiantly, though the poet is at pains to point out that this is the result of *furor* and *ira*. The impression this book conveys is that Aeneas' natural impulse is to fight in total disregard of his usual circumspection and deliberation. In the Latin war in the second half of the epic, Aeneas' skill as a fighter is, of course, emphasized even more strongly and culminates in the final scene of the poem where Aeneas kills his opponent Turnus. Aeneas' eagerness for battle is described with such forcefulness and his enemies are portrayed with such sympathy that the martial means by which the Trojan finally arrives at establishing the first *pax Romana* have often been looked upon as an ironic contradiction of the hero's *pietas*. It is also significant that the Sibyl, the prophetic seer, introduces him as *pietate insignis et armis (Aeneid* 6.403) and thereby explicitly modifies the hero's self-characterization in Book 1.378: *sum pius Aeneas*, as well as his characterization in the prologue as *insignem pietate virum* (1.10). Similarly, the words of the Homeric hero Diomedes, who was well qualified to speak on Aeneas and Hector, recall the Homeric tradition and are also entirely consistent with Aeneas' portrayal in the *Aeneid*:[35]

> ambo animis, ambo insignes praestantibus armis;
> hic pietate prior.

The most revealing instance of Vergil's stressing this traditional aspect of the hero is perhaps the very description of Aeneas' flight from Troy. The scene, which is supposed to be so emblematic of *pietas*, is described as follows (*Aeneid* 2. 721-725):

> haec fatus latos umeros subiectaque colla
> veste super fulvique insternor pelle leonis,

[35] *Aeneid* 11.291-292; cf. 1.544-545.

succedoque oneri; dextrae se parvus Iulus
implicuit sequiturque patrem non passibus aequis;
pone subit coniunx.

It is remarkable that Aeneas here dons the lion's skin. There
is no literary or artistic precedent for this connection of the
Trojan with the symbol of Hercules. In the *Aeneid*, however,
Aeneas is associated several times with the great warrior. When
he sees the monsters which Hercules fought in Hades, Aeneas
draws his sword and wants to attack them.[36] Deiphobe therefore has good reasons for introducing him as *Troius Aeneas
pietate insignis et armis* (6.403). In the Hercules-Cacus episode in *Aeneid* 8, this identification of Aeneas and Hercules is
worked out in detail. Wherever Hercules is alluded to in the
Aeneid, he appears as the warlike hero. The passage which
most clearly echoes the description of Aeneas' departure from
Troy is, significantly enough, his departure from Rome, when
Aeneas is setting out with the army of his allies into battle
against his foes (*Aeneid* 8.552-553):

ducunt exsortem Aeneae, quem fulva leonis
pellis obit totum praefulgens unguibus aureis.

"Aeneas marches into battle against Turnus as a second Hercules."[37] This is already anticipated in the *"pietas"* scene in
Book 2.

This traditional portrayal of Aeneas in the Roman epic
literature has its counterpart in Roman art. On a circular base
or altar from Città Castellana there is represented an armed
figure performing a sacrifice in the presence of Mars, Venus
Genetrix, and Vulcan (Fig. 16).[38] A winged Victory whose

[36] *Aeneid* 6.285-294. The identification of Hercules with Aeneas in the
Aeneid is discussed, with particular reference to Book 8, by Buchheit,
Sendung 116-132, and by me, *AJP* 87 (1966) 18-51.

[37] Buchheit 125.

[38] The two most important discussions are R. Herbig, *MDAI(R)* 42
(1927) 129-147 with pls. 15-18, and Ryberg, *Rites* 27 and fig. 16; cf. C. L.
Seltman, *CAH Plates* 4 figs. 90b-c.

drapery and touseled hair indicate her hurried approach, holds a laurel wreath above the warrior's head and evidently intends to crown him. In her left hand Victory carries a palm branch. The sacrifice thus is clearly defined as a thank offering for victory in war. The famous Venus of Arkesilaos (Fig. 17), which influenced the representation of Venus on this base, gives a *terminus post quem* for this sculpture, i.e. the year 46 B.C. For reasons of style and because the cult of Mars enjoyed a revival at that time, Reinhard Herbig and Inez Scott-Ryberg have both dated the base to about 40 B.C. As for the interpretation of the scene represented, Mrs. Ryberg has rightly observed that "a legendary hero offering such a triumphal sacrifice could hardly in this period be other than Aeneas, who might very fitly, after his victory over Turnus, bring a thank offering to Mars as god of war, to Venus his goddess mother, and to Vulcan who fashioned the armor for the combat."[39] She further makes the point that the bearded face and the bare feet of the sacrificant mark him as a legendary rather than as a contemporary hero. Bare feet, however, are not uncommon even for a still living man during the performance of ritual; the Prima Porta Augustus is a good example of this. The beard, on the other hand, provides a positive iconographic clue, for the best parallel in this respect is furnished by the Aeneas figure on the Ara Pacis frieze (Fig. 8).[40] Another iconographic detail which indicates that the interpretation of the warrior as Aeneas is correct is his Phrygian helmet. This helmet type, with its two wings, is best known from the Republican coins with the head of Rhome, a Trojan woman closely associated with the legend of Rome's foundation.[41] Furthermore, the cuirass, which is worn by the sacrificant and by Mars and which lacks the leather straps that

[39] *Rites* 27.

[40] This was noticed by Herbig 147, who, however, did not reach any conclusions about the identity of the figure.

[41] See the well-documented interpretation of Alföldi, *Urahnen* 9 with pls. 8 and 9; cf. Chapter IV, pp. 188-189 with Figs. 131a and b.

usually cover up the tunic, reflects a type known from Etruria, where it is found in the paintings of the François tomb and in the sculptures of a sarcophagus in the church of San Severino in Orvieto.[42] This Etruscan gear may well be a reflection of the Etruscan heritage of Rome's Aeneas legend. The figure therefore is Aeneas, and he is portrayed as a mighty warrior, clenching a spear and resplendent with the glory of a freshly won victory.

As the Città Castellana base can be considered an artistic epilogue to the *Aeneid*, so a scene on the Belvedere Altar reflects the prologue of the epic, and in particular the prophecy of Jupiter, which anticipates the entire epic and is the culmination of its beginning (Fig. 18).[43] On this Augustan monument, Aeneas is shown facing a bearded *vates*. The theme of the composition is the storied prophecy received by Rome's Trojan ancestor. Two principal events from the *Aeneid* are combined: the white sow with her litter of thirty piglets is to recall the prodigy described in *Aeneid* 7, while the more predominant figure, the *vates*, suggests the prophecy read from the scroll of fate to Venus in *Aeneid* 1.261-296. The emphasis in that prophecy distinctly is on the *imperium* which Aeneas' descendants will establish first over Italy and then over all the world (1.278-279):

> his ego nec metas rerum nec tempora pono:
> imperium sine fine dedi.

They will finally take revenge on the Greeks for the fall of Troy (1.283-285):

---

[42] So Herbig 146 n. 1. A good reproduction of the pertinent painting from the François tomb is found in M. Pallottino, *Etruscan Painting* (Skira 1952) 115.

[43] The principal discussions of this monument are W. Amelung, *Die Sculpturen des Vaticanischen Museums* 2 (Berlin 1908) 242-247 with pl. 15.87b; J. Carcopino, *Virgile et les origines d'Ostie* (Paris 1919) 716-720; L. R. Taylor, *AJA* 29 (1925) 299-310, and *Divinity of the Roman Emperor* 186-190; J. Gagé, *MEFR* 49 (1932) 61-71; Moretti, *APA* 259-262; Ryberg, *Rites* 56-58.

veniet lustris labentibus aetas
cum domus Assaraci Phthiam clarasque Mycenas
servitio premet ac victis dominabitur Argis.

The prophecy culminates in a description of the exploits of
Augustus, Caesar's son, who will give Rome's *imperium* its
greatest expansion and finally will be deified. Accordingly, the
apotheosis of Caesar is represented on one of the adjoining
sides of the altar. Thereafter there will be a period of peace.
Pulchra Troianus origine, Augustus is the true heir of Aeneas
and his achievement is merely the completion of the mission
begun by his Trojan ancestor. And Aeneas' task is to wage
war (1.263-264):

bellum ingens geret Italia populosque ferocis
contundet.

This is the prophecy Aeneas receives on the altar relief. His
association with an essentially warlike task, the expansion of
Rome's *imperium*, recurs on the Great Cameo of Paris (Fig.
124) which will be discussed later.[44] This theme is the official
Roman adaptation of the traditional subject of Aeneas the
great warrior. Its presence on the Belvedere Altar is accounted
for by the fact that this monument, although it was influenced
by the plans for the Ara Pacis, was on a level much closer to
popular art than the latter monument.

This warlike appearance of the sacrificing Aeneas also
influenced his representation in the sacrifice, whose martial
aspects had been eliminated on the Ara Pacis frieze: his landing in Italy. On the Ara Pacis (Fig. 8) the hero performs the
rite with his toga arranged in the *cinctus Gabinus*, and this
underlines his peaceful intentions. On a sarcophagus fragment
in the Palazzo Camuccini (Fig. 20), which served as the
prototype of a fourteenth century relief in the Uffizi in Florence (Fig. 21),[45] Aeneas appears as a warrior in complete

[44] See Chapter IV, pp. 166-167.

[45] The Camuccini relief has been described in detail by G. Q. Giglioli,
BCAR 67 (1939) 109-117. For earlier discussions of the Uffizi relief and

armor. He wears a tunic with short sleeves, a cuirass with a sword belt, high boots, and the *paludamentum*, the general's cloak. Three unarmed men in tunics accompany him, as does Ascanius with his Phrygian cap, while a female figure, probably Virtus, is looking on. The Camuccini relief dates from the time of Trajan and became the model for a similar representation on a sarcophagus in Torre Nova, which in turn was closely imitated by the Renaissance sculptor of the relief in the Uffizi. In contrast to his companions, Aeneas is portrayed as the *imperator*. The representation of the Trojan under this aspect is consistent with the reissue of the Caesarean denarius by Trajan (Fig. 3), as it may have been modeled on a Julio-Claudian relief of which a fragment is preserved in the Capitoline Museum.[46]

Both the Belvedere Altar, an example of popular art, and the Camuccini relief, which was part of a private sarcophagus, show Aeneas as a warrior rather than as being merely *pius*. And to find out which representation of Aeneas, the warrior or the *pius*, was privately preferred among the people, we need only take a look at the Aeneas theme in Pompeian painting.

One of the finest examples of the continuing influence of Homeric themes in Roman art is the so-called Casa Omerica or Casa del Criptoportico in Pompeii.[47] The name of the house is derived from its cryptoporticus, the frieze of which consists of a continuous narrative sequence of scenes from Homer's

---

the Torre Nova sarcophagus fragment see also G. E. Rizzo, *MDAI(R)* 21 (1906) 289-306, 398-402, and J. Sieveking, *MDAI(R)* 32 (1917) 168-171.

[46] S. Reinach, *Répertoire de reliefs grecs et romains* 3 (Paris 1912) 204 no. 1; H. Stuart Jones, *A Catalogue of Ancient Sculptures Preserved in the Municipal Collections of Rome* 1 (Oxford 1912) 33 no. 23a, with pl. 8.

[47] A comprehensive bibliography is listed in Schefold, *Wände* 17. The best description of the Casa and its paintings is that by Spinazzola, *Pompei* 437-593, where S. Aurigemma also discusses the painting with the combat of Aeneas and Achilles (935-936 with figs. 942-945). Another painting on the north wall of the north wing of the cryptoporticus may represent the clash between Diomedes and Aeneas; see Aurigemma, *ibid.* 912-913 with figs. 907-910. More probably, however, Diomedes' combat with Ares (*Iliad* 5.850-861) is shown there.

Iliad. The scenes on the west wall of the east wing start with Thetis' visit in Hephaestus' workshop and continue, among other episodes, with the return of Achilles to battle and the combat between Achilles and Aeneas (Fig. 22). As in *Iliad* 20, Aeneas is shown to be the courageous fighter who holds his ground against the greatest warrior of the Greeks, for against him rages

> expers terroris Achilles
> hostibus haud tergo, sed forti pectore notus
> (Catullus 64.338-339)

The same subject matter is represented on a Pontic amphora from Etruria (Fig. 99), which will be described in more detail later.[48] The difference between the two representations is revealing. The Roman artist added to Aeneas' portrayal as a warrior the very aspect we found emphasized on the Belvedere Altar: the beginning of the *imperium Romanum* with the Trojan ancestor. For this reason Poseidon appears in the Pompeian painting. For it is he, the protector of Aeneas, who issued the famous prophecy (*Iliad* 20.307-308):

> And now the might of Aeneas shall rule over the Trojans,
> and his sons' sons, and those who are born thereafter.

> νῦν δὲ δὴ Αἰνείαο βίη Τρώεσσιν ἀνάξει
> καὶ παίδων παῖδες, τοί κεν μετόπισθε γένωνται.

We know from Strabo (13.608) that this wording of the prophecy was changed to

> "And now the race of Aeneas shall rule over *all* men."

> Αἰνείαο γένος πάντεσσι ἀνάξει

For in the *Aeneid* (3.97-98), where Augustus' favorite god, Apollo, utters the prophecy, Vergil had translated the words of Apollo as follows:

[48] See Chapter III, pp. 126-127.

27

hic domus Aeneae *cunctis* dominabitur oris
et nati natorum et qui nascentur ab illis.

The Iliadic prediction of the supremacy of Aeneas and his family "is converted into the promise of the Roman empire."[49] The legendary founder of this empire is the warrior Aeneas.

The painter of a scene in the exedra behind the small peristyle of the Casa del Centauro was inspired even more by the *Aeneid*. The painting on the north wall of that part of the house is no longer extant, but a drawing by Marsigli reproduces its original state before its destruction.[50] Aeneas is shown receiving the armor from Venus. Following Vergil's description in *Aeneid* 8, Aeneas is given the armor, the vision of which resolves his last doubts about his military mission in Latium (*Aeneid* 8.533-540):

ego poscor Olympo.
hoc signum cecinit missuram diva creatrix,
si bellum ingrueret, Volcaniaque arma per auras
laturam auxilio.
heu quantae miseris caedes Laurentibus instant!
quas poenas mihi, Turne, dabis! quam multa sub undas
scuta virum galeasque et fortia corpora volves,
Thybri pater! poscant acies et foedera rumpant.

Again the glory of Rome's empire is hinted at, for Aeneas' shield is the *fama et fata nepotum* (*Aeneid* 8.731).

A wall painting in the triclinium fenestratum in the Casa di Sirico shows a more generic scene, which might have been inspired either by the *Iliad*, or more probably, by the Twelfth Book of the *Aeneid*: the wounding of Aeneas (Fig. 23).[51] No

---

[49] Conington-Nettleship, *The Works of Virgil* 2 (Hildesheim 1963) *ad loc.*

[50] Helbig, *Wandgemälde* no. 1382; Schefold, *Wände* 115.

[51] Museo Nazionale, Naples, inv. 9009; Helbig, no. 1383; O. Elia, *Pitture murali e mosaici del Museo Nazionale di Napoli* (Naples 1932) 12; G. E. Rizzo, *La pittura ellenistico-romana* (Milan 1929) 86 and fig. 195b; Schefold, *Wände* 165. A painting with the same subject was found in the

opponent is visible, but Aeneas is bleeding profusely from a wound in his thigh. A physician, perhaps Iapyx, is attending to him in the presence of the crying Ascanius/Iulus, while Venus descends from heaven to comfort her son. Two warriors in the background lend an even more martial note to the picture. The painting places the heroism of the Trojan in sharp focus. As in the *Iliad* or the *Aeneid*, Aeneas is no shirker who stays out of battle. He fights even at the risk of being seriously wounded. In so doing he gains great glory without bringing his life into real jeopardy. For "ancestors have to survive."[52]

Another painting which emphasizes the heroic exploits of Aeneas rather than his flight with Anchises from Troy has been preserved on the right wall of the tablinum in the Casa di Laocoonte.[53] Aeneas' encounter with Polyphemus (Fig. 24) is represented. The inspiration of the *Aeneid* again is evident to a surprisingly detailed degree. The Trojan's encounter with Polyphemus in the Third Book is part of the Achaemenides episode (3.588-691). The latter is a different recasting of the Sinon story in the Second Book,[54] which is closely connected with the Laocoon episode. This correspondence between the two episodes in the epic finds its artistic expression in the Casa di Laocoonte: the Polyphemus-Aeneas scene is the visual counterpart of the painting with the Laocoon group in the atrium. True to the description in the epic—*trunca manum pinus regit . . . lanigerae comitantur oves* (3.659-660)—

Domus Transitoria under Domitian's Palace on the Palatine; see K. Bulas, *AJA* 54 (1950) 116.

[52] So K. Reinhardt, *Die Ilias und ihr Dichter* (Göttingen 1961) 380.

[53] Museo Nazionale, Naples, inv. 111211. Published by A. Sogliano, *Le pitture murali Campane* (Naples 1879) no. 603; Reinach, *Répertoire des peintures grecques et romains* (Paris 1922) 172 no. 9; Herrmann, *Denkmäler der Malerei des Altertums*, pl. 206; Schefold, *Wände* 135. A. Mau, *Geschichte der dekorativen Wandmalerei in Pompeji* (Leipzig 1882) 426, is the only scholar who has identified the figure with Odysseus.

[54] *Aeneid* 2.57-233. For the relation between the two passages see *AJP* 89 (1968) 161-164.

Aeneas and his companions are juxtaposed with a barbaric, inhuman enemy.

Another episode from the *Aeneid* which appealed to the Pompeians was Aeneas' meeting with Dido. This scene adorned the west wall of the tablinum of a house in Regio IX. The picture is not well preserved, but the inscriptions "Aeneas" and "Dido" still are clearly visible (Fig. 25).[55] In a painting in the triclinium of a house in Regio IX the inspiration of the Fourth Book of the *Aeneid* is also evident (Fig. 26).[56] Aeneas and Dido are sitting in front of the cave, the *spelunca*, which is to be their marriage chamber. Dido is dressed as a huntress, and she passionately caresses the still reluctant Aeneas. It is significant that Aeneas is not only represented as a hunter but also as a warrior. The mythical hunters in Campanian painting commonly carry two spears, whereas Aeneas is armed with a sword. The two Cupids hint at the eventual success of Dido's efforts. This motif is very appropriate since Cupid in the *Aeneid* approaches her in the guise of Ascanius.

In contrast to these six representations of Aeneas as a warrior or lover, only two show him carrying his father from Troy. Whereas the paintings with the martial Aeneas have received virtually no attention, the Aeneas group from the shop of Fabius Multitremulus on the Via dell'Abbondanza has so often been published that a detailed description here is not necessary (Fig. 27).[57] What is important is that this painting is paired

[55] Sogliano, *op.cit.*, no. 602; Schefold, *Wände* 151.

[56] Schefold, *Wände* 151. The interpretation of A. Rumpf, *Festschrift Bernhard Schweitzer* (Stuttgart 1954) 341-344, seems to me most cogent; cf. A. Sogliano, *RAAN* 21 (1900/1901) 67-77. The doubts voiced by R. Herbig, *MDAI(R)* 66 (1959) 209-211, do not substantially weaken the arguments of Rumpf and Sogliano. Rizzo, *La pittura ellenistico-romana* 86, and others go too far in denying any traces of Vergilian influence in these paintings, although the Roman epic was very popular with the Pompeians; see, e.g., M. della Corte, *Epigraphica* 2 (1940) 171-178, and M. Gigante, "La cultura letteraria a Pompei," in *Pompeiana. Raccolta di studi per il secondo centenario degli scavi di Pompei* (Naples 1950) 111-143.

[57] The best discussion, with excellent bibliography, is Spinazzola, *Pompei* 150-154 with figs. 183 and 184. See also Rizzo, *La pittura ellenistico-romana*

with that of Romulus carrying the *spolia opima* of the slain
Acron. This combination of the Trojan and Roman ancestors
is a solid reflection of the imperial ideology. In the official
poetry of the Augustan age as well as the imperial monuments
the two mythical heroes were given prominence and linked to
each other. The attitude of the private citizen to the imperial
theme is reflected, to some extent, by Propertius' (4.10) rather
perfunctory and extraordinarily brief "praise" of Romulus'
deed.

It should be noted that this painting of the Aeneas group
appears on the outside of the house—virtually as the shop
sign of a loyal fuller and an outward documentation of his
patriotism. Within the private quarters of a Pompeian house
this theme, painted in a straightforward way, is found only
once: in the west wing of the cryptoporticus of the Casa
Omerica (Fig. 28).[58] The painting has been diligently as-
sembled from more than twenty fragments and shows Aeneas,
Anchises, and Ascanius leaving Troy under the guidance of
Hermes. This representation is similar to a scene with the
same group on the *Tabula Iliaca* in the Capitoline Museum,
which will be discussed in more detail below (Fig. 29).[59] Perhaps, as has been suggested, this painting in the Casa del
Criptoportico is based on an earlier prototype which belonged
to a cycle like the one in the Casa and was composed of scenes
from Homer's *Iliad*, Arctinus' *Aithiopis*, and Stesichorus'
Iliupersis. Naturally, when this Stesichorean group appeared
in Roman art, it was "to recall and exalt the Trojan origins
of Rome."[60] But it cannot be ruled out altogether that the
scene in the Casa del Criptoportico also had a rather down-
to-earth meaning. It is located on the south wall right next

85-86 with fig. 194; A. Alföldi, *MH* 8 (1951) 193 with fig. 2; A. Mau,
Führer durch Pompeji[6] (Leipzig 1928) 136 with fig. 64.

[58] Spinazzola, *Pompei* 592-593 with fig. 644; 955-956 with fig. 971.

[59] See Chapter III, p. 106.

[60] So S. Aurigemma in Spinazzola, *Pompei* 956.

to the exit to the street and thus provides an ennobling mythological parallel to the ordinary, everyday act of leaving the house.

It is not surprising that the only extant parody of the Aeneas/Anchises theme in art also is found in Pompeian painting. This is a small rectangular picture, which probably was part of a narrative frieze (Fig. 30). It is an obvious caricature of the compositional scheme of the Aeneas/Anchises/Ascanius group. The three characters are represented in the form of dogs or, according to others, apes. Instead of the *cista sacra* with the Penates, Anchises holds a dice box, which is best explained as an allusion to one of Julius Caesar's favorite pastimes. Ascanius wears the familiar Phrygian cap and exchanges a soulful look with his father. While all scholars are agreed on the parodic intent of the picture, different explanations have been offered for its exact meaning. According to Professor Maiuri, the phalloi and the animal costume provide positive iconographic clues that the painting was inspired by a theatrical farce in the tradition of the phlyax or the *fabula Atellana*.[61] Attractive as it may be, this suggestion is beyond proof. It is a more reasonable assumption, therefore, that this parody had political overtones and reflects the attitude of the native Pompeian element to the new Augustan colonists and their Julio-Claudian sympathies.[62] This is very much in keeping with the Pompeian preference for the less officially sanctioned representations of the Warrior or Lover Aeneas.

Aeneas also was given much prominence in the *Tabulae*

[61] A. Maiuri, "La parodia d'Enea," *BA* 35 (1950) 111. No Atellan character, however, is known to have worn animal masks. The painting is now in the Museo Nazionale in Naples, inv. 9089; see the descriptions by A. Ruesch, *Guida illustrata del Museo Nazionale di Napoli* (Naples 1908) 291 no. 1295 and Elia (note 51, above) 18 no. 18.

[62] See W. McDermott, *The Ape in Antiquity* (Baltimore 1938) 278-280; W. Binsfeld, *Grylloi* (Cologne 1956) 31 n. 11; Spinazzola, *Pompei* 623 n. 135.

Iliacae, which date from the time of Augustus and Tiberius.[63] The famous scene on the *Tabula Iliaca* in the Capitoline Museum (Fig. 29) which shows Aeneas rescuing his family from Troy has been given considerable attention, but it is just as important to note that Aeneas appears no less than three times in the Homeric part of this *Tabula*. In fact, his combat against Aphareus, which is mentioned in only four lines in the *Iliad* (13.541-544) concludes the series of representations of the Homeric frieze (Fig. 32). On the third frieze band from the bottom, Hector and Aeneas, both armed as archers, are the conspicuous protagonists in the battle by the ships. Both tower over the other fighters because they stand on elevated ground. In the eighth band from the bottom, Poseidon is shown coming to the rescue of Aeneas. This theme is repeated on the fragment of a *Tabula Iliaca* in New York (Fig. 31).[64] On the right is Achilles who is covered by his shield and attacks the Trojan. On the left Aeneas has sunk on his knee and supports himself with his right hand, while Poseidon intervenes and pushes Achilles back.

The other episode with Aeneas, of which we have two examples on *Tabulae Iliacae*, is his combat with Diomedes, which had attracted the attention of several Greek vase painters. A frieze band from a *Tabula* in Paris shows Aphrodite carrying off the inert body of Aeneas (Fig. 33).[65] On the

---

[63] Detailed discussions of the iconography and purpose of the *Tabulae* may be found in Sadurska, *Les tables iliaques* 9-17, and E. Lippold, *RE* 4A (1932) 1892-1896. For reproductions of the *Tabula Iliaca Capitolina* see our Figs. 32, 85, and 86.

[64] Metropolitan Museum of Art 24.97.11. For the details see Sadurska 37-40.

[65] Paris, Bibliothèque Nationale, Cabinet des Médailles 3318; Sadurska 40-43. Diomedes and Aeneas also appear in the drawing of a *Tabula Iliaca* fragment by E. Sarti (Sadurska 49), and on the "Zenodotean" *Tabula Iliaca* in Paris (Sadurska 53-54). The sculptor of the *Tabula Iliaca "Tarentina,"* which shows Achilles dragging the body of Hector, may have introduced Aeneas as Hector's defender into the representation of this scene; see Sadurska 67-68. Aside from the Capitoline *Tabula*, the motif of Aeneas

33

left, through a vaulted gate, a helmeted Athena hurries to protect Diomedes as she did on the Greek vases. Diomedes has placed his left foot on Pandarus who is lying on the ground. The scene on the right is less clear although Apollo may be shown there protecting Aeneas.

Like the Pompeian paintings, the *Tabulae Iliacae* were intended for private use and enjoyment. In this private art the representation of Aeneas as a warrior again prevails. This conception of Aeneas, however, was certainly not incompatible with official Roman customs. This is brought out very clearly by the earliest appearance of this subject on a Praenestine cista which dates from the end of the second century B.C. or before.[66] It commemorates the greatest and most Roman honor that could be bestowed on a warrior: a triumph. The front of the cista (Fig. 34) shows the victorious triumphator, who pours a libation over a lighted tripod. The general wears a laurel wreath and holds a standard with an eagle or hawk devouring a fish—the badge of a Latin city. He is distinguished by the decorated leggings. This Phrygian costume is an indication that he represents a Trojan ancestor, very probably Aeneas. The cista is from pre-Vergilian times, and the emphasis is on the military success of the Trojan. This military aspect is intensified by his wearing, contrary to Roman custom, a military cloak instead of the usual *toga picta* during the performance of the sacred ritual.

This brief survey, which is not meant to be exhaustive, shows that Aeneas as a warrior was a well-known theme in ancient art. It is no coincidence that unlike any of the scenes with Aeneas and his father, this motif was chosen for mythological "program" representations such as the Siphnian frieze.

and Anchises appears only once—on the *Tabula Iliaca* Thiérry, though the present condition of the work is too bad to allow any definite conclusions (Sadurska 51-52).

[66] More detailed arguments concerning the date and iconography of the cista are found in L. Bonfante Warren, *AJA* 68 (1964) 35-42; cf. Ryberg, *Rites* 20-22.

It may not be entirely accidental either that the Aeneas/ Anchises group is conspicuously missing, for instance, from Polygnotus' painting of the Iliupersis, the destruction of Troy, in the Lesche of the Cnidians at Delphi (Paus. 10.25-27). The literary evidence makes it clear that Aeneas was primarily known as a warrior. At Rome, this portrayal of the Trojan was adapted for national purposes *ad maiorem Romae gloriam*. And while the Aeneas/Anchises group was connected with *pietas* and became a theme in imperial propaganda, it is revealing to see that those artistic representations, which most indisputably reflect the private predilections and tastes of the populace, the wall paintings from Pompeii, show a marked preference for the time-honored theme of Aeneas as a warrior. Although this characterization of Aeneas has its roots in the *Iliad*, it is emphasized also in Vergil's epic. Therefore it is not always possible to determine conclusively whether the Pompeian painters followed Hellenic rather than Roman inspiration in their treatment of this theme.

To overstress the contrast between the warlike Aeneas and his *pietas* would be to confuse a modern concept with an ancient one. In ancient times the two could well coexist. On the Praenestine cista (Fig. 34), for instance, the triumphant Aeneas is engaged in a religious act and accompanied by a bearded man who, with his veiled head, resembles the Aeneas on the Ara Pacis (Fig. 8). On the Augustan monument, Aeneas' *pietas* is the dominating and exclusive aspect, whereas both are combined once more on the Camuccini relief (Fig. 20). The final scene of the *Aeneid* suggests that these two aspects of his character could clash and Vergil did not try to offer a facile solution for Aeneas' dilemma. The *Aeneid* as a whole, however, does not convey the impression that *pietas* and martial fervor are mutually exclusive and the modern misconception[67] that they are has, in no small measure,

[67] A recent example is M. C. J. Putnam, *The Poetry of the Aeneid* (Cambridge, Mass. 1965), esp. 151ff., and a more graphic one, a favorite

contributed to obscuring the traditional character of Aeneas.

The second most outstanding characteristic of Aeneas in the *Iliad* is his levelheadedness. His first appearance in Book Five again sets the tone. Whereas the first characterization of Aeneas in the Augustan epic is the programmatic *insignem pietate virum* (1.10), he is introduced in the *Iliad* by Pandarus' calling him "counselor of the Trojans" (Τρώων βουληφόρε 5.180). This epithet is applied to Aeneas more frequently than to any other hero in the *Iliad*. Aeneas has already lived up to his characterization as βουληφόρος for the advice he gives Pandarus is pragmatic and realistic (5.174-178):

> Come now, shoot him with an arrow! this man who is
> mighty among us
> and has brought about all this ruin, taking the life of
> our heroes
> many and brave. But first lift up to Zeus your hands in
> prayer
> lest there might be some god who is angry with the
> Trojans
> for some neglected rite, and who wreaks such vengeance
> upon us.

His analysis of the situation turns out to be correct. This is evident from Pandarus' reply: there is indeed a god who is angered (5.191) and helping Diomedes (5.185-188). It is worth noting that it is Aeneas who urges Pandarus to let go the arrow. This is bound to recall the last time Pandarus had done so: when he nefariously broke the truce between the Trojans and the Greeks. Yet Aeneas has no scruples to avail

---

anecdote of William Butler Yeats (as quoted by Ezra Pound, *ABC of Reading* [New Haven 1934] 31): A plain sailor man took a notion to study Latin and his teacher tried him with Vergil; after many lessons he asked him something about the hero. Said the sailor: "What hero?" "Why, Aeneas, the hero." Said the sailor: "Ach, a hero, him a hero? Bigob, I thought he was a priest." In the Middle Ages, *Pius* was thought to be a part of Aeneas' name; see E. H. Alton, *CR* 32 (1918) 156 n. 1.

himself of Pandarus' talents. This alone should caution us against taking his comment on the gods as an expression of sententious "piety." Rather, it shows, on Aeneas' part, the pragmatic realization of their power. This same attitude, mingled with pride in his descent from Zeus, is also reflected in what Aeneas says after informing Achilles of his genealogy (20.241-243):

> Thus I have traced my descent through a line of gods and of heroes.
> It is Zeus, however, who grants strength and power to man
> as he pleases. For he is the mightiest of all gods.

The practical illustration of this again follows soon—Zeus weighs the scales of Hector and Achilles.

This trait which differentiates Aeneas from others, appears even more clearly in the description of his encounter with Achilles. Achilles is foolish ($\nu\acute{\eta}\pi\iota o\varsigma$ 20.264) whereas Aeneas is clearheaded ($\delta a\acute{\iota}\phi\rho o\nu o\varsigma$ 20.267). But Aeneas knows it would be madness to fight against the raging Achilles (20.87-102; cf. $\nu\eta\pi\acute{\upsilon}\tau\iota o\nu$ 20.200) and Poseidon later agrees with him ($\nu\acute{\eta}\pi\iota o\varsigma$ 20.296). He is not provoked by Apollo-Lycon's taunts, but answers with the most prudent arguments possible. He knows Achilles from experience and knows also that the gods make the Greek invincible.

A comparison between Hector's and Aeneas' going into battle against Achilles suggests that their characterization is deliberate and not the result of formulaic accident. Whereas a god makes Aeneas fight against Achilles because of the very vague boasts ($\dot{a}\pi\epsilon\iota\lambda a\acute{\iota}$ 20.83), Hector has to fight against Achilles because of his own recklessness ($\dot{a}\tau a\sigma\theta a\lambda\acute{\iota}\eta\sigma\iota\nu$ 22.-104). There can be no return for Hector; his unabated fury ($\ddot{a}\sigma\beta\epsilon\sigma\tau o\nu$ $\mu\acute{\epsilon}\nu o\varsigma$ 22.96) compels him to go. Thus he becomes an easy prey for Achilles and the machinations of the goddess. The contradistinction between Aeneas' deliberation and the

3 7

foolish and reckless behavior of Achilles and Hector is worked out as carefully as is the contrast between Odysseus and his companions in the *Odyssey* prologue. It is therefore not surprising that as early a mythographer as Hellanicus depicts Odysseus and Aeneas as allies in Italy.[68] The Vergilian Aeneas whose travels, after all, parallel those of Odysseus, embodies certain significant traits of Homer's Odysseus. Both heroes had a reputation for sagacity, and whereas the pre-third century tradition of Aeneas' *pietas* is uncertain, Odysseus is the most god-fearing of all heroes in Homer, a trait which often recurred in the subsequent literary tradition.[69] That Odysseus was not viewed with any hostility in Rome is evident also from the coin issues of the *gens* Mamilia, which claimed to have descended from Odysseus and placed the hero on the reverse of their coins in the second and first centuries B.C. (Fig. 35).[70] Before the *Aeneid* became the national epic of Italy this honor had belonged to the *Odissia Latina* of Livius Andronicus.[71] Even if the cultured thumbed their noses at it, the *Odissia* remained popular in the schools and Vergil's friend Horace still recalled the days when he studied this epic under the watchful eye and rod of *plagosus* Orbilius (*Ep.* 2.1.69-75).

Homer's emphasis on the mental faculties and the prudence of Aeneas was clearly recognized by the ancients. Lycophron praises the hero as "outstanding in counsel" (βουλαῖς ἄριστος *Alex.* 1235). One of the Philostratoi is even more explicit

68 *FGH* 4 F 84; cf. Lycophron 1242-1245. For details, see Chapter III, p. 103.

69 For Odysseus' piety see below, p. 43; for the similarities between Odysseus and Aeneas, W. B. Stanford, *The Ulysses Theme*[2] (New York 1963) 136; B. E. Levy, *Vergilius* 7 (1961) 25-26. Cf. Phillips, *JHS* 73 (1953) 57-58, and my articles in *AJP* 89 (1968) 164, and *Latomus* 28 (1969) 3-18.

70 *BMC Coins Rep.* 1.97 no. 725, with pl. 22.7; 1.343 nos. 2716-2722, with pl. 40.9; Sydenham nos. 369 and 741.

71 See F. Altheim, *A History of Roman Religion* (London 1938) 298-299, and my article in *Latomus* 28 (1969) 15-16.

and gives the clearest expression yet of the distinction between Hector and Aeneas:[72]

> They say that Aeneas was somewhat less of a fighter than that man [Hector], but that in intelligence and sagacity he was the best of the Trojans. He was esteemed as much as Hector. He was very much aware of the divine prophecy concerning his fate after the fall of Troy. He was not stricken with any fear, and he never ceased reasoning and calculating even in the most frightful circumstances. The Greeks thus called Hector the arm of the Trojans, but Aeneas, their mind, and they put greater stock in Aeneas' wisdom than in Hector's raging.

This characterization of Aeneas is even more trustworthy since the *Heroicus*, according to Arthur Darby Nock, whose terminology fits in well with this discussion of *pius* Aeneas, is characterized by "a clear rise in the tension of piety."[73] The work, which was written in the third century A.D., tendentiously appealed to credulity and superstitious hero worship. Clearly, if any aura of mysticism had surrounded Aeneas in Philostratus' Greek sources, the *Heroicus* would be the work in which we should expect an intensification of it. The emphasis, however, is on Aeneas' λόγος, νοῦς, σωφροσύνη, and πράγματα.

Even at the very time when the *Aeneid* was written Dionysius of Halicarnassus, who may have been quoting Hellanicus, stressed Aeneas' determination to fight, and especially, his sagacity prior to his departure from Troy. At a time when

---

[72] Flavius Philostratus 2 (ed. Kayser) 316: Αἰνείαν δὲ μάχεσθαι μὲν τούτον ἧττον, συνέσει δὲ περιεῖναι τῶν Τρώων. ἀξιοῦσθαι δὲ τῶν αὐτῶν Ἕκτορι, τὰ τῶν θεῶν εὖ εἰδέναι, ἅ δὲ ἐπέπρωτο αὐτῷ Τροίας ἁλούσης, ἐκπλήττεσθαι δὲ ὑπ' οὐδενὸς φόβου, τὸ γὰρ ἔννουν καὶ λελογισμένον ἐν αὐτοῖς μάλιστα τοῖς φοβεροῖς ἔχειν. ἐκάλουν δὲ οἱ Ἀχαιοὶ τὸν μὲν Ἕκτορα χεῖρα τῶν Τρώων, τὸν δὲ Αἰνείαν νοῦν, καὶ πλείω παρέχειν αὐτοῖς πράγματα Αἰνείαν σωφρονοῦντα ἢ μεμηνότα Ἕκτορα.

[73] *Conversion* (London 1933) 129.

Aeneas' *pietas* must have been proverbial, the Greek historian emphasized his subtle contrivances (μηχάνημα), reasoning (λογισμός), and deliberation (νοῦν 1.46.2); and the first quality is intentionally contrasted with the Greeks' failure to come up with a successful stratagem: οὐδὲν προεμηχανῶντο (1.46.3).

These passages, to which more could be added, provide the most convincing proof that there was a well-established literary tradition which stressed the hero's sagacity and presence of mind. This literary tradition doubtless was inspired by and originated with the portrayal of Aeneas in the *Iliad*.

It was for these very qualities that Aeneas was chosen to be the trusted confidant and accomplice of young Paris on the latter's expedition to abduct Helen from Sparta. The story is told in the *Cypria*, one of the poems of the epic cycle. The son of Aphrodite was ordered by his mother to accompany Paris, who had favored the goddess because she promised him marriage with Helen. A recent study has shown that the rape of Helen was a very popular theme in ancient art, and Aeneas frequently appears in its representations.[74]

One of the most illuminating examples is a Pontic oinochoe from Etruria, in the collection of the Bibliothèque Nationale in Paris (Fig. 36a).[75] On the right side of its main frieze we see Helen, who artfully gathers up her robe. Paris, Aphrodite—πότνια θήρων—and Aeneas are approaching her. Paris is completely stunned by Helen's beauty and has to shade his eyes with his left hand. Aeneas, however, is the clearheaded, plotting βουληφόρος. He pays no attention to the lovers but surveys the terrain behind him for the best way to escape (Fig. 36b). "Whereas Paris is completely entranced by Helen, Aeneas has to keep a cool head in order that the scheme to

[74] Ghali-Kahil, *Enlèvements*; see the index s.v. "Enée."
[75] *CVA* France fasc. 7 (=Bibl. Nat. fasc. 1) pl. 27.5-7 and pl. 28.2,3,7; A. de Ridder, *Catalogue des vases peints de la Bibliothèque Nationale* 1 (Paris 1902) no. 178; Pfuhl, *Malerei und Zeichnung der Griechen* fig. 159; Hampe-Simon, *Griechische Sagen* 41-44 with pl. 28 and fig. 8.

abduct her may succeed."[76] In this composition he is the counterpart of Helen; both frame the scene, and both are poised and self-assured.

The painting of Makron on a skyphos in Boston combines the motifs of Aeneas, the accomplice of Paris, and Aeneas, the warrior (Fig. 37).[77] On this vase Aeneas does not form the rearguard but marches in front of the group and protects Paris and Helen with a shield. The diadem which Aeneas holds on the Pontic oinochoé in Paris is now placed on Helen's head by Eros and Aphrodite. Again Aeneas turns his head back, this time in the direction of Paris and Helen, as if to admonish them not to tarry. The presence of Aeneas and Aphrodite shows that the *Cypria* served as the poetic source for this painting also.

The participation of Aeneas in the abduction of Helen has rightly been called an act of impiety.[78] The same feeling is expressed in Horace's Ode on this theme which was written before the concept of Trojan descent was given in the *Aeneid* the halo of such sacrosanctity that it could no longer be connected with any adverse notions (*Odes* 1.15.1-5):

> pastor cum traheret per freta navibus
> Idaeis Helenen perfidus hospitam,
> ingrato celeres obruit otio
>   ventos, ut caneret fera
> Nereus fata.

It is worth noting that Nereus appears on the Pontic oinochoe directly beneath the scene with Paris, Helen, and Aeneas.

There is no indication in the *Iliad* that Aeneas was more god-fearing or dearer to the gods than other Greek or Trojan

---

[76] Hampe-Simon 42.

[77] Boston 13.186; Beazley, *ARV*² 458 no. 1; G. Richter, *A Handbook of Greek Art*² (New York 1960) 330-331 with fig. 445; Ghali-Kahil, *Enlèvements* 53 no. 11, with pl. 4.

[78] Ghali-Kahil 52: ". . . cet acte d'*asébeia*, cette impiété majeure parmi les impiétés." Cf. Juno's harsh words in *Aen.* 10.92.

heroes. It is true that in 11.58 the Trojans are said to have honored Aeneas like a god, but the phrase θεὸς δ'ὣς τίετο δήμῳ recurs four times in the epic, referring to various Greek and Trojan heroes.[79] In 20.347 Aeneas is called "dear to the gods" (φίλος ἀθανάτοισι θεοῖσιν) but the line has to be read in context. For it is the intentional echo of line 334 where Achilles is described as being even dearer to the gods—φίλτερος ἀθανάτοισι. Furthermore, it is essential to take into account the foreshadowing function of the Achilles-Aeneas episode in Book Twenty and the parallelism between Hector and Aeneas. For Zeus will later say of Hector (24.66-67): "He was dearest of the gods" (ἀλλὰ καὶ Ἕκτωρ/φίλτατος ἔσκε θεοῖσι). The word φίλτατος here harks back to Achilles, who, as we have seen, is only φίλτερος ἀθανάτοισι (20.334). The "piety" of Aeneas thus should not be looked at as isolated; if we take the meaning of the epithets as literally as most scholars have interpreted them, Aeneas' being φίλος ἀθανάτοισι θεοῖσιν would actually denote that his piety was considered inferior to that of Achilles, and, even more so, to that of Hector.

Aside from the Homeric passages which have been mentioned thus far, the sources that are cited in support of the view that piety was Aeneas' outstanding characteristic from the very beginning are these:

1. *Iliad* 20.297-299

> Why does this man, who is blameless, suffer hardships
> all in vain, just because others are in distress?
> Always he gives pleasing gifts to the gods who hold
>   the wide heaven.

> ἀλλὰ τίη νῦν οὗτος ἀναίτιος ἄλγεα πάσχει,
> μὰψ ἕνεκ' ἀλλοτρίων ἀχέων, κεχαρισμένα δ' αἰεὶ
> δῶρα θεοῖσι δίδωσι, τοὶ οὐρανὸν εὐρὺν ἔχουσιν;

---

[79] *Iliad* 5.78 (Dolopion); 10.33 (Agamemnon); 13.218 (Andraimon); 16.605 (Onetor).

When we compare this one passage which makes mention of Aeneas' generosity toward the gods, to the numerous instances where Homer extols the piety of Odysseus it becomes clear that Aeneas does not significantly differ from Odysseus in this respect in the pre-Vergilian tradition. What is more, of all Homeric heroes it is precisely Odysseus whose piety the poet sets most strongly in relief. "More than any other mortals has he offered sacrifices to the immortal gods," Zeus says of "god-like" (δῖος) Odysseus in the *Odyssey* (1.66-67). Odysseus' behavior in the Doloneia as well as his actions throughout the *Odyssey* illustrate his personal piety. "Even in his worst sufferings he never blames the gods . . . or accuses them of 'envy' as others do."[80] This contrasts strongly, for instance, with Achilles' threats against Apollo (*Iliad* 22.15-24) and his defiance of the river god Scamander (21.130-135). Yet Achilles is "dearer to the gods." Whereas the piety of Odysseus is one of his most important character traits, the same is not true of the Homeric Aeneas.

2. Pseudo-Xenophon, *Cynegeticus* 1.15:

> Aeneas saved the gods of his ancestors. Then he saved his father and acquired a reputation for piety. As a result, even his enemies let him pass as the only one of all the people whom they had captured in Troy.

> Αἰνείας δὲ σώσας μὲν τοὺς πατρῴους καὶ μητρῴους θεούς, σώσας δὲ καὶ αὐτὸν τὸν πατέρα δόξαν εὐσέβειας ἐξηνέγκατο, ὥστε καὶ πολέμιοι μόνῳ ἐκείνῳ ὧν ἐκράτησαν ἐν Τροίᾳ ἔδοσαν μὴ συληθῆναι.

The passage is unique in that it attests outright Aeneas' claim to a reputation of piety, which even appears to be the sole reason the Greeks permitted the Trojan to depart from Troy. However, while there is considerable disagreement about the date and authorship of the *Cynegeticus*, the proem is gen-

---

[80] Stanford (note 69, above) 250 n. 6.

erally recognized to be a later addition.[81] Estimates of its
date have ranged from the middle of the third century B.C.
to the time of the Second Sophistic, i.e. the second century
A.D. Even if we accept the former date for the proem, it would
coincide with the active propagation of the Trojan legend by
the Romans for political and cultural reasons. By that time,
the Romans had taken the shaping of the legend and its
manipulation into their own hands. A reference to Aeneas'
εὐσέβεια in a Greek source of the period thus can hardly be
interpreted as being based on an early tradition of Aeneas'
piety. It is more likely to reflect a Roman-inspired notion
which presumably was current by the second half of the third
century, although it was to receive stronger emphasis only
later.

3. A similar reference to Aeneas' εὐσέβεια can be found
in the Vatican *Epitome* (21.19) of Apollodorus' *Bibliotheca*:

Aeneas lifted up his father Anchises and fled, and the Greeks
let him pass because of his piety.

Αἰνείας δὲ Ἀγχίσην τὸν πατέρα βαστάσας ἔφυγεν, οἱ δὲ Ἕλληνες
αὐτὸν διὰ τὴν εὐσέβειαν εἴασαν.

Like the *Cynegeticus* prologue, the *Epitome* is a spurious
work, which has wrongly been ascribed to Apollodorus. Its
idiom suggests that it is most probably a work of the first
century A.D.[82] The earliest date that has been assigned to it is
the second half of the first century B.C. By that time, as is
shown by a passage from the *Rhetorica ad Herennium* (4.46)
there was a Roman tradition of *pius* Aeneas.

4. The reference in Lycophron, *Alex.* 1270, to a man
"judged to be most pious by his enemies" (παρ' ἐχθροῖς
εὐσεβέστατος κριθείς), doubtless applies to Aeneas. Again

---

[81] The various scholarly views are summarized by A. Lesky, *A History
of Greek Literature* (New York 1966) 622.
[82] See M. van der Valk, *REG* 71 (1958) 167.

there has been a lively scholarly controversy about the date of the composition of the *Alexandra*.[83] Even if a mid third century date is accepted, this would again be too late to enable us to conclude that the Romanophile Lycophron in this instance was drawing on earlier Greek sources. He apparently made considerable use of Timaeus in his prophecy of Rome's rise (1226-1280) although Lycophron's originality in this instance should not be underestimated. Moreover, fragments from Timaeus' *Troika*, which cannot have been composed before the outbreak of the First Punic War, are, above all, a reflection of Roman customs and tendencies. The scholia, the earliest stratum of which is dated to the first century of our time, give the version familiar from 2 and 3. Significantly enough, the only version of Aeneas' fate referred to in the scholia, which is demonstrably earlier than the third century B.C., contains no allusion whatever to Aeneas' εὐσέβεια but relates his departure with Andromache to Neoptolemus' court.[84]

References to Aeneas' εὐσέβεια in authors such as Diodorus (7.4.1-4) and Aelian (*V.H.*3.22) belong to a period too late to justify the conclusion that there was a literary tradition stressing Aeneas' piety independently of Roman influences. Diodorus, for instance, clearly follows a Roman-inspired tradition in connecting Aeneas with Venus Erycina (4.83.4).[85]

5. Nor is the account in the *Posthomerica* (13.334-349) of Quintus of Smyrna conclusive in this respect. Quintus, who wrote in the fourth century A.D., is sometimes said to have drawn on early Greek epic source, which is otherwise not

---

[83] For a summary see A. D. Momigliano, *RSI* 71 (1959) 551 n. 71. Jacoby, *FGH* III b *Noten zum Kommentar*, p. 332 n. 317, criticizes the assumption that Lycophron merely versified Timaeus' information.

[84] Schol. ad Lycophr. 1270 (ed. Scheer, p. 360): Λέσχης δ' ὁ τὴν μικρὰν Ἰλιάδα πεποιηκὼς Ἀνδρομάχην καὶ Αἰνείαν αἰχμαλώτους φησὶ δοθῆναι τῷ Ἀχιλέως υἱῷ Νεοπτολέμῳ καὶ ἀπαχθῆναι σὺν αὐτῷ εἰς Φαρσαλίαν τὴν Ἀχιλέως πατρίδα. Simmias (cf. below, p. 112) returned to Lesches' version.

[85] See Chapter II, p. 64.

extant.[86] When Aeneas is leaving the burning city of Troy
(13.300-333) and the Greeks try to attack him, Calchas re-
strains them by issuing the prophecy that Aeneas is fated to
establish a sacred city by the Tiber and become the founder
of a new nation. The Greeks are further told not to harm
Aeneas because he is the son of a goddess.

All this has little to do with εὐσέβεια of which no mention
is made. Roman authors had emphasized Aeneas' divine descent, but Poseidon's prophecy and Aeneas' genealogy in *Iliad*
20 provide a strong precedent. The distinctive characteristic
of *pius* Aeneas, i.e. his rescuing the *sacra patriosque penates*,[87]
is conspicuously missing from this account whose Vergilian
echoes are considered inconclusive even by the staunchest
advocates of Quintus' dependence on Vergil.

A theme which had greater continuity in the literary tradition
than Aeneas' εὐσέβεια is the antagonism between Aeneas and
Priam. It finds its clearest expression in *Iliad* 13.459-461.
Priam, unlike the other Trojans, does not honor Aeneas
(οὔ τι τίεσκεν) although Aeneas is a good (ἐσθλός) man. This
very theme is reemphasized in *Iliad* 20, where Aeneas appears
almost as a dynastic rival (178-182), and Poseidon, using
the very words that recur in the *Hymn to Aphrodite* (197-
198), predicts that Aeneas and his descendants will rule over
the Trojans (*Il.* 20.307-308).

Although a few authors described Aeneas' escape without
any bias, others viewed it in connection with the opposition
between the past and the future ruler of Troy, and it therefore
developed implications that were distinctly unfavorable for
the hero. As early as the end of the sixth century B.C., the
logographer Akusilaus asserted that the Trojan War was
instigated by Aphrodite for the sole purpose of establishing
Aeneas in power (*FGH* 2 F 39). In Arctinus' *Iliupersis*, the

---

[86] See, most recently, F. Vian, *Récherches sur les Posthomérica de
Quintus de Smyrne* (Paris 1959) 55-61, 72-76, 96-101, 105-106.

[87] See pp. 59-60, below.

hero cowardly escapes from Troy after watching the serpents attack Laocoon.[88] After giving the account of Aeneas' flight as told by Hellanicus, which he calls "most trustworthy" (πιστότατος), Dionysius of Halicarnassus, in spite of his Roman sympathies, nonetheless feels compelled to devote an entire chapter to summarizing other versions of the same story. He then leaves it up to the reader to decide which of these interpretations is most reliable (1.48). Prominent among these versions is that of Menecrates of Xanthus, who probably lived in the fourth century B.C. After describing the funeral of Achilles, Menecrates relates this:

> The Achaeans were overcome with grief and believed that the army had had its head cut off. Nonetheless, they celebrated his funeral feast and made war with all their might until Ilium was taken by the aid of Aeneas, who delivered it up to them. Because Aeneas was scorned by Alexander and excluded from his prerogatives, he overthrew Priam; and after he accomplished this, he became one of the Achaeans.

Substantially the same version recurs in the *Ephemeris Belli Troiani* of the Cretan Dictys. As the Greeks are about to conquer the city, the Trojans hold a council *ubi multa ab Aenea contumeliosa ingesta sunt* (4.22). Finally, he arranges for the betrayal of the city to the Greeks under the condition that *si permanere in fide vellet, pars praedae et domus universa eius incolumis* (4.22). Ironically enough, Dictys has often been cited by the advocates of a pre-Roman tradition of Aeneas' *pietas*. A closer look, however, shows that in these chapters (4.17 and 18) Aeneas is never called *pius*, and his "pious" actions spring, to a considerable extent, from his opposition to Priam's son Paris. Whatever Dictys' sources may have been,

---

[88] *Epicorum Graecorum Fragmenta* (ed. Kinkel), p. 49. For a more detailed discussion and further testimonia see Förstemann, *Zur Geschichte des Aeneasmythus* 4ff.

his treatment of Aeneas' character shows that, even as late as in the second or third century A.D., the *pius* tradition could easily be subordinated to that of Aeneas the rival of the Priamids and the traitor of Troy, and that no contradiction was seen between the two. Similarly, Aeneas appears as a traitor in the Phrygian Dares' *De Excidio Troiae Historia* (40-41).

Dares and Dictys do not constitute an isolated instance. There are numerous references in post-Vergilian writers that are critical of Aeneas.[89] Furthermore, the Vergilian scholiasts broach the question of Aeneas' treason openly. There can be little doubt that this tendency of post-Vergilian *literati* reflects a literary tradition which did not spring up in reply to Vergil's portrayal of Aeneas, but had its roots in the pre-Vergilian literary tradition. Almost all of the writers in whose works this critical tendency is found were highly erudite people such as Seneca, Tertullian, Porphyrio, and the Vergil scholiasts, and they were familiar even with the more recondite earlier literature.

That this tradition of Aeneas *proditor* was historiographical rather than epic and is frequently found in post-Vergilian sources detracts neither from its authenticity nor from its strength and influence. As a concluding example, which typifies the situation, we may cite the author of the treatise *Origo Gentis Romanae*. In this work, which was composed around A.D. 360, Vergil is used as a source in the early chapters on Italy before Aeneas' arrival, and quotations from the *Aeneid* abound. As soon as the author deals with Aeneas, his method changes and Vergil is replaced by Republican historians as the main source of information. The reason, as Professor Momigliano has rightly pointed out, is that "Vergil on Aeneas was not history."[90] From that point onward the author of the *Origo*

---

[89] The most judicious discussion of the sources is V. Ussani, *Eneide libro II. Introduzione e commento* (Rome 1952) vii-xviii. See also G. Walter, *Untersuchungen zur antiken Aeneiskritik* (Weida 1930), and the works listed in note 3.

[90] *JRS* 48 (1958) 71. References to the relevant bibliography are found

freely elaborated on a book written under Augustus and Tiberius which contained references to earlier writers. One of these was Lutatius Catulus, the consul of 102 B.C. and author of a *communis historia*, who related that Aeneas betrayed Troy (*Or.Gent.Rom.* 9.2). The events are told in reverse order from Pseudo-Xenophon's and Apollodorus' accounts: Aeneas first is permitted to leave (because of his treason) and to take with him whatever he can carry. Then he chooses the Penates and Anchises, and the Greeks, moved by this display of *pietas*, allow him to take along all his possessions (*Or.Gent.Rom.* 9.3-4). As can be seen, the *pietas* and the *proditor* version had coalesced by the second century B.C., even though this source is quoted only by an author in the fourth century A.D.

There is no reflection of Aeneas' *proditio* in ancient art. Too many cities claimed the Trojan as their founder, and even for the mainland Greeks, vase paintings with that subject would not have held any appeal since it would have reminded them of the dishonorable way in which Troy was finally overcome. Besides, this version probably did not belong to the early epic tradition. In mediaeval times, however, the story of Aeneas the traitor finally found its way into art. The mediaeval romances, which were based mostly on Dares and Dictys, linked Aeneas with the story of the stolen Palladium and subtly implicated him in treacherous acts. An artistic representation of this is found, for instance, on a late fifteenth century Franco-Flemish tapestry in Madrid (Fig. 38).[91] Aeneas is so prominent that he appears in three scenes. In the conference scene on the left, Priam is shown standing by an

in Momigliano (pp. 56-73), whose conclusions I have accepted. According to E. Bickel, *RhM* 100 (1957) 201-236, the *Origo* is the epitome of the *Libri Augurales* of C. Lucius Caesar, consul in 64 B.C. The *Origo* is part of F. Pichlmayr's Teubner edition of *Sexti Aureli Victoris Liber de Caesaribus* (1911).

[91] From the Collection of the Duke of Alba. Described by G. L. Hunter, *The Practical Book of Tapestries* (Philadelphia 1925) 80, and M. R. Scherer, *The Legends of Troy in Art and Literature* (New York 1964) 108-109 with fig. 87.

altar and image of Zeus, and he is facing Odysseus who gesticulates vividly. Diomedes and Aeneas, whose names are inscribed on their hats, stand farther back. "The latter looks up sideways from under his downswept brim, his parted lips seeming to convey a surreptitious message to Diomedes."[92] Antenor is a little farther to the right.

The scene in the upper right part of the composition takes place in Minerva's temple. Antenor bribes his former wife Theano, who has been metamorphosed into the priest of Athena, into giving him the Palladium. Aeneas and an unnamed man are shown holding the image in a Gothic shrine in the background. Prior to this treacherous action, Aeneas and Antenor are shown consulting with each other at the entrance of the temple.

A fragment from Naevius' *Bellum Punicum* (23 Strzelecki) may be said to constitute the earliest literary testimony of the reaction to this unfavorable tradition. Aeneas' host, whoever he or she may be,

> blande et docte percontat, Aenea quo pacto
> Troiam urbem liquerit.

The speaker is scrutinizing Aeneas in a sly and shrewd manner; *blande* and *docte* in old Latin is typical of the attitude of those persons who approach someone else with some ulterior and hidden purpose in mind.[93] Aeneas doubtless replied that he had left Troy honorably and thus proved the suspicions of his host to be unfounded. But it is important to note that the hero evidently had to justify himself. In Ennius, Venus herself had to intervene to induce Aeneas to flee, as the hero was reluctant to do so in spite of the prayers of his father (*Ann.* 17-22 Vahlen). It was Vergil who finally created the truly *pius* Aeneas and even turned the hero's flight from Troy to his praise: *fato profugus* (*Aeneid* 1.2). Some of the most

[92] Scherer 108.
[93] See H. Haffter, *DLZ* 58 (1937) 660.

perceptive remarks on Vergil's intent are still those by Tiberius
Claudius Donatus:[94]

> For his task was to present Aeneas in such a way that he
> might prove to be a worthy parent and ancestor of Augustus
> in whose honor the epic was written. Because Vergil was
> to convey to posterity that this very man, Aeneas, had
> emerged as the founder of the *imperium Romanum*, he
> doubtless had to present him, as he did, as being free from
> all blame and as the worthy object of great praise . . .

> By his magical art Vergil clears Aeneas of these accusa-
> tions (of treason). This he does not only with a program-
> matic declaration in the very first lines of the epic, but his
> justification is interspersed throughout all books. Finally—
> and this is the hallmark of a man greatly skilled in rhetoric
> —he openly states the things that could not be denied,
> eliminates the accusation, and then turns it into praise, in
> order to make Aeneas in numerous ways outstanding for the
> very reasons which could give rise to his detraction.

*Ut dignus Caesari, in cuius honorem haec scribebantur, parens
et auctor generis praeberetur*—this explains, more than anything else, why Aeneas was portrayed as *pius* in the epic, and
why *pius* Aeneas became so important a theme in the artistic
and numismatic imperial propaganda. Nor is it coincidental
that the iconography of Pietas did not take on definite form
until the Principate.[95] As Aeneas throughout the epic is in

---

[94] Ed. H. Georgii (Leipzig 1905-1906) 2-3: *talem enim Aenean monstrare
debuit, ut dignus Caesari, in cuius honorem haec scribebantur, parens et
auctor generis praeberetur; cumque ipsum secuturae memoriae fuisset tra-
diturus extitisse Romani imperii conditorem, procul dubio, ut fecit, et
vacuum omni culpa et magno praeconio praeferendum debuit monstrare . . .*

*purgat ergo haec mira arte Vergilius, et non tantum collecta in primis
versibus, ut mox apparebit, verum etiam sparsa per omnis libros excusabili
adsertione, et, quod est summi oratoris, confitetur ista quae negari non
poterant et summotam criminationem convertit in laudem, ut inde Aenean
multiplici ratione praecipuum redderet unde in ipsum posset obtrectatio
convenire.*

[95] See Liegle, *ZfN* 42 (1932-1935) 71. The point that Aeneas' *pietas*

many ways identified with Augustus, so Aeneas' *pietas* typifies that of the ruling monarch. Augustus proudly relates in the *Monumentum Ancyranum* (34) that a golden shield had been set up in his honor in the Curia Iulia because of his *virtus, clementia, iustitia,* and *pietas.* The presentation of this shield was made in 27 B.C.—the very year in which Vergil began composing the epic whose hero was the Julian ancestor. The eagerness of Augustus, *templorum omnium conditor aut restitutor* (Livy 4.20.7), to be considered as *pius* is reflected even in Tacitus' terse account of the emperor's reign. The mention of Augustus' *pietas* is the very first point made in the enumeration of the emperor's praiseworthy deeds (*Annals* 1.9) as well as in their rebuttal: some charged that Augustus assumed his *pietas erga patrem* merely as a mask (*Annals* 1.10). Tacitus here "records faithfully the diverse attitudes to Augustus that were current at the time of his death."[96]

Of course this is not to affirm the romantic prejudice that Vergil was merely an imperial propagandist. Rather, the salient fact with which we are here concerned is that his choice of Aeneas as the official ancestor of Rome was not, in the first century B.C., the matter of course it has been regarded in retrospect. We will return to his adoption—in the fourth and third century—in Chapter IV. Meanwhile, it suffices to say that by the end of the first century B.C., Trojan descent had been the jealously guarded prerogative of a few noble families, the *familiae Troianae,* for the better part of two centuries. Therefore there was at least the possibility that another hero, like Hercules, Odysseus, or Evander, might have been ac-

---

was intended to reflect, above all, the *pietas* of Augustus, was made first by N. Moseley, "Pius Aeneas," *CJ* 20 (1925) 398-400. Cf. Pease, *Liber Quartus,* p. 335, with more bibliographical references, and D. L. Drew, *The Allegory of the Aeneid* (Oxford 1927) 79: "In Augustus' life there is nothing more startling perhaps than his persistent attempt, not indeed to placate the gods—for that is comprehensible enough—but to be really thought pious."

[96] D. C. A. Schotter, *Mn* 20 ser. 4 (1967) 174.

cepted as the popular ancestor of all the Roman people. [97] But since it was Octavian, a member of the Julian family, who asked Vergil to write the epic, Aeneas was selected because of his assumed connection with the *gens* Julia, and "once the choice was made, all the power of Augustan propaganda was used to publicize it and make the Aeneas legend popular."[98] This effort in no way detracts from Vergil's achievement; the popularity, for instance, of the *Odissia Latina* made it a necessity and without it the *Aeneid* might have become no more than the family bible of the Julian *gens*.

We can see now, however, why Aeneas was meant to prefigure Augustus. *Pietas* was the final of the virtues mentioned on Augustus' Golden Shield, and perhaps the most important and inclusive. It reminded the Romans—as did the *pius* Aeneas—that the emperor, *divi filius*, was at once the object of *pietas* from his subjects, and an example to them of *pietas* toward the gods.[99] For this reason the emperors continued to place programmatic emphasis on the *pietas* theme; among the most conspicuous examples are the Ara Pietatis, built by Claudius, Commodus' title *Pietatis Auctor*, and the coins with Aeneas and Anchises, and with Livia as *Pietas*.[100]

Finally, it may be helpful to clarify somewhat more the actual meaning of *pietas* and its iconographic reflections. One assumption, which is implicitly taken for granted in many interpretations of the Aeneas theme in art, is that the representation of Aeneas carrying Anchises inherently serves to convey, above all, the Trojan's *pietas* regardless of the period of its

[97] See H. Hill, *JRS* 51 (1961) 90.

[98] Hill, *loc.cit.*, with reference to Norden's important article in *NJA* 7 (1901) 249ff.; cf. Buchheit, *Sendung* 168. All this also strengthened the relatively late claim of the Julian family to Trojan descent, which is not attested before the first century B.C.; see Münzer, *RE* 10 (1919) 106-107.

[99] See M. P. Charlesworth, *JRS* 33 (1943) 7.

[100] For the Ara Pietatis and its reflection on coins see Ryberg, *Rites* 65-66; the coin with Livia is found in *BMC Coins Emp.* 1.133 no. 98, with pl. 24.7.

occurrence. For the early period, however, i.e. the Greek vase paintings with this motif from Etruria and elsewhere, there is nothing that would enable us generically to interpret this representation in terms of *pietas* or εὐσέβεια. The literary evidence for this particular act of *pietas* is two passages from post-Augustan writers. One is a rather rhetorical discussion by Seneca in *De Beneficiis*.[101] In the light of other comments by Seneca on the character of Aeneas it is difficult to avoid the conclusion that the last sentence is not entirely sincere. The description of Aeneas, who is staggering under the weight of Anchises and the *sacra Troiana*, suggests that Seneca had in mind one of the ever increasing representations of a theme that had received the imperial blessing. Whatever Seneca's feeling may have been, it is worth noting that, in typical Roman fashion, a nexus is immediately established between this act of *pietas* and the foundation of the *imperium Romanum*.

The second testimonium is from a handbook of mythology, the so-called *Fabulae* of Hyginus, which is dated to the time of the Antonines. Aeneas there is grouped with one of two Sicilian brothers, who carried his father on his shoulders from a fiery outburst of Mt. Aetna.[102] In the *pietas* catalogues of Valerius Maximus (5.4-6) and Pliny (*N.H.* 7.121-122) Aeneas is not even mentioned.

Given the absence of early testimonia of this kind and of an early Greek tradition of *pius* Aeneas, a more natural reason for the choice of this theme suggests itself. It expresses best what, in the eyes of the Greeks, was Aeneas' most distinctive achievement: his escape from Troy. The emphasis is on his flight rather than any spiritual qualities that might be

[101] 3.37: *vicit Aeneas patrem, ipse eius in infantia leve tutumque gestamen, gravem senio per media hostium agmina et per cadentis circa se urbis ruinas ferens, cum complexus sacra ac penates deos religiosus senex non simplici vadentem sarcina premeret; tulit illum per ignes et—quid non pietas potest?—pertulit colendumque inter conditores Romani imperii posuit.* Cf. *Ben.* 6.36.1, quoted in note 3.

[102] Hyginus 254.4: *Aeneas item in Ilio Anchisem patrem humeris et Ascanium filium ex incendio eripuit.*

associated with it. To some extent, this may be indicated by
his association, on some vases, with Antenor, although this
pairing with a known traitor might have evoked the dubious
circumstances to which some mythographers had attributed
Aeneas' survival. On the Iliupersis kalyx-krater of the Alta-
mura Painter in Boston, Antenor is shown leading the way
for Aeneas and Anchises (Fig. 39).[103] He encouragingly beck-
ons to them, and Aeneas is obviously cheered by this gesture.
Another example is a late black-figure vase where Antenor,
in Phrygian attire, accompanies Aeneas.[104]

A further indication that Aeneas' piety was not the pre-
ponderant aspect of the Aeneas/Anchises theme in Greek art
is the representations which show Aeneas leading, and not
carrying, his father out of Troy. According to one version of
the familiar story of Jupiter's ire, Anchises was not paralyzed,
but merely blinded by the god's lightning. The earliest iconographic evidence for the connection between *pietas* and the
act of carrying a parent is a coin struck by the Herennian
family shortly after 100 B.C. (Fig. 40a.).[105] A female head,

103 Boston 59.176; described by C. Vermeule in the *Illustrated London
News*, Oct. 10 (1959) 398-399, and by Beazley-Caskey, *Attic Vase Paintings
in the Museum of Fine Arts, Boston* 3.12-15 with suppl. pl. 23; cf. Alföldi,
Early Rome 283. The point should not be overstressed, however, since it
is open to question whether the tradition of Antenor as a traitor goes back
as early as the sixth century; see Perret, *Origines* 172-175, and A. Wlosok,
Die Göttin Venus in Vergils Aeneis (Heidelberg 1967) 42-52.

104 From a private collection in Hamburg. Published by Alföldi, *Early
Rome* 284 with pl. 24.

105 *BMC Coins Rep.* 1.195 nos. 1231-1285 with pl. 30.19-20. T. Mommsen, *Histoire de la monnaie romaine* 2 (Paris 1870) 391 n. 2, and Babelon,
Monnaies 1.539, have plausibly argued that there may be an allusion to the
loyalty of M. Herennius, the grandfather of the magistrate who struck the
coin, to C. Gracchus. *Pietas* on coin issues thus may have had political
overtones from the very beginning. The similarity of this coin to the aureus
issued by Octavian (see note 6) suggests that the former served as the
model for the latter (Fig. 40b). The intent of Octavian's coin certainly was
political. Boyancé (*La religion de Virgile* [Paris 1963] 60-61) and Alföldi
(*Hermes* 65 [1930] 375 n. 1) assume that the Herennius coin represents
Aeneas, but they fail to provide an explanation and overlook Hyginus 254.4
where the two brothers are *singly* compared to Aeneas. Hence there was no
need to represent both.

identified by the legend *Pietas,* is shown on the obverse, whereas the reverse shows a nude male figure bearing a man on his shoulder. The type is considered to refer to a legend of Catana, and to represent Amphinomus or Anapias rescuing his father from an eruption of Aetna. This story is told by Valerius Maximus (5.4.4), who also points out the limits of their *pietas: neutris pro spiritu parentium expirare propositum fuit,* and contrasts this attitude with the unselfish filial devotion of the Scythians. By the first century B.C., then, *pietas erga patrem* was identified with bearing the parent on the shoulder.

It is doubtful that this was the primary meaning of the early representations of Aeneas, let alone the representations in which Aeneas merely leads his father. Again it is important to note that this second type was chosen for a metope of a building which, like the Siphnian frieze, aimed to be emblematic of Greek mythology—the Parthenon. Within the cycle of scenes from the Iliupersis the flight of Aeneas, Anchises, and Ascanius is shown on Metope XXVIII of the north side of the building (Figs. 41a and b).[106] The emphasis once more is on Aeneas the mighty warrior. He wears a tall helmet which is very similar to the one worn by him on an Etruscan statuary group (Fig. 111). With the huge orb of his shield, he is protecting his son, and not his father. Ready to strike any moment, he holds a drawn sword in his right hand, while exchanging a look with his wife Creusa. Aeneas cannot carry his father because this burden would prevent him from using the weapon.

A similar representation recurs on a white lekythos from the Navarra collection in Gela (Fig. 41c).[107] Aeneas, who looks very youthful and is fully armed, carefully leads the blind and slightly stooping Anchises. The contrast between old age

---

[106] See the discussions by F. Brommer, *Die Metopen des Parthenon* (Mainz 1967) 220-221 with pls. 118-122, and C. Praschniker, *Parthenonstudien* (Augsburg 1928) 108-110 with fig. 79.

[107] Benndorf, *Vasenbilder* 99 with pl. 46.1; Beazley, *ARV*² 385 no. 223.

and youth evidently interested the painter most. From a krater in the British Museum (Fig. 42)[108] it is even clearer that the escape of Aeneas' family is what really mattered. The subject once more is the Iliupersis. Aeneas is missing from this painting. Instead, Anchises, who is groping his way with a cane, is leading the little Ascanius from the scene of destruction. The simple fact of the Aeneadae's escape, and not Aeneas' *pietas*, accounts for the adoption of this legend by many cities around the Mediterranean and the popularity of this theme in art.

The early literary and iconographic evidence, therefore, does not make it possible for us to conclude that Aeneas' flight from Troy with his father was taken, at that early a time, as primarily symbolizing *pietas* in general or *pietas erga patrem* in particular. Even in as late a writer as Aelian, Aeneas' *pietas erga patrem* is of secondary importance only. In his moralizing account of Troy's fall (*V.H.* 3.22), the Greeks sympathize with the misfortune of the Trojans and in true Greek fashion (πανὺ Ἑλληνικῶς) give the survivors the choice of carrying off their dearest belongings. Aeneas promptly chooses the ancestral gods. Because of his demonstration of εὐσέβεια, he is given a second choice and only then does he carry off his father. Similarly, when Dido speaks about Aeneas' *pietas*, she first mentions Aeneas' carrying the Penates and then, his father (*Aen.* 4.596-599):

> infelix Dido, nunc te facta impia tangunt?
> tum decuit, cum sceptra dabas. en dextra fidesque,
> quem secum patrios aiunt portare penatis,
> quem subiisse umeris confectum aetate parentem!

These two actions are listed in the same order in Pseudo-Xenophon (*Cyn.* 1.15) and the *Origo Gentis Romanae* (9.2).

This close connection between the ancestral gods and the *pietas* of the hero is important for an understanding of the meaning of *pietas* in Italy. We can be sure that *pietas* in the

---

[108] London F 160; Praschniker, *op.cit.* 109 n. 2.

late sixth and the early fifth century B.C., which is the time of
the first representations of Aeneas on Italian soil, did not have
the same vastly extended meaning which it had at the time
of Augustus and Vergil, when it had become the programmatic
quality of the first citizen, Augustus, and the ideal Roman
citizen, Aeneas. Almost all scholars who have written on this
subject have stressed the fact that the meaning of this term
was subject to various extensions, changes, and reinterpreta-
tions.[109] Because the conclusion that *pietas* by the time of the
early fifth century was a fully developed and almost national
concept cannot be supported by a study of *pietas* itself, the
example of *fides* is often cited as a presumably analogous case.
But this method of analogies rarely works in the study of
Roman religion; what holds good for one cult hardly ever
applies to another, different one. For instance, a temple of
Fides was built between 254 B.C. and 250 B.C., whereas none
was built for Pietas until seventy years later.[110] *Fides*, in contrast to *pietas*, appears to have been a concept which reached
its full development at an earlier time and, so far as we know,
was subject to few changes. *Fides* also appears on coins significantly earlier than *Pietas*. The use of this concept in
Roman policy is well reflected by the famous didrachm of
Locri celebrating the *Fides* of Rome, who is shown crowning
the seated Roma (Fig. 43). The coin is commonly dated to
the time of Pyrrhus and, more conservatively, to the Second
Punic War.[111]

[109] See, for instance, Pease, *Liber Quartus* 333-336; Koch, *RE* 20 (1941)
1221-1232; Liegle, *ZfN* 42 (1932-1935) 59-100; Charlesworth, *JRS* 33
(1943) 1-10; H. Wagenvoort, *Pietas* (Groningen 1924); E. Burck, *Gymnasium* 58 (1951) 174-180; Latte, *RRG* 39-40; H. Doerrie, *AU* 4.2 (1961)
5-27; cf. P. Fécherolle, *LEC* 2 (1933) 167-181.

[110] See Chapter IV, pp. 178-179, and consult the references in Platner-
Ashby, *A Topographical Dictionary of Ancient Rome* (Oxford 1929) 209
and 390. For the tradition of an early Fides shrine in Rome see Wissowa,
RuK[2] 133-134; cf. Alföldi, *Urahnen* 11-12.

[111] Head, *HN*[2] 104 with fig. 57; *BMC Coins Italy* 365 no. 15; the later
date has been advocated by H. Mattingly, *NC* 6th ser. 17 (1957) 288. For

It is better, therefore, to take *pietas* in the more limited meaning with which Aeneas was associated at this early time. A study of the Aeneas legend in Ennius, Cato, Cassius Hemina, Piso, and Varro, and other pre-Vergilian Latin authors, has shown that all these writers emphasized his divine parentage and, in particular, his rescuing the Penates from Troy and bringing them to Italy.[112] This is also Vergil's definition of the purpose of Aeneas' coming to Italy—*inferretque deos Latio* (*Aen.* 1.6)—and it is this aspect of his mission that is emphasized above all others in the *Aeneid*.[113] Aeneas himself programmatically announces this relation between the Penates and his *pietas* when he introduces himself in the epic (*Aen.* 1.378-379):

> sum pius Aeneas, raptos qui ex hoste penatis
> classe veho mecum.

Ovid, finally, simply calls Aeneas *penatiger* (*M.* 15.450).

It is not impossible that a Greek writer before the third century B.C. may have mentioned Aeneas' εὐσέβεια. For lack of evidence, this matter is beyond proof, although the emphasis on this detail strongly suggests that this was something specifically Italic. Because the Aeneas legend in Italy stressed this function of the hero especially, it gained preeminence over other legends:[114]

> It was customary in historical migrations to take the πατρῷοι θεοί to one's new homeland. Because the Aeneas legend in Italy emphasized this aspect in particular, it acquired sacral character and outstanding importance.

There is a close correspondence between the literary tradi-

---

fides as a concept in propaganda see E. Badian, *Foreign Clientelae* (Oxford 1958).

[112] Förstemann, *Aeneasmythus* 49-93.

[113] *Aen.* 1.68; 2.293-295, 717, 747-748; 3.12, 148-159; 4.598; 5.632; 7.120-122; 8.10-13, 39; cf. 12.192: *sacra deosque dabo.*

[114] S. Weinstock, "Penates," *RE* 19 (1937) 456.

tion and some of the earliest artistic representations of Aeneas that were made on Italian soil. On an Etruscan scarab that can be dated to the late sixth century B.C., Aeneas is shown carrying Anchises, who in turn solemnly holds up the *cista mystica* containing the sacred cult objects (Fig. 44).[115] A similar representation recurs on an Etruscan amphora; instead of the *cista*, the wife of Aeneas carries the *doliolum*, the earthen jar, in which, according to several authors, the *sacra* were kept and brought to Italy (Figs. 45a and b).[116] When the motif of Aeneas' flight from Troy had its great revival in the first and second centuries A.D., the *cista*, even on small art objects such as coins and lamps, was almost always represented. It is significant that there is not a single known representation of the *cista* in Greek art, and this, together with the complete lack of an early *pius* Aeneas tradition, indicates that the Greeks, aside from having a part in transmitting the Aeneas legend, were not instrumental in its adoption in Italy. Aeneas carrying the *sacra*—this is the original meaning of the figure of *pius* Aeneas, and we should be careful not to read back into the early days of Rome the vastly more developed and inclusive concept of the *pietas* of the later Republic and the Augustan age.

It may even be suggested that *pietas erga patrem* was only a late, though direct, extension of this original meaning of *pietas*. For Anchises was the bearer of the *sacra* and the *penates* and thus came to share in the *pietas* accorded to them. In the passage quoted earlier,[117] Seneca singles out Aeneas' *pietas* not so much because he carries his father, but because

---

[115] Furtwängler, *Die antiken Gemmen* 1, pl. 20.5, and 2.181; R. Texier, *RA* n.s. 14 (1939) 15 with fig. 1. M. Pallottino, *SE* 26 (1958) 337, dates the scarab to the early decades of the fifth century, but the conclusions reached about the date by Furtwängler, Texier, and Alföldi (*Urahnen* 16; *Early Rome* 284-286) are better supported.

[116] Munich 3185; Beazley, *EVP* 195; Alföldi, *Urahnen* 16 with pl. 14; Schauenburg, *Gymnasium* 67 (1960) 181 no. 58; Riis, *EFH* 13 (1967) 70-72.

[117] See note 101.

the father is a *religiosus senex* who holds the household gods. Ovid implies the same when he says (*Fast.* 1.527-528):

> tum pius Aeneas sacra et, sacra altera, patrem
> adferet.

The fact that most authors mention the rescue of the Penates prior to that of Anchises points in the same direction. Roman writers seem to have been more acutely aware of the original implications of Aeneas' *pietas* than their Greek counterparts although by the end of the first century B.C., as is shown by the Herennius coin, the meaning of *pietas* could be extended to any son carrying his father.

Vergil's portrayal of Aeneas, therefore, has its roots in Italy. It is no coincidence that the Roman poet was the first and only writer who made Italy the native land of Aeneas. The poet gave this *pietas* infinitely more connotations than it had had originally and thus was able to adapt a hero, whose character had been rather contradictory, to his own purposes. *Pius* Aeneas is essentially his creation and this phrase certainly is much more than "a protest against the accusation of treason."[118] But we should be aware that besides a rather positive tradition concerning the hero, there was another, quite influential one which was distinctly hostile to the Trojan. This ambiguity with which not only Aeneas but the Trojans in general were viewed, is a factor that we have to take into account when we turn our attention to Sicily.

---

[118] J. van Ooteghem, *LEC* 20 (1952) 288. The function of the epithet *pius* in the *Aeneid* has been analyzed by U. Knoche in *Festschrift Snell* (Munich 1956) 89-100.

1. Map of Sicily

CHAPTER II

THE LEGEND OF THE

TROJAN LANDING

IN SICILY

ERYX, Polybius (1.55.7) writes, "is a mountain near the sea on that side of Sicily which looks toward Italy." From a geographical point of view, this statement may be debatable (text fig. 1),[1] but it is a good reflection of the successful attempt of the Romans to bring this site in a close relation with their homeland. From the First Punic War onwards the mountain, called San Giuliano today, had definite connotations for the Romans. The precinct of the temple of Aphrodite, protected by huge walls which were said to have been built by Daedalus (D.S. 4.78.4), had been the scene of the most savage fighting of the war from 249 B.C. until its end. In his description of the struggle, which he fittingly characterizes as a *psychomachia*, Polybius compares the two opponents to gamecocks (1.58.7-8) and boxers (1.57.1). Perhaps this episode, coupled with the fact that Eryx was by far the most famous sanctuary in Sicily and its conquest presaged victory, explains the curious mystique and almost magic appeal this place was to have for the Romans.[2] Some Gallic mercenaries, who had capitalized on their desertion

---

[1] By contrast, the orientation of the mountain towards Africa was the basis of Strabo's (6.267; cf. Pliny, *N.H.* 7.85, and Aelian, *V.H.* 11.13) exaggerated claim that one could see the ships in the harbor of Carthage from that part of Sicily on a clear day; cf. the tradition of the ἀναγώγια and καταγώγια (see below) and the Erycina cult in the African Sicca Veneria (Sol. 27.8; Val. Max. 2.6.15; Dessau *ILS* 5505); see also note 26. For detailed topographical discussions see Hülsen, *RE* 6 (1902) 602-604, and Kienast, *Hermes* 93 (1965) 478 n. 1.

[2] This has been suggested by Schilling, *Vénus* 241.

from the Carthaginian to the Roman side by looting the sanctuary, were prevented by the outraged Romans from entering Italy at the end of the war (Polyb. 2.7.9-10). In 217 B.C., in an hour of grave national peril, the cult of the goddess was introduced into Rome and installed on the Capitol, to be followed in 184 B.C. by the temple of Venus Erycina outside the *pomerium* near the Colline Gate.[3] Meanwhile, Eryx in Sicily had become an officially recognized cult center. Diodorus (4.83.4-7) relates that

> the Romans, when they had brought all of Sicily under their domination, surpassed all people before them in the honors they paid to the goddess. They did so for good reasons. For since they traced back their ancestry to her and therefore were successful in all their enterprises, they were only repaying her, the cause of their aggrandizement, with the proper gratitude and honor that were her due. The consuls and praetors who visit the island and all Romans who travel there on state business, embellish the sanctuary with magnificent sacrifices and honors whenever they come to Eryx. They lay aside the austere attitude that goes with their business. Instead, they enjoy themselves and frequent with the women there amid much gaiety. The Roman senate has so earnestly concerned itself with the honors of the goddess that it has decreed that the seventeen cities of Sicily which are most faithful to Rome shall pay a tax in gold to Aphrodite, and that two hundred soldiers shall serve as a guard of her sanctuary.

After Diodorus had cautiously spoken of Aeneas' coming to Eryx and embellishing the sanctuary (4.83.4), and after Cicero had mentioned Segesta's foundation by Aeneas (*Verr.* 4.33), Vergil incorporated the story of the goddess' sanctuary into the story of the origins of Rome (*Aen.* 5.759-760):

---

[3] See Chapter IV, pp. 174-180.

tum vicina astris Erycino in vertice sedes
fundatur Veneri Idaliae.

This version was to survive in later authors as the official one.

Cult provides a convenient point of departure for discussing the tradition of the Trojan landing and settlement in the northwest of Sicily, which is attested especially by Thucydides (6.2.3). According to Dionysius (1.53.1), Aphrodite Aineias had an altar on the summit of Mt. Eryx. The cult of this goddess has often been credited with contributing to the diffusion of the Aeneas legend throughout the Mediterranean.

The extreme scantiness of the evidence suggests that it was not a widespread and ancient cult. No archaeological or epigraphic finds have come to light to enable us positively to identify a sanctuary anywhere with that of Aphrodite Aineias. Our only literary source is Dionysius, who mentions four sanctuaries founded by Aeneas in honor of Aphrodite Aineias at Leucas, Actium, Ambracia (1.50.4), and Eryx, but Dionysius' own sources of information about the cult are unreliable.[4] At the time of Augustus, when Dionysius lived, the epithet "Aineias" was doubtless taken as referring to Aeneas. It is more than unlikely, however, that this cult existed and that Aeneas was associated with it in the early centuries after the fall of Troy. Jean Perret therefore concluded that the appellative "Aineias" was invented in Roman times because the inhabitants of certain Greek towns wished to connect the beginnings of a local cult with the deeds of Rome's legendary founder.[5] A good parallel is found in the title "Goddess Aphro-

[4] Dionysius drew on Hegesianax of Alexandria in the Troad, who wrote a historical novel, the *Troika*; see Ciaceri, *Studi Storici* 4 (1895) 521. His other source was the novelist Hegesippus, on whom see F. Jacoby, *RE* 7 (1912) 2610-2611.

[5] *Origines* 60-61. His view that Varro created the fiction of this cult is not supported. For other theories, most of which assume the existence of the cult in early times see, e.g., Farnell (Chapter I n. 17) 638-642; E. Meyer, *Geschichte des klassischen Alterthums* 2 (Stuttgart 1893) 428-429; G. J. Laing, *CJ* 6 (1910-1911) 59-64; Malten, *ARW* 29 (1931) 46; J. A. Brinkman, *CJ* 54 (1958-1959) 27. Cf. Chapter V, p. 218.

dite Anchiseias" with which the inhabitants of the Troad later honored Livilla, the wife of Drusus.[6] This example suggests that an epithet of this kind could easily be invented without having any basis in cult. Numerous instances show that this kind of intentional appeal by Greek cities to the Trojan sentiment of the Romans was politically profitable and even could lead to freedom from taxation. The date of the only piece of evidence that has been adduced in support of the cult of Aphrodite Aineias, besides Dionysius' four references to it, coincides with the period of political and cultural manipulation of the Trojan legend by both Greeks and Romans,[7] and further suggests that political reasons were instrumental in the creation of this cult.

This evidence is the coins of Leucas which were struck around 167 B.C., after Leucas, like all of Greece, had come under Roman domination. The coins (Fig. 46)[8] show a composite type of goddess with symbols such as an aplustre, a stag, a crescent, ears of grain, a dove, and an owl, although the identity of the last two has been disputed because of the bad condition of the specimens. The goddess represented has a hieratic appearance; the arrangement of her hair resembles a turban, and she is crowned with a wreath of laurel or myrtle. Since all these symbols, with the possible exception of the aplustre, are not uncommon for Artemis, most numismatists identified the figure with that goddess until Ernst Curtius proposed interpreting her as Aphrodite Aineias.[9] This interpretation generally has been accepted.

It is implausible to assume that the "Aphrodite Aineias"

[6] *IGRR* 4.206=Dessau *ILS* 8787; Ehrenberg-Jones, *Documents Illustrating the Reigns of Augustus and Tiberius*[2] (Oxford 1955) no. 93. Cf. H. Seyrig, *RA* n.s. 4 (1929) 93-94.

[7] See Chapter IV.

[8] Head, *HN*[2] 330-331; *BMC Coins Thessaly* 179-180 nos. 78-103, with pl. 28.15-16; G. Macdonald, *Catalogue of the Hunterian Collection* 2 (Glasgow 1901) 25 nos. 5-7, with pl. 32.7; *SNG* 11-15, *Epirus and Acarnania*, pl. 9, nos. 377-384.

[9] *Hermes* 10 (1876) 242-243.

cult at Leucas was created overnight without any local precedents on which it could graft itself.[10] This is also true of the Eryx "Aphrodite Aineias," whose forerunners included the Phoenician Astarte. What, then, were the local precedents at Leucas?

The female head which appears on Leucadian coins issued around 330 B.C. (Fig. 47) has been identified by several scholars as that of Aphrodite, whereas others have interpreted the figure merely as a local nymph.[11] The iconography indeed is too little specific to point to a particular cult of Aphrodite such as the Aphrodite of seafaring, Aphrodite Pelagia.[12] On the reverse of the Leucadian Aphrodite coins appears a trident or a rudder, but these symbols are found on the reverse of most Leucadian coins and therefore cannot be considered as specific attributes of the Leucadian Aphrodite.

The proximity of Leucas to Cephallenia seems to have been part of the reason the goddess of Roman Leucas was endowed with the symbols of Artemis and was called "Aineias." Cephallenia had a long-established cult of Zeus Ainesios, which took its name from Mt. Ainos and is attested as early as Hesiod.[13] This Cephallenian Ainesios cult may well have provided the "Aeneadic" environment for the Aphrodite cult at Leucas. The latter thus could credibly be linked to Aeneas, for both the hero's name and the epithet "Ainesios" were thought of in antiquity as being derived from αἰνός, i.e. "terrible."

The reason for the Leucadians' decision to borrow from the cult of Artemis on Cephallenia is somewhat different. The

---

[10] This is the opinion, e.g., of R. Texier, *RPh* 60 (1934) 159-164.

[11] *BMC Coins Thessaly* 175 nos. 26-31, with pl. 28.5; *SNG* 11-15, *Epirus and Acarnania*, pl. 8 nos. 362-366; F. Imhoof-Blumer, *NZ* 10 (1878) 130 no. 37.

[12] Pace Texier, *loc.cit.*, who believes that the Leucadians revived an ancient seafarers' cult of Aphrodite and purposely connected it with Aeneas to please their Roman masters.

[13] Hesiod *Catal.* fr. 67 (Marckscheffel); Schol. Apoll. Rhod. 2.297; Strabo 10.456; *Etym. Magn.* 153.41. See also the remarks of R. H. Klausen, *Aeneas und die Penaten* 1 (Hamburg und Gotha 1839) 394-395 with note 628, and Bürchner, *RE* 11 (1921) 210.

most plausible explanation is the striking coincidence between the cult environments at Leucas and Eryx.[14] Both cults centered around the worship of Aphrodite. In addition, however, Cicero (*Verr.* 4.33-34) relates the existence of an ancient and much revered cult statue of Artemis at Segesta. According to him, it was *summa atque antiquissima praeditum religione* and one of the city's main sights:

> All this proves only that this was one of the most important cults of Segesta and suggests that this Diana is none other than the goddess of the city which is shown on the coins.[15]

Both the Leucadian coins and the Segestan ones share in the crescent as a common symbol of Artemis (Fig. 48). Like the Leucadian Aphrodite coins, the Segestan coins have been considered to represent a local nymph rather than Artemis, although an identification with Aphrodite Urania has also been proposed.[16] It is possible, therefore, that the composite and somewhat ambiguous older types of the "Trojan" Segesta, which claimed Aeneas as her founder since the First Punic War (Fig. 49) and was closely associated with the Eryx sanctuary in Roman times,[17] may have served as a model for the Leucadians. For while the cult of Erycina was widespread even prior to their arrival, the Romans enhanced its prestige even more by associating it with the legend of their origins and

[14] Cf. Texier, *RPh* 60 (1934) 163: "L'existence . . . d'un culte d'Aphrodite Ainéias était certes un argument profitable, surtout si l'on identifiait à l'Erycine, protectrice vénérée des Romains." Texier does not develop this point further.

[15] Ziegler, *RE* 2A (1921) 1069, with further ancient and modern sources.

[16] For the crescent on Segestan coins see G. F. Hill, *Coins of Ancient Sicily* (Westminster 1903) 213; Rizzo, *Monete* pl. 61.4-5 (Fig. 48); cf. *BMC Coins Sicily* 130 nos. 65-66 (the Augustan coin with Aeneas and Anchises). Rizzo 283 argues in favor of the nymph Segesta, Ziegler 1068 in favor of Aphrodite Urania, whose cult is attested by *IG* 14.287. E. Gabrici, *Problemi di numismatica greca della Sicilia e Magna Grecia* (Naples 1959) 12-14, has some sound comments on nymphs in Sicilian coinage, including the coinage of Eryx and Segesta.

[17] See Chapter IV, pp. 172-174. The coin was issued soon after 241 B.C.; see Head, *HN*[2] 167, and *BMC Coins Sicily* 137 nos. 59-61.

giving it an important part in their political and cultural campaign to demonstrate their Greek-mindedness.[18] With the help of borrowings from Cephallenia, the Leucadians may have been able to create a believable, composite "Aphrodite Aineias" type, which was reminiscent of the cults and the Aeneadic environment of the Sicilian northwest. The local Aphrodite could cleverly be transformed into an Aphrodite Aineias, and the similarities with Eryx and Segesta were apt to give more credence to the claim that Aeneas had founded the Leucadian sanctuary.

The ears of grain which appear both on the coins of Zeus Ainesios[19] and the Leucadian Aphrodite Aineias issues are a further indication that Leucas may have drawn on Cephallenian cults to legitimize its new goddess. The same symbol is found on the coins of Eryx and Segesta (Fig. 50).[20] Further similarities between the Segestan and Cephallenian coinages include the recurrent representation of a hunter with spear and dog, who has been identified with Cephalus on Cephallenia (Fig. 51) and Aigestus in Segesta (Fig. 52).[21] Nor is the adoption of Sicilian coin types by the Acarnanians without precedent. The crowned female head, for instance, which appears around 370 B.C. on the obverse of the Cephallenian coins with Cephalus on the reverse, was copied from Syracusan types.[22]

In sum, ill-attested as it is, the existence of a particular cult of Aphrodite Aineias can be proved by no numismatic in-

[18] Cf. Chapter IV. The testimonia for the Eryx cult outside of Sicily have been collected by Jessen, *RE* 6 (1907) 564-565.

[19] Head, *HN*[2] 428. For the Leucadian coin see also *AJA* 70 (1966) pl. 54 fig. 19.

[20] Eryx: Head, *HN*[2] 138; Rizzo, *Monete* pl. 64.8-10. Segesta: Head 165-166; Rizzo, pl. 62.6, 9, 11; pl. 63.7, 8, 9; *BMC Sicily* 134-135 nos. 36-39.

[21] Cephallenia: *BMC Coins Pel.* 84-85 nos. 1-23, pl. 17.9-20; Head, *HN*[2] 427-428. Segesta: Rizzo, *Monete* 290, with pls. 61.18-21; 62.14-15; 63.7-9; Head 166; *BMC Coins Sicily* 133-134 nos. 30-34.

[22] Head, *HN*[2] 428. The Syracusan coinage at various times also influenced the Eryx issues; see, most recently, S. Consolo Langher, *Contributo alla storia della moneta bronzea in Sicilia* (Milan 1964) 83.

genuity. By using this title, Dionysius seems to refer to some local cults of Aphrodite which were brought into a connection with Aeneas in Roman times. A connection of this kind certainly imposed itself at Actium. Dionysius' mention of such a cult at Eryx reflects the close association which the Romans, ever since the First Punic War, had endeavored to establish between the Sicilian sanctuary and the story of their origins. It is, however, a completely inadequate basis for the hypothesis that a migration of real Trojans to Sicily ever took place. The extent to which the Sicilian cult may have inspired the Leucadian one is an additional indication of the popularity and importance in the western Mediterranean of Erycina worship, the political overtones of which were well recognized in Roman times.

The Eryx goddess had been worshiped for many centuries before her cult was connected with Aeneas.[23] Unfortunately, the archaeological remains of the site give us little information about the architecture of the ancient sanctuary. Today the temenos is dominated by a castle built in Norman times (Fig. 53), when the northwest of Sicily took as independent a development from the rest of the island as it did in antiquity. Of the pre-Roman temple no trace has been found, except for a triglyph which may have belonged to the primitive temple and been used again in its reconstruction by Claudius. This lack of material supports the local tradition of a deliberate destruction of the temple *ab imis fundamentis*. The orientation of the temple, so far as it can be reconstructed, was not east-west, but northeast-southwest, which would suggest a non-Hellenic origin.

[23] The Erycina cult has been the subject of several detailed discussions, in particular those of Jessen, *RE* 6 (1907) 562-567; Ciaceri, *Culti e miti* 76-89; Holm, *Geschichte Siciliens* 1.86-91; Schilling, *Vénus* 233-266; Pace, *Sicilia antica* 3.630-647; Manni (Chapter I n. 1) 79-91, 233-236.

For the report on the most recent systematic excavations of the sanctuary in 1930-1931 see G. Cultrera, *NSA* n.s. 11 (1935) 294-328. A summary is given by U. Zanotti Bianco, *JHS* 56 (1936) 218-221.

The architecture of the building followed Hellenic conventions. This we can gather from its representations, simplified and schematic as they may be, on the coins of C. Considius Nonianus (Fig. 54a).[24] On top of a rocky elevation appears a small tetrastyle temple, which in reality may have been amphiprostyle. If the triglyph belonged to the actual temple building, the shrine of Eryx would have had a front of about 33 to 48 ft., and thus was well suited for the discovered ditches and embankments which measure about 75 ft. in length.[25]

The cult at Eryx was an ancient one. The numerous legends concerning the city and the sanctuary point to an early period of habitation, as do the neolithic finds that have been discovered at the site and now are in the Trapani and Erice Museums. The earliest stratum of the cult, that of the native Sicanian population, which is attested by Diodorus (4.83.4), is no longer open to scrutiny. The Phoenicians, who may have arrived at Eryx as early as the 12th century B.C., and who worshipped the goddess under the name Ashtoreth Erech, were not the earliest occupants of the Eryx site. However, many aspects of the cult are so permeated by Phoenician characteristics that it is virtually impossible to draw any detailed inferences about the nature of any pre-existing worship at Eryx. The strongest indication of this Phoenician influence is the annual rites of ἀναγώγια and καταγώγια when the pigeons sacred to Erycina disappeared and then returned after nine days. This was interpreted as the goddess' annual visit to her "sister sanctuary" in the Libyan Sicca Veneria.[26] On some

[24] *BMC Coins Republic* 1.473 nos. 3830-3832, with pl. 47.21; Sydenham 147 nos. 886-889. See also T. L. Donaldson, *Architectura Numismatica* (Chicago 1965) 110-115.

[25] Cultrera 312; Zanotti Bianco 220.

[26] Aelian, *N.A.* 4.2; cf. Athenaeus 9.394-395 (quoting Aristotle). Solinus 27.8 identifies the Siccan Astarte with the Erycinian Aphrodite; cf. note 1.— The frequently voiced assumption that the Eryx goddess originally was a Mediterranean fertility goddess rests on no positive evidence besides the presumed similarity between the doves of the former (Figs. 50, 55b) and those

of the huge fortification walls at Eryx (Fig. 56) this influence is still attested by the Punic mason's marks although Diodorus, as we saw earlier, ascribed the walls of the sanctuary proper to the time of Daedalus and King Minos.

Consequently it is not surprising that the symbols found on the coinage of Eryx and Segesta, such as the dog (Figs. 48, 50, 55a), the wheel, and the ears of grain (Fig. 50), as well as the practice of sacred prostitution at the sanctuary, have been regarded as testimonies to the Phoenician influence. Although alternative interpretations have been suggested,[27] this explanation is for the most part correct and receives new confirmation from the picture that especially recent finds have given us of the considerable influence of the Phoenicians on the civilizations of Sicily from the eleventh to the eighth century B.C.[28] Scholarly speculation has regarded the oriental character of the cult as proof of an Anatolian-Trojan migration to Sicily.[29] More probably, however, it reflects the century-long domination of the cult by the Phoenicians and later, the Carthaginians.

---

of the Minoan "Dove Goddess" (Fig. 57); see, ultimately, Evans, *Palace of Minos* 4.960. The identity, however, of the Minoan "doves" is far from clear, and the existence of a syncretistic Mediterranean *koine* of cults is purely conjectural; see M. Nilsson, *The Minoan-Mycenaean Religion and its Survival in Greek Religion*[2] (Lund 1950) 336-338, 392-396.

[27] For the dog, see Ciaceri's plea for "il cane come elemento indigene, e non simbolo di riti religiosi asiatici" (*Culti e miti* 126), and, somewhat more judiciously, Pace, *Sicilia antica* 3.633. For the wheel, see Schilling, *Vénus* 237 ("un vieil héritage mediterranéen"), and Pace 633 (an indication of "il patrimonio indigene"). The hieroduleia at Eryx is placed in the wider context of this phenomenon by F. Cumont, *The Oriental Religions in Roman Paganism* (New York 1956) 118 with notes 40 and 41 on pp. 246-248; for its Phoenician manifestations, including on Cyprus, see G. Garbini, *Kokalos* 10-11 (1964-1965) 59.

[28] For an excellent, judicious summary see L. Bernabò Brea, *Kokalos* 10-11 (1964-1965) 12-23; cf. V. Tusa, *ibid.*, 589-602, and *Eretz-Israel* 8 (1967) 50-57. See also below, pp. 100-101.

[29] As was posited by Malten, *ARW* 29 (1931) 46; cf. Dunbabin, *The Western Greeks* 336, and F. Altheim, *Italien und Rom* 2 (Amsterdam 1943) 34. The Phoenician aspects of the cult have most recently been stressed by Garbini (note 27, above) 59 although one must be aware of "il fatto della pluralità delle componenti." (62).

Nonetheless, the ancient notices about the rites at Eryx show that they were sufficiently different from the other Phoenician and the Greek cults on the island to merit special attention. The goddess was not worshiped in a roofed temple, but all sacrifices took place in the open air on an altar which was surrounded by an enclosure. Aelian (*N.A.* 10.50) relates that

> upon it [the altar], many sacrifices are offered, and all day long and into the night the fire is kept burning. The dawn begins to brighten, and still the altar shows no trace of embers, no ashes, no fragments of half-burned logs, but is covered with dew and fresh grass which comes up again every night.

The finest architectural monument to these rites has been preserved not at Eryx, but at nearby Segesta. This is not surprising as both cities belonged to the same cultural environment, that of the Elymians. The so-called temple at Segesta (Fig. 58) is Doric and dates from the last quarter of the fifth century B.C. The Segestan temple is distinguished from many others by the extreme diligence of its workmanship, by the regularity of its square stones, by the perfection of its forms, and by its large dimensions. It therefore has been called a splendid monument to the complete Hellenization of the architecture of a barbarian city.[30] The Greek influence, however, seems to have been restricted to the outer form of the building. No trace has been found of the cella and its foundation, and the peristasis formed only the decorative enclosure for an altar which, like the altar at Eryx, stood under the open sky.[31] The deity to

[30] So R. Koldewey and O. Puchstein, *Die griechischen Tempel in Unteritalien und Sizilien* 1 (Berlin 1899) 132.

[31] So Pace, *Sicilia antica* 2.236-237; L. von Matt, *Das antike Sizilien* (Würzburg 1957) 172; L. Bernabò Brea, *Musei e monumenti in Sicilia* (Novara 1958) 114; H. Berve and G. Gruben, *Greek Temples, Theatres, and Shrines* (New York 1963) 443; V. Tusa, *AA* (1964) 771 n. 105. The opinion that the temple was left unfinished had most recently been repeated by A. Burford, *CQ* n.s. 11 (1961) 87-93. Burford's arguments are (a) a

which the temple was dedicated is not known, and the data about the place of discovery of a dedicatory inscription to Aphrodite Urania (*IG* 14.287) are too imprecise to be related to this building.

An earlier sanctuary at Segesta may have set the pattern. Remains of a large precinct (83.4 by 47.8 meters) are in the course of being excavated on a hillside to the south of the Monte Barbaro, the so-called Contrada Mango. The walls are Greek (Fig. 59) and architectural remains such as capitals of at least three Doric buildings have been discovered at the site. The earliest architectural remains date from the first half of the sixth century B.C., and the sanctuary apparently was abandoned in the fifth, in favor of the new "temple" that had been built. What is striking is the total lack of any Greek sherds; only the native, Elymian ware, dating from the eighth and seventh centuries, has been found there. The preliminary conclusion, which of course has to be confirmed by further excavations, is that Greek architectural forms were borrowed for a precinct in which Elymian rites were performed.[32]

The closest parallels to the peculiarities of the cults at Eryx and Segesta are found on Cyprus. The Aphrodite at Paphos also

---

building inscription from Epidaurus (*IG* 4². 1.102), but the crucial passage is a lacuna restored by Burford; (b) some building blocks shown in J. I. Hittorff and L. Zanth, *Architecture antique de la Sicile* (Paris 1870), pls. 3 and 4, which cannot be shown to have belonged to a cella; (c) that the Segestans built the temple around 416 in a flourish of Hellenizing to impress the Athenians. There was no need for this: Greek influence on Segestan pottery starts as early as the eighth century B.C. (see below), copious Corinthian and Attic sherds were found at Segesta, the honors the Elymians accorded Philip, a companion of Dorieus, in 510 were as Greek as can be (Herod. 5.47), and a treaty between Segesta and Athens had already been concluded in 458/457 (see A. E. Raubitschek in *TAPA* 75 [1944] 10-15), and now there is the further evidence of the archaic sanctuary.

[32] Preliminary discussions have been published by V. Tusa in *Kokalos* 3 (1957) 85-89; *Atti del Settimo Congresso Internazionale di Archeologia Classica* (Rome 1961) 31-40; and *AA* (1964) 766-771. Cf. M. Guido, *Sicily: An Archaeological Guide* (New York 1967) 69.

was worshiped on altars under the open sky, and Aelian's description of the cleanliness of the sacrifices to Erycina is paralleled by Servius' and Tacitus' accounts of the sacrifices at Paphos.[33] Furthermore, the legends associate the Eryx sanctuary closely with the sea. The eponymous hero Eryx appears as the son of Poseidon or of the Argonaut Butes who, in turn, is but a hypostasis of the sea god.[34] Butes was indispensable for explaining the nature of the cult. Therefore he, and not his son Eryx, who received his name from the Greek transcription of the indigenous name of the site, is the reigning monarch in Diodorus' account of Heracles' coming to Sicily (4.24.2). In this legend, which dates from Mycenaean times, the hero Eryx does not personify any of the essentials of the cult. His death, therefore, does not greatly matter because Butes-Poseidon, the sea god and real cult hero, will still survive.

Given the legendary and, of course, geographical connection between the Eryx sanctuary and the sea, the Eryx goddess is likely to have been that Venus Marina—the Greek Aphrodite of seafaring—whose cult in the western Mediterranean is mentioned by Avienus. It is attested by other authors also, and Avienus' own sources are generally believed to be early as well as reliable.[35] This goddess again appears to be the same kind of Aphrodite who was worshiped as a sea goddess on Cyprus at Amanthus and Paphos.[36] It is also worth

[33] Servius, *Aen.* 1.335: *Paphiae Veneri quae Cypri colitur, ture sacrificatur et floribus*; Serv. auct., *ibid.*: *ture calent arae, sertisque recentibus halant.* Tac., *Hist.* 2.3.5: *sanguinem arae obfundere vetitum; precibus et igne puro altaria adolentur.* I owe this point to Schilling, *Vénus* 237 and note 6, who suggests the reading *floribus* for *precibus* in the Tacitean passage.

[34] See Apoll. Rhod. 4.912-919; Apollod. 1.9.25; Schol. Theocr. 15.101; D.S. 4.83.1; Servius, *Aen.* 1.570; 5.24, 412; Steph. Byz. s.v. "Ἔρυξ"; and Wernicke, *RE* 3 (1897) 1080-1081.

[35] Avienus *Ora Maritima* 158, cf. 315, 437. For further sources and discussions see A. Schulten, *Klio* 23 (1929-1930) 424-427.

[36] See R. Dussaud, *RHR* 73 (1916) 245-258, where additional documentation for the Paphian Aphrodite Pelagia can be found; cf. Schmidt, *RE* 18 (1949) 959-963.

noting that the Sicilian poets Theocritus and Calpurnius readily associate the Eryx goddess with the Cyprian Aphrodite.[37]
Since the Paphian Venus originally was not a manifestation
of the Phoenician Astarte and a Greek cult was never super-
imposed on the Elymian-Phoenician cult at Eryx, the common features of the Cypriote cult and the Sicilian one may
thus go back to pre-Phoenician times, although Phoenician
influences came to be dominant at Eryx and perhaps at Paphos
also. In the seventh and sixth centuries B.C. terracotta statuettes
of a female deity (Fig. 60), most probably the Eryx goddess,
follow the Cypriote style, but the type is not uncommon in
Sicily and belongs to a period too late to allow any conclusions
about the origin of the cult in prehistoric times. We will see
shortly, however, that the Phoenicians are likely to have ef-
fected the connection between Cyprus and the northwest of
Sicily.

Eryx and Segesta were cities of the Elymians. As in the
case of the Etruscans, it would be utterly futile and even pointless to scrutinize the available evidence pertaining to this people with the purpose of solving the enigma of its origins,
although most scholarly studies of the Elymians have been
devoted to this one objective. Rather, the Elymian problem
is an Etruscan problem *in parvo*, i.e. a problem of formation
rather than origins. As in Etruscology, the historical notices
about the Elymians, which are preoccupied with the question
of origins as is most of the ensuing scholarship, have recently
been supplemented by archaeological and linguistic finds
which set in relief the uniqueness of their civilization in the
northwest of Sicily. It therefore is our task to study the historical tradition and the archaeological evidence, and to see

---

[37] Calpurnius calls the Erycina Dione (*Ecl.* 9.56-57), which was one of
the favorite titles of the Cyprian goddess; see A. S. F. Gow, *Theocritus* 2
(Cambridge 1950), *ad Id.* 15.106. Theocritus speaks of Κύπρι Διωναία after
calling on the Eryx goddess (*Id.* 15.106), and in *Id.* 7.116, the phrase
ἕδος αἰπὺ Διώνας suggests that he was thinking of Erycina; cf. *iuga celsa
Erycis* (Calp., *Ecl.* 9.58).

whether an analysis of both combined sheds some light on the reason this people was said to have descended from Trojan immigrants.

The two earliest sources for the origin of the Elymians are the Greek historians Hellanicus and Thucydides. According to Hellanicus, who is quoted by Dionysius of Halicarnassus, the Elymians were part of the Sikels who migrated from Italy to Sicily around 1270 B.C.:[38]

> In this manner, the Sikel nation left Italy, according to Hellanicus of Lesbos, in the third generation before the Trojan War, and in the twenty-sixth year of the priesthood of Alcyone of Argos. But he says that two Italian expeditions passed over into Sicily, the first consisting of Elymians, who had been driven out of the country by the Oenotrians, and the second, five years later, of the Ausonians, who fled from the Iapygians.

Hellanicus' account of the Elymian migration was almost immediately corrected by Thucydides, who based his version on that of the historian Antiochus of Syracuse and who was followed by virtually all later authors.[39]

> After the fall of Troy, some of the Trojans, who had escaped the Achaeans, came in boats to Sicily. They settled

[38] D.H. 1.22.3 - *FGH* 4 F 79b: τὸ μὲν δὴ Σικελικὸν γένος οὕτως ἐξέλιπεν Ἰταλίαν, ὡς μὲν Ἑλλάνικος ὁ Λέσβιός φησι, τρίτῃ γενεᾷ πρότερον τῶν Τρωικῶν, Ἀλκυόνης ἱερωμένης ἐν Ἄργει κατὰ τὸ ἕκτον καὶ εἰκοστὸν ἔτος, δύο δὲ ποιεῖ στόλους Ἰταλικοὺς διαβάντας εἰς Σικελίαν. τὸν μὲν πρότερον Ἐλύμων, οὕς φησιν ὑπ' Οἰνώτρων ἐξαναστῆναι, τὸν δὲ μετὰ τοῦτον ἔτει πέμπτῳ γενόμενον Αὐσόνων Ἰάπυγας φευγόντων.

[39] Thuc. 6.2.3: Ἰλίου δὲ ἁλισκομένου τῶν Τρώων τινὲς διαφυγόντες Ἀχαιοὺς πλοίοις ἀφικνοῦνται πρὸς τὴν Σικελίαν, καὶ ὅμοροι τοῖς Σικανοῖς οἰκήσαντες ξύμπαντες μὲν Ἔλυμοι ἐκλήθησαν, πόλεις δ' αὐτῶν Ἔρυξ τε καὶ Ἔγεστα. προσξυνῴκησαν δὲ αὐτοῖς καὶ Φωκέων τινὲς τῶν ἀπὸ Τροίας τότε χειμῶνι ἐς Λιβύην πρῶτον, ἔπειτα ἐς Σικελίαν ἀπ' αὐτῆς κατενεχθέντες. Philistus of Syracuse (*FGH* 556 F 46) also denied that the Elymians participated in the Italian migration to Sicily. The Trojan origins of Segesta and the Elymians are further attested by Lycophron 951-977 with the scholia; Apollod., *FGH* 244 F 167, Cicero, *Verr.* 4.33; Strabo 6.272; 13.1.53 p. 608, Vergil, *Aen.* 1.549-550 and 5, passim, with Servius' scholia; D.H. 1.52-53.1; Silius, *Pun.* 14.220; Plutarch, *Nic.* 1.3; Festus 458L.

as neighbors of the Sicanians and they all together were called Elymians, and their cities were Eryx and Segesta. With them settled some Phocians who had come from Troy and had been driven by a storm first to Libya and from there to Sicily.

Both authors agree that the Elymians, or at least a part of them, came from abroad, although their views about the exact provenience of this people are different. Thucydides gives a more precise account of the ethnic composition of the Elymians. He views them as a mixed people of native Sicanians and ethnic elements from the eastern Mediterranean, who for certain reasons were called Trojans. A third cultural component of the Elymi was the Phocians, who lived very closely nearby, and Thucydides' phrasing implies a similarity of manners and customs between them and the "Trojanized" Sicanians.[40]

Hellanicus is less precise because his notice reflects the political situation in Sicily in the sixth century B.C. At that time, the Elymians' state had reached the stage of its greatest territorial expansion and occupied most of the Sicanian territory. Therefore the Sicanians were not even mentioned by Hellanicus, because they were indistinguishable, at the time, from the Elymians.[41]

Hellanicus' version was not accepted by anyone else, and the archaeological finds also support Thucydides' account rather than Hellanicus'. There is no evidence that the Sikels,

[40] For this use of ὅμοροι, cf. Arist., *Eth. N.* 3.5.2. For the interpretation of the Thucydides passage in the light of the archaeological finds see especially Bovio Marconi in *La ricerca archeologica nell'Italia meridionale* (Naples 1960) 233. The older literature on the Elymians is vast, and only the most pertinent discussions may be mentioned here: Bérard, *Colonisation*[2] 352-364, 456-458; Pais, *Storia della Sicilia e della Magna Grecia* 1.123-145; Pace, *Sicilia antica* 1[2].116ff.; Holm, *Geschichte Siciliens* 1.86-90; Freeman, *The History of Sicily* 1.542-559; Dunbabin, *The Western Greeks* 335-338, and especially R. van Compernolle, *Phoibos* 5 (1950-1951) 183-228.

[41] So van Compernolle 216.

whom Hellanicus partially identified with the Elymians, brought any culture of their own to Sicily. If they came from central or southern Italy soon after 1270 B.C., we should expect to find in Sicily traces of a sub-Apennine or post-Apennine civilization. None have been found to date that would relate to the migration of the Sikels. Beginning with the thirteenth century, however, the inhabitants of the southeast of the island abandoned the coastal plains and fled to the least accessible hill country so as to be better protected from invaders. But whereas these Sikel invaders prevailed politically, their culture was absorbed by the superior one of the natives, and no distinctly Siculan culture is revealed by the archaeological finds.[42]

The archaeological picture in the Eryx-Segesta region is different. The inhabitants of that region shared in the Conca d'Oro culture, the beginnings of which can be traced approximately to 1500 B.C.[43] This was the culture of the native Sicanians, and its characteristic, incised pottery style persisted into the late Bronze Age, i.e. ca. 1000 B.C. A typical example of this culture is a glossy vase, found at Segesta, with a tall, cylinder-shaped neck and a somewhat globular body (Fig. 61). In technique and decoration it is very similar to a cup from Isnello (Fig. 62), which is to the east of Palermo (text fig. 1). Both pots are made of the same dark material and have the same glossy red coating. The surface of both vases is divided into horizontal zones by incised bands, which are plain, while the zones themselves are decorated by groups of four or six oblique lines, which alternately converge and diverge.

At a later period, especially the eighth and seventh centuries B.C., the *facies* in the northwest of Sicily again was not

---

[42] The problems of Siculan archaeology are discussed in more detail by Bernabò Brea, *Kokalos* 10-11 (1964-1965) 24-33, and *Sicily*[2] 141-144.

[43] This culture has been discussed in detail by Bovio Marconi, *MAL* 40 (1944) 1-170; see *ibid.* 74 for the examples listed in the text.

self-contained, but its incised pottery belongs to the Sant'Angelo Muxaro style.[44] Typical of this ware are small pots with incised or impressed geometric designs such as small concentric circles, triangular patterns, lozenges, and stipple decorations (Fig. 63). The same kind of pottery has been found throughout western Sicily—for instance, at Motya, Eryx, Polizzello near Mussomeli, and Prizzi—but also as far east as Morgantina (text fig. 1).

While the incised pottery from the Elymian territory shows a general affinity to the pottery decoration of Sant'Angelo Muxaro, "which is altogether different from eastern Sicily,"[45] the ceramic finds also have several features which are peculiar to Eryx and Segesta. From Segesta have come vases, native ware of the eighth, seventh, and perhaps even ninth centuries, with stylized handles shaped like the faces of humans and animals (Fig. 65).[46] They have no parallels elsewhere in Sicily. The same schematization appears on the bronze fibulae found at Segesta. Several specimens show a modification of the usual Sicilian elbow fibula in that the spiral, which supports the pin, is shaped like an animal's head with two horns or feelers (Fig. 64).

On the basis of this evidence, the scantiness of which should be stressed, Professor Iole Bovio Marconi, the former Superintendent of Antiquities in Palermo, has come to rather far-reaching conclusions. "Anthropomorphic" stylized vases are known from pre-Mycenaean sites of the eastern Mediterranean, notably Troy, where they were found in strata II to V (Fig.

[44] For the Sant'Angelo Muxaro ceramic style see P. Orsi, *Atti Acc. Palermo* 3rd ser. 17 (1932) fasc. 3, and Bernabò Brea, *Sicily*[2] 173-174, and *Ampurias* 15-16 (1953-1954) 207-208. I cannot agree with Bovio Marconi, *Ampurias* 12 (1950) 79-90, and Tusa, who call this style "Elymian."

[45] Bernabò Brea, *Sicily*[2] 174, though see E. Sjöqvist, *AJA* 62 (1958) 157 with pl. 29, fig. 9 g-h, for the finds from Morgantina.

[46] More detail in Bovio Marconi, *Ampurias* 12 (1950) 82-83 with pls. 2a, 3b, 4b; id. (note 40, above) 232-233 with pl. 47; cf. Bernabò Brea, *Sicily*[2] 176-177 with fig. 42; *Kokalos* 10-11 (1964-1965) 11, 28.

66),[47] and Cyprus. According to Professor Bovio Marconi, the closest parallels to the anthropomorphic schematizations and the incised patterns of the Eryx-Segesta pottery are the flat, red-polished idols from a tomb of the necropolis of Lapithos on Cyprus (Fig. 67). In her view the similarities seem to extend to the very arrangement of the incised decorations.[48] Some similarities are undeniable, but if we accept the most recent chronology that has been proposed for Middle Cypriote I, the Cypriote finds belong to the period of ca. 1800 B.C., the latest date ever proposed for the end of Middle Cypriote I. Moreover, Lapithos had lost all its importance by the beginning of Late Cypriote I, which is dated to either 1600 B.C. or 1550 B.C.,[49] whereas the earliest Elymian finds date to the eighth century. Because of the lack of intermediary evidence, it would be a hazardous hypothesis to argue in favor of cultural dependence, let alone continuity.

Recent excavations at Segesta have given us a somewhat better picture of the Elymian ware and its tradition. A truly enormous number of ceramic fragments, at times more copious than the very soil, has come to light in the middle of the northeast slope of the Monte Barbaro (Fig. 68, cf. text fig. 1). The site is directly beneath the top of the mountain on which

[47] See R. Dussaud, *Les civilisations préhélléniques*[2] (Paris 1914) 132-134, figs. 96 and 97 (Troy) and 366, figs. 271 and 272 (Cyprus); C. W. Blegen *et al.*, *Troy* 1 (Princeton 1950) pt. 1.236 and 353; pt. 2 fig. 370b C 30; for the Cypriote evidence, also see the following note.

[48] *Ampurias* 12 (1950) 84, 88-89; followed by Pace, *Sicilia antica* 1[2].562. The Lapithos idols have been published by E. Gjerstad, E. Sjöqvist, and A. Westholm, *The Swedish Cyprus Expedition* 1 (Stockholm 1934) 93 nos. 20, 21, 40, with pl. 26 (Lapithos Tomb 313B); P. Astrom, *The Middle Cypriote Bronze Age* (Lund 1957) 152 fig. 16.1; National Museum Copenhagen, Dept. of Oriental and Classical Antiquities, *Catalogue of Terracottas* pl. 1.1 and 2 (inv. 6534 and 6535); cf. Karageorghis, *ND* 47 no. 109 (from the Pendayia Necropolis).

[49] Astrom 273 has proposed the latest date for the end of Middle Cypriote I, whereas most scholars date it 300 years earlier. On Lapithos, see *ibid.* 278. For the date of the beginning of Late Cypriote I see E. Gjerstad, *Studies on Prehistorical Cyprus* (Uppsala 1926) 332-333 (1600 B.C.), and E. Sjöqvist, *Problems of the Late Cypriote Bronze Age* (Stockholm 1940) 193 (1550 B.C.).

stood the ancient city of Segesta. A Hellenistic city was built over the old,[50] and its most splendid monument is its theater dating from the third century B.C.

The ceramic finds come from an unstratified deposit and it is therefore impossible to establish a precise chronology. The bulk of the finds comprises sherds of local painted ware, but there also are some fragments of local incised pottery, and a goodly number of fragments of imported Corinthian and Attic ware. The fragments seem to come from varied and numerous types of vases. The latest finds are datable to the middle of the fourth century, which thus gives us a *terminus ante quem*. It can be assumed that all this material was thrown from the top of the mountain during an at least partial destruction of the city in that century. The historical event which fits the situation best is the devastation Segesta suffered at the hands of Agathocles' army in 307 B.C. (D.S. 20.71).

The incised pottery mostly consists of Sant'Angelo Muxaro ware (Fig. 69), and there were further finds of "anthropomorphic" vase handles. Another motif, which in Sicily so far has been found only on the incised ware from Segesta, is concentric circles connected by a diagonal line. This motif is found frequently on Mycenaean painted vases.[51]

Several of the patterns on the painted pottery from Segesta are Geometric and belong to the style of decoration whose distribution in the western Mediterranean has been well described by Alan Blakeway.[52] Prominent among the designs

[50] Cf. the remarks by Tusa, *Kokalos* 3 (1957) 85-88. I am indebted to Soprintendente Tusa for permission to use his paper entitled "La questione degli Elimi alla luce degli ultimi rinvenimenti archeologici," a summary of which has appeared in *Atti e Memorie del Primo Congresso Internazionale di Micenologia* 2 (Rome 1968) 169-170. My conclusions, however, on both details and the general problem, are somewhat different from his.

[51] Furumark, *MP* motive 46; Karageorghis, *ND* fig. 50.5 (Kition); F. H. Stubbings, *Mycenaean Pottery from the Levant* (Cambridge 1951) 27 fig. 3 (Enkomi), 63 fig. 18 (Gezer). The motif, however, also occurs on Geometric ware: *NSA* 6 (1928) pl. 9; *ABSA* 33 (1932-1933) pl. 29.63; A. Akerstrom, *Der geometrische Stil in Italien* (Uppsala 1943) pl. 16.24.

[52] *ABSA* 33 (1932-1933) 170-208 with pls. 22-35.

of this style is a thick, wavy line between two horizontal lines, which is usually found at the neck or handle zone of the vase (Fig. 70.9-10).

Other patterns, however, are local imitations of decorations that originated in Mycenaean times and are found predominantly on Mycenaean and Submycenaean pottery. A good example is the schematized drawing of a bull (Fig. 70.8), moving from the left to the right with horns butting against an unidentified object. This motif was a common one on Mycenaean and, more generally, Aegean pottery. The Mycenaean specimens[53] are drawn with greater care whereas the Segestan bull, a late reminiscence of this common Mycenaean motif, is sketched more in outline fashion. Several fragments (Figs. 71.1, 72.4 and 8) show a stylized floral motif that is known as "parallel chevrons." This pattern also was very common on Mycenaean pottery.[54] Similarly, the tassel type of decoration beneath the meander pattern in Fig. 71.5 occurs on Mycenaean vases especially of the late and Submycenaean period, and the running spiral underneath it recalls yet another Mycenaean motif.[55] Another floral decoration, resembling a stylized star, is very similar to the Mycenaean "sea anemone" motif (Fig. 72.4, 73.3 and 5).[56]

Whereas the preceding motifs are not paralleled in Geometric pottery, other patterns on the Segestan sherds have decorations for which it is possible to find Mycenaean antecedents but which also, to some extent, continued during the Geometric style. This does not permit us to state conclusively whether the Elymians, in these instances, drew directly on Mycenaean traditions or whether they imitated Geometric

[53] Furumark, *MP* motive 3.27-28; Karageorghis, *ND* figs. 53-54, pls. 23.5 and 27.6.

[54] Furumark, *MP* motive 58, esp. 58.28-29; Stubbings 62 figs. 17 and 19; Karageorghis, *ND* fig. 48.3; Taylour, *Mycenean Pottery* pl. 6.22 and 25.

[55] Tassel: Furumark, *MP* motive 72.12-13, also found on another Segestan fragment: *AA* (1964) 767 fig. 74. For the running spiral see note 51.

[56] Furumark, *MP* motive 27, esp. 27.13; Stubbings 50 fig. 2; 55 fig. 12.

decorations. A prominent example of this kind of decoration is the bundles of thin, wavy lines (Figs. 71.2 and 4; 74.3, 4, 6, 7, 9; 75.6). The motif is well attested for the late Mycenaean period, but it also occurs on Geometric vases, including those found in the western Mediterranean.[57] Much the same can be said of the zigzag pattern (Fig. 75.11), the concentric circles (Figs. 70.1 and 6; 72.6; 73.2), and the paneled patterns consisting mostly of six thin vertical lines perpendicular to one or several lines extending around the body of the vase (Figs. 70.3, 72.1 and 2).[58]

Many parallels to this latter group and the Mycenaean-inspired group of decorations can be seen on pottery found on Cyprus and, to a much smaller extent, in the Levant and Anatolia.[59] The continuing interest of the Segesta region in the artistic traditions of the eastern Mediterranean is attested by the decoration on one sherd (Fig. 70.2) which is clearly reminiscent of the lotus motif. The best parallels date from the orientalizing style of approximately the middle of the seventh century.[60] The same kind of artistic influence is evident from another find, the head of a small female terracotta statuette

[57] Furumark, *MP* motive 53; F. Biancofiore, *La civiltà micenea dell'Italia meridionale* 1, *La ceramica* (Rome 1963) 107 fig. 14.1, pls. 12.73, 21.205, and 31; Taylour, *Mycenean Pottery* pl. 2.2 ("Local" Mattpainted ware from Lipari), pl. 15.20 (Iapygian Geometric); V. R. d'A. Desborough, *The Last Mycenaeans and their Successors* (Oxford 1964) pl. 2b and 8 (Late Helladic III B and C). Geometric: *ABSA* 33 (1932-1933) pl. 26.43, pl. 31.71, 75, 77; Akerström, *Der geometrische Stil in Italien* pl. 6.12, 15, 16; pl. 16.10, 13, 16, 19; K. Kübler, *Kerameikos* 5.1 (1954) pl. 135.

[58] Zigzag: Furumark, *MP* motive 61, esp. 61.2 and 4; Akerström pl. 6.22; 16.14 and 17; 21.2; 23.26. Concentric circles: Furumark, *MP* motive 41. 12-16; Akerström pl. 6.7; 16.15; 23.20; *ABSA* 33 (1932-1933) 185 fig. 9. Metopal pattern: Furumark, *MP* motive 75.15 and 28; Karageorghis, *ND* fig. 11.19, 31, 94; Desborough pl. 2a. The meander (fig. 71.5) is common on Protogeometric and Geometric vases: J. K. Brock, *Fortetsa* (Cambridge 1957) pl. 19.301; *ABSA* 33 (1932-1933) pl. 27.52; Akerström pls. 2.2; 16.8; 18.3 and 4; 23.12; E. Akurgal, *Die Kunst Anatoliens* (Berlin 1961) fig. 45; Kübler, *Kerameikos* 5.1, passim.

[59] See especially the references to Karageorghis, Akurgal, and Stubbings in the previous notes.

[60] Gjerstad (above, note 48) 4.2, fig. 18; Brock pl. 89.1318; pl. 122.

(Fig. 76). It was made of reddish clay and perhaps is an ex-voto. Peculiar to this head are the bulbous irises of the eyes, which are further accentuated by the pieces of clay that outline the eyes. Rhodian and Cypriote parallels of the late seventh century can be adduced although the closest resemblance, especially to the eyes and the arrangement of the hair, is found in Anatolian statuette heads of the late eighth century.[61]

Before trying to explain why the inhabitants of Segesta and Eryx were called "Trojans," we must place the Segestan finds in their proper perspective and in the context of our knowledge about Sicily before the Greeks. Contacts with and reminiscences of other cultures are not uncommon for civilizations in other parts of Sicily also and they are documented by both literary tradition and archaeological evidence. For instance, the legend of Heracles' exploits in Sicily (D.S. 4.23) is a reflection of Mycenaean trade contacts with the island.[62] Mycenaean sherds have come to light especially in the Syracusan area. The finds mostly date from the Mycenaean III B period (1300-1230 B.C.) and are of Cypriote provenience.[63] The Sicilian Castelluccio culture of the early Bronze Age and the Thapsus culture of the Bronze Age are permeated by Aegeo-Anatolian elements "which would speak in favor of their eastern origin."[64] The parallels that have been discerned between the script of the Aeolian islands and the Cypro-Minoan one[65] also testify to eastern Mediterranean influences in the Sicilian region which, even if they were trans-

[61] Akurgal figs. 17-28, esp. 19; cf. V. Müller, *Frühe Plastik in Griechenland und Vorderasien* (Augsburg 1929), pls. 31.342 and 49.452; R. A. Higgins, *Catalogue of Terracottas in the British Museum* (London 1954) figs. 21 and 23.

[62] See E. Sjöqvist, *Opusc. Rom.* 4 (1962) 117-123; cf. F. H. Stubbings, *CAH* 2² (1963) ch. 14, 29-30; Taylour, *Mycenean Pottery* 189-190.

[63] The evidence has been collected and discussed by Taylour 54-80.

[64] Bernabò Brea, *Sicily*² 142.

[65] See L. A. Stella, *ArchClass* 10 (1958) 283 and note 5.

mitted by merchants or navigators, also were cultural in the wider sense of the term.

The finds in the Elymian region take on their full significance in the light of the literary tradition, which recognizes that the integrity of the Elymians is not only cultural but ethnic. A goodly part of their pottery consists of local imitations of late Mycenaean and Submycenaean patterns of decoration. It appears that for such a tradition to continue, more than sporadic trade contacts were necessary. This sets the territory of Segesta, Eryx, and Entella[66] apart from Sant' Angelo Muxaro. There splendid gold rings were found which date from the sixth century B.C., but clearly presuppose an earlier cultural tradition. Most of them are decorated with Geometric patterns except for two rings, one of which shows a cow suckling her calf (Fig. 78a), the other a strange feline animal, or perhaps a wolf (Fig. 78b). Concerning these representations one scholar recently summarized the opinion of many by stating: "Perhaps here again we have a far distant echo of the Mycenaean world."[67] Again it would be hazardous, on so tenuous a basis, to postulate the existence of a Mycenaean settlement or continuous Mycenaean cultural traditions at Sant'Angelo Muxaro, which at least one scholar has tried to identify with the ancient Kamikos, the court of the legendary Sicanian king Kokalos.[68] In contrast to Eryx and Segesta, the archaeological evidence at Sant'Angelo Muxaro, which is reminiscent of Mycenaean traditions, is not corroborated by any literary tradition.

At the other extreme are the interpretations that have been given to the legend of Minos and Daedalus. According to Diodorus (4.79), Daedalus fled to king Kokalos in Sicily, who

[66] Where several sherds, now at the Soprintendenza alle Antichità in Palermo, were found in a mountain cave without a formal excavation.

[67] Guido (note 32, above) 130. Cf. P. Orsi, *Atti Acc. Palermo* 3rd ser. 17 (1932) 273 with fig. 3, and 279 with fig. 8; Pace, *Sicilia antica* 1² 164-165 with figs. 78-79; Bernabò Brea (note 44, above) 197 with fig. 30.

[68] P. Griffo, *Ricerche intorno al sito di Camico* (Agrigento 1948).

had the pursuing king Minos of Crete suffocated in the bath. Some of Minos' Cretans stayed on at Minoa, where they built a splendid monument to their dead king, which was connected with a temple of Aphrodite. The building is said later to have been destroyed by Theron, the tyrant of Acragas. Our only sources for it are literary, but nonetheless Professor Dunbabin, followed by most scholars, has come to the following conclusion:[69]

> The discovery of the Temple-Tomb at Knossos provides the most convincing proof that the tradition of a Minoan colony in Sicily is genuine. It corresponds so closely with Diodorus' description of the double building the front part of which was a Temple of Aphrodite and the hidden back part the tomb that there need be little doubt that a similar building existed at Minoa. The Temple-Tomb had been lost to sight for centuries before Theron discovered the tomb at Minoa, which must genuinely have been a tomb of the same sort, and Minoan. The view that the Minos story is no older than the Greek colonization of Sicily cannot explain this monument. The name Minoa must have the same origin as the Minoas in the Aegean, in a colony or trading post from Crete.

In the absence of any supporting archaeological evidence this argument has to remain rather tenuous and hypothetical, especially as the monument in Knossos is no tomb.

The contrast with Sant'Angelo Muxaro and Minoa sets in relief the coincidence between the literary tradition, composed of Thucydides and later writers, and the archaeological evidence pertaining to the Elymians. It is remarkable that the notice about this people is the first passage in Book Six

[69] *PBSR* 16 (1948) 8-9. G. P. Carratelli, *Kokalos* 2 (1956) 89-104, has tried further to corroborate the historicity of this legend with Linear B evidence; cf. M. P. Nilsson, *Opuscula Selecta* 3 (Lund 1960) 504-509. I share, however, the skepticism of G. Becatti, *MDAI(R)* 60-61 (1953-1954) 30-32, and Taylour, *Mycenean Pottery* 188-189.

which Thucydides does not qualify by saying "as is reported" (λέγονται) or "as it seems" (φαίνονται) and thus affirms as the truth, the ἀλήθεια. Nonetheless, Thucydides' reference to the Trojans, like references to Trojan settlements in all of ancient literature, cannot be taken literally but is best understood as concerning ethnic elements from the eastern Mediterranean.[70] Their exact provenience is not known nor is the exact time of their migration, although some answers may be suggested. Incomplete as it is, however, the evidence establishes beyond any doubt that by the eighth century, if not by the ninth, a people lived at Segesta and Eryx which had its own artistic traditions, different from the rest of Sicily, its own language and its own cult. Future excavations, it is hoped, will give us a fuller picture of many details.

The affinity of several decorative patterns on the Segestan pottery with Mycenaean ware chiefly from Cyprus should not lead us to conclude that the ethnic influx from the east actually came from Cyprus. Cyprus was instrumental in the Mycenaean overseas trade with Sicily, i.e. especially the area around Syracuse, and Apulia, and Cypriote influence can once more be traced in Sicily during the Geometric period.[71] As for western Sicily, it is possible, if not likely, that the connection between Cyprus and the Eryx-Segesta region may have operated through the Phoenicians. The Mycenaean motifs that are imitated on the Segestan finds date mostly to the twelfth and eleventh centuries, which would coincide with the beginning of Phoenician colonization of the west.[72] Nor is this incon-

[70] Cf. Bovio Marconi, *loc.cit.* (note 40 above). Pais, *Storia della Sicilia* 139 already differentiated somewhat less precisely: "E storico l'elemento indigeno dei Sicani . . . mitico è invece l'arrivo dei Troiani."

[71] Taylour, *Mycenean Pottery* 187.

[72] For a summary of the various scholarly views on the beginning of the Phoenician "colonies" in the west see V. Tusa, *Eretz-Israel* 8 (1967) 50-51, and especially G. Garbini, "I Fenici in Occidente," *SE* 34 (1966) 111-137. The earliest Phoenician find on the coasts of Sicily dates from the twelfth or eleventh century; see S. Chiappisi, *Il Melquart di Sciacca e la questione*

sistent with Thucydides' statement that the migration took place after the fall of Troy, although the Thucydidean passage should not be pressed for a precise chronology and may indicate merely that these events took place before the beginning of the Greek colonization of Sicily in the eighth and seventh centuries B.C. Moreover, from the end of the ninth century the Phoenicians had a firm foothold in Kition on Cyprus. This is the earliest time to which the Mycenaeanizing sherds from Segesta can actually be dated, although most of them seem to come from the next two centuries. This chronological retardation of Mycenaeanizing motifs, especially from the Submycenaean period, is not unparalleled.[73]

Unlike the Greek colonization later, the Phoenician one was largely restricted to trading ports or *emporia*. Segesta had a flourishing emporium in today's Castellamare (text fig. 1) and here the Phoenicians, for once, may have penetrated the hinterland and intermingled with the natives. The predilection of the Phoenicians for Greek artistic traditions is well attested by the remains of their colony at Motya where they modeled virtually everything, except for religious and funeral rites, on Greek examples.[74] It therefore does not seem impossible that the Phoenicians might have been carriers of a late Mycenaean tradition, but the earliest evidence at Motya dates from the seventh century and of course is not Mycenaean. Besides, Thucydides, who speaks of the close association between Phoenicians and Elymians after the arrival of the Greeks (6.2.6) never identifies the two with each other. This, however, does not preclude the possibility that Antiochus and

---

fenicia in Sicilia (Rome 1961). G. L. Huxley, *PP* 12 (1957) 209-212, argues that Thucydides and Hellanicus placed the Trojan War in the middle of the thirteenth century.

[73] See Gjerstad (note 60, above) 436-442 on the Phoenician colony at Kition. At Vrokastro on Crete, Mycenaean and Submycenaean motifs survived into the eighth and seventh centuries; see P. Demargne, *La Crète dédalique* (Paris 1947) 98-100, 106; cf., on this general question, Biancofiore (note 57, above) 92-99, and S. Wide, *MDAI(A)* 22 (1897) 233-258.

[74] G. Whitaker, *Motya. A Phoenician Colony in Sicily* (London 1921).

Thucydides may have known that the Elymians at least in part were Phoenicians; we shall see shortly that there were compelling reasons for a Greek writer to call them "Trojans" rather than Phoenicians.

The third ethnic and cultural component of the Elymians, i.e. the Phocians, further testifies to the early date of the contacts and influences of Greek civilization on the Elymian one. Here the archaeological finds again support the literary sources, although they are of course not sufficient to prove the immigration specifically of Phocians to the Sicilian northwest. Besides the architectural evidence from the archaic sanctuary at Segesta this eagerness of the Elymi for Hellenism is also borne out by the early imitation, which we have noted, of Greek geometric patterns on the painted pottery of the Eryx-Segesta region. Another, most splendid testimony to the Hellenic tendencies of the Elymians is the sequel to the Spartan Dorieus' unsuccessful attempt to gain a foothold at Eryx in 510 B.C. He was slain with his companions, among whom was Philip of Croton, an Olympian victor and the most beautiful Greek of his time. The Segestans honored him by building a heroon over his grave and making sacrifices to appease his spirit and to secure his favor. Herodotus (5.47) says explicitly that the honors accorded Philip were without parallel, because of his beauty.

The definition of the Elymian question as an Etruscan question *in parvo* applies particularly to the linguistic evidence. It is comprised of the early coin legends of Eryx and Segesta, especially the puzzling legend appearing on Fig. 77, and some one hundred and thirty graffiti (Fig. 79), many of which were found in the deposit on the slope of the Monte Barbaro (Fig. 68). The inscriptions so far have defied decipherment and have been considered both Greek and, more probably, non-Greek—but, at any rate, Indo-European.[75] Like the arguments

[75] The graffiti have been published by Tusa, *Kokalos* 6 (1960) 34-48 and *Kokalos* 12 (1966) 207-220. Meanwhile several more have been found which

from toponymy, the interpretations of the scant linguistic evidence are conflicting and have been used to postulate a descent of this people from almost every region between Anatolia and the Pillars of Heracles. The true value of this evidence once more is not the encouragement of largely inconclusive speculations about the origin of the Elymians, but it is an additional strong proof of the distinctiveness of their culture. This disproves, for instance, the theory that "Elymian" was not an ethnic term, but a political one, denoting the Phoenician-oriented cantons of the Sicanians.[76] The Segestans probably imported their alphabet, which has many Corinthio-Megarian characteristics, from Selinus. In view of the marked interest of the Elymians in Hellenic civilization and of the close, though fluctuating, relationship between Segesta and Selinus, this is not surprising.

The Thucydidean tradition and the material aspects of Elymian culture as revealed by archaeology agree that they were a people which evolved *in situ* by the admixture of elements from the eastern Mediterranean and Greek immigrants to a native, Sicanian substratum. It remains to analyze why it was exactly this small and somewhat obscure people that was credited with Trojan descent.

The legend of Trojan descent is not limited to the Elymians but is found in many parts of the Mediterranean. Although each of these foundation legends has to be treated on its own

---

still await publication. The controversy about the Elymian language dates back to K. F. Kinch, *ZfN* 16 (1888) 187-207, who tried to demonstrate that the Elymians were Phocaeans. Recent discussions, with references to the older literature, include U. Schmoll, *Die vorgriechischen Sprachen Siziliens* (Wiesbaden 1958) 4-19; cf. Pisani, *Gnomon* 34 (1962) 192-193; Schmoll, *Sprache* 7 (1961) 104-122 and *Kokalos* 7 (1961) 67-80; R. Arena, *AGI* 44 (1959) 17-37; M. Durante, *Kokalos* 7 (1961) 81-90. The toponomastic-linguistic speculations underlying Malten's theory of a migration of Trojan Elymians, led by Aeneas (*ARW* 29 [1931] 56-59; cf. Bömer, *Rom und Troia* 29-30; Büchner, *RE* 8A [1958] 1443), are a product of the scientific optimism that was typical of classical scholarship early in this century, and they are completely untenable.

[76] This was posited by U. Kahrstedt, *WJA* 2 (1947) 16-32.

merits, some general considerations apply to all of them.[77]
The most obvious of these is that the Trojans were the most
famous fugitives of the ancient world and therefore readily
suggested themselves as the founders of settlements elsewhere.
A more detailed attempt to explain the origin of local Trojan
legends was made by Ettore Pais, and is in some respects a
somewhat more specific elaboration of a similar theory advanced by Mommsen.[78] Pais contends that wherever Greek
colonists from Asia Minor settled, they tended to identify the
indigenous populations with their former neighbors, the Trojans. According to Pais, this was especially the case when
their contacts with the natives were hostile. To make this
theory work in Sicily, Pais, like so many other scholars, converted Thucydides' Phocians into Phocaeans. The latter were
well known for their daring voyages to the western Mediterranean from the end of the seventh century onward when
they founded several colonies, among them Massalia. This
is much too late a period, however, to make sense in Thucydides' passage, and it is questionable that five hundred years
after the fall of Troy colonists from Asia Minor still considered the Trojans, whom they knew only from hearsay, as
their chief adversaries. In contrast to the Phocaeans, the
Phocians participated in the Trojan War and the subsequent
nostos, and the Phocian settlements in the western Mediterranean are mentioned by other authors also.[79] By adopting a
different reading, therefore, Pais actually weakened his own
case. As for the main point of his theory, i.e. the identifica-

[77] The *locus classicus* for Trojan legends is J. Perret's monumental study,
Les origines de la légende troyenne de Rome. Despite its main thesis, which
has generally been rejected, it represents the most comprehensive collection
of the evidence to date. For the legendary Trojan diaspora in the western
Mediterranean see also Bérard, *Colonisation*[2] 323-384.

[78] Pais, *Storia della Sicilia* 451-452, 470-471. For a summary of Mommsen's and also de Sanctis' views see Boas, *Arrival* 10-12.

[79] Pausanias 5.25.6; Strabo 6.1.14; Steph. Byz. s.v. "Λαγάρια"; Ephorus
FGH 70 F 141; Pliny *N.H.* 3.72; Vell. 1.1.1; Justin 20.2.1. Cf. F. Zucker,
WJA 4 (1949-1950) 335-339.

tion of native peoples elsewhere with tribes in Asia Minor by Greek colonists from Asia Minor, it has rightly been objected that this assumption does not explain the genesis of Trojan legends everywhere. Such legends were current, for instance, in Epirus and Cyrene where no Greek colonists from Asia Minor ever settled.[80] Pais tried to support this theory by adducing the analogy of the Bebrycians in Spain who were named after the Bebrycians of Asia Minor by the Phocaeans.[81] The Trojan legend, however, was more widespread and the instrumental role in its genesis cannot be restricted to the Greeks of Asia Minor.

The basis of the identification of barbarians with Trojans was certainly not, as a famous scholar once asserted, an attitude of implacable enmity on the part of the Greeks toward the Trojans.[82] The Greek attitude to the Trojans was more complex, for although the Trojans had been their enemies, they also had Greek ancestry. While the Trojans by some were regarded as *barbaroi* they had, by the time of Homer, come to be considered as belonging "to the most venerable and widely-known of Greek sagas," and for this reason "were accepted by the Greeks as a portion of their common past."[83] The arts provide further examples of the conception that the Trojans were merely other Greeks.

The oldest preserved vase painting which doubtless was inspired by the Trojan War is a polychrome Rhodian plate (Fig. 80) representing the fight of Hector and Menelaos over the slain Euphorbus.[84] It dates from the last quarter of the seventh century. The representation of the two Trojans differs

---

[80] Perret, *Origines* 6-7.

[81] *Studi Storici* 4 (1895) 80-104.

[82] U. von Wilamowitz-Moellendorff, *Herakles* 1[2] (Berlin 1895) 32-33. Against this widely accepted argument see, for instance, the judicious remarks of P. Boyancé in *REA* 45 (1943) 278.

[83] Bickerman, *CW* 47 (1943-1944) 95.

[84] British Museum A 749; discussed by A. Schneider, *Der troische Sagenkreis in der ältesten griechischen Kunst* (Leipzig 1885) 12-17, and Johansen, *Iliad* 77-80 with fig. 18.

in no respect from that of Greek hoplites. Only the inscriptions serve to distinguish the combatants. The same holds good of the representations of the Trojans in sculpture and vase painting which have been discussed in the preceding chapter.

Even at the time of the Persian Wars, the Trojans were not differentiated from the Greeks in combat scenes. On a cup in the manner of Douris, which dates from ca. 475 B.C., Hector and Achilles are represented almost identically (Fig. 81).[85] Outside of Iliadic scenes, however, the Trojans began to appear in Phrygian costume on the stage as well as in vase painting. This is illustrated by the cover of a pyxis in Copenhagen, which shows the arrival of the three goddesses on Mt. Ida for the judgment of Paris (Fig. 82).[86] Whereas Paris in red-figure vase painting before the Persian Wars was dressed in a himation, chiton, or chlamys, he now appears increasingly often in a gaudy Phrygian dress (cf. Fig. 34) and the Phrygian cap which is familiar to us from the representations of Ascanius in the Aeneas-Anchises groups (Figs. 1, 6, 27, 29, 30).

Whereas the Trojans were not represented differently from the Greeks before the Persian Wars, other nationalities appeared in their native "barbarian" costume even in black-figure vase painting. This applies especially to the Cimmerian and Scythian archers, who were distinguished by their characteristic pointed caps. Regardless of whether they were allied with the Greeks, they were always differentiated from the latter by their native insignia. A good example is the scene with the Calydonian boar hunt on that compendium of Greek mythology, the François Vase (Fig. 83),[87] where one of the

[85] Beazley, *ARV²* 449 no. 2.

[86] *CVA Denmark* fasc. 4 (*National Museum Copenhagen* fasc. 4) 125-126 with bibliography and pl. 163.1; also, C. Clairmont, *Das Parisurteil in der antiken Kunst* (Zurich 1951) 54 with pl. 35. Clairmont discusses the change in Paris' appearance on pp. 104-106. References to the costume of the Trojans on the Attic stage can be found in H. H. Bacon, *Barbarians in Greek Tragedy* (New Haven 1961).

[87] Florence 4209; *ABV* 76 no. 1. A. Minto, *Il vaso François* (Florence 1960), discusses the representation of the Calydonian hunt on pp. 27-36

archers is identified as Κιμεριος. Bý contrast, on the black-figure amphora showing the battle over the body of Achilles (Fig. 96), Paris' weapon also is the bow, but his dress is that of an Ionian hoplite.

Art and literature make it abundantly clear that the Trojans could be viewed both as Greeks and as non-Greeks. The latter attitude has been emphasized by Professor Bérard in his explanation of the genesis of the legendary Trojan diaspora.[88] Because the Trojan War, he argues, was depicted from early times as a crusade of the Achaean Greeks against the pre-Hellenes, the *barbaroi*, some of the most ancient populations of Italy could be regarded as having Trojan ancestry. The same would apply to the Elymians, who by Thucydides and others expressly are called βάρβαροι. But Bérard's theory again is only partially valid. It does not explain why it was only certain *barbaroi* that were identified with Trojans and why there were no Trojan legends in many other places where Greek colonists or traders came into contact with pre-Hellenic populations. More importantly, Bérard overlooks two further basic factors that were at work in the creation of Trojan foundation legends. One is that the Greeks craved Greek ancestry for the barbarians.[89] Settlements in the western Mediterranean were traced back not only to the Trojans but also to the Argonauts, Heracles, Odysseus, Philoctetes, Epeios, some companions of Nestor, and others. The second is that the barbarians, in turn, eagerly accepted the Greek or Trojan interpretation of their origins.[90] This gave them the opportunity to share in the splendor of the Homeric poems and in the cultural respectability that was Greece. Their efforts were matched by the desire of the Greeks to represent the entire

---

with pl. 23. I follow the interpretation of M. F. Vos, *Scythian Archers on Archaic Attic Vases* (Groningen 1963) 56-62.

[88] *Journal des savants* (1944) 127-128.

[89] T. Mommsen as quoted by Boas, *Arrival* 12.

[90] Cf. Bickerman, *CW* 37 (1943-1944) 95 and, with more detail, *CP* 47 (1952) 65-86.

barbarian world as subdued by or originating from the Greeks. To a Greek, to overstate it somewhat, the barbarians basically were Greeks, who had been so unfortunate as to take a somewhat different development, which had made them second-class Greeks. This was best exemplified by the Trojans, who, as the vase paintings show, could be accepted as Greeks fully or partially, and this ambiguity explains the frequent occurrence of "Trojans" in the western Mediterranean.

The basis of this Trojan identification of peoples, who were neither totally identical with the Greeks nor totally different from them, was not political enmity, but a cultural distinction. Even when the Trojan image, under the impact of the Persian Wars, was more than ever associated with that of the βάρβαρος and the Trojans appeared in Phrygian costume on stage and in the arts, the distinction was primarily a cultural one: that between uncivilized βάρβαρος and civilized Hellene. In the fourth century Isocrates inveighs against the Persian and Trojan barbarians and calls them "enemies by nature" (φύσει πολέμιοι; *Panegyricus* 158), but in the preceding chapters (150-155) he discusses the cultural influences that have made the φύσις of the Persians inferior to that of the Greeks. It was only much later, after the Romans had started utilizing the Trojan legend for political purposes, that the distinction between Greek and Trojan could be divested, by a man like Pyrrhus, of its cultural meaning and be used in a predominantly political sense.[91] In sum, the identification of other peoples with "Trojans" corresponded most fortuitously to the

[91] H. Diller, *EFH* 8 (1961) 46, speaks of the "political" connotations of "barbarian" in the fifth century, but his very documentation shows that this is not the case. An exception would be the so-called decree of Themistocles (line 45), which was published first by M. H. Jameson in *Hesperia* 29 (1960) 198-223. Its authenticity is doubtful; see the bibliography listed by Jameson in *Historia* 12 (1963) 385 n. 1. C. Habicht, *Hermes* 89 (1961) 7-8, singles out the mention of βάρβαρος as one of the anachronisms of the decree. The word βάρβαρος belongs to the literary sphere; it is a rather emotional term. On the passage in the *Panegyricus* cf. E. Buchner, *Der Panegyrikos des Isokrates* (Wiesbaden 1958) 143.

Greeks' wish to view these peoples as Greeks although they were culturally inferior.

Although there is no clear-cut evidence for Bérard's assumption that the Trojans were viewed as barbarians from early times even before the Persian Wars, it is clear that some blemish was inherent in Trojan ancestry as is shown, for instance, by a passage in Plutarch (*Nicias* 1.3):

> Heaven indicated to them [i.e. the Athenians] in advance
> . . . that it was fitting that Heracles should aid the Syra-
> cusans but should be angry with the Athenians. For they
> were trying to come to the aid of the Segestans, although
> the Segestans were descendants of the Trojans whose city
> he had once destroyed because of the wrong done to him
> by Laomedon.

The emphasis here is not, as has often been contended, on the contrast between the Doric Heracles and the Segestan Trojan legend. For at the very moment the Segestans decide to "go Roman" and put Aeneas and Anchises on the obverse of their coins (Fig. 49), Heracles appears on the reverse of other Segestan coins:[92] the two legends co-exist. The contrast in Plutarch's statement is between the noble city of Syracuse, worthy of aid, and the Trojan-founded Segesta, which shares in the perjuries of Troy.

The ambiguity with which the Trojans were viewed—now as Greeks, now as barbarians—perhaps is reflected best in Nonnus' *Dionysiaca*. In Dionysus' army he has the Sicilian Trojans fight against the "barbarian" Indians, but they are grouped with the Killyrians, fifth class citizens, who were the serfs of the Syracusans: Κιλλυρίων τ' Ἐλύμων τε πολὺς στρατός (13.311). Similarly, in Apollodorus' notice about the founding of Segesta[93] we have the only mention of a Greek sending

[92] Head, *HN*² 167; A. Holm, *Storia della moneta siciliana* (Rome 1964) 236 no. 611a.
[93] *FGH* 244 F 167; cf. n. 39.

help to the Sicilian Trojans and Aigestus. This Greek is Philoctetes, who was best remembered in antiquity for being treated by the Greeks like an outcast. It is difficult to avoid the conclusion that this was the reason he could readily become an ally of the Trojans.

It should be noted that all these passages specifically deal with the Sicilian Trojans. The ambiguous notions that were associated with the Trojans persisted even in Vergil's time, when the Romans prided themselves on their Trojan descent.[94] For instance, when Aeneas comes to Africa, it is, ironically enough, the barbarian king Iarbas who brands the Trojans as effeminate and impious barbarians (*Aen.* 4.215-218) and he singles out the Phrygian cap, which Ascanius wears so often on the monuments, as the epitome of barbarianism:

> et nunc ille Paris cum semiviro comitatu,
> Maeonia mentum mitra crinemque madentem
> subnexus, rapto potitur: nos munera templis
> quippe tuis ferimus famamque fovemus inanem.

As for Sicily, it may be suggested that it was either the Phocians, whom Thucydides explicitly mentions as coming from Troy, or the Selinuntines that were instrumental in causing the legend of a Trojan landing to spring up in the Sicilian northwest. As we have seen, the Phocian *nostos* and their settlement in Magna Graecia are well attested. Besides Thucydides, Pausanias (5.25.6) knows of their existence in Sicily also. Pausanias is careful to differentiate between Greeks and non-Greek barbarians in Sicily and naturally, he groups the Phocians with the former. This reflects what was already

---

[94] Among the Roman sources for the "barbarian" Trojans are Cic., *Off.* 3.99; Vergil, *Aen.* 2.504, 11.777; Horace, *C.* 2.4.9; *Ep.* 1.2.7; Prop. 3.8.31; Ovid, *M.* 14.163, *Her.* 1.26, 8.12, 16.64; Sen., *Ag.* 185; Stat., *Ach.* 1.954. Aeneas is called "Phrygian" in Vergil, *Aen.* 12.75, 99; Prop. 4.1.2; Ovid, *Fasti* 4.274. For a fuller discussion see J. Jüthner, *Hellenen und Barbaren* (Leipzig 1923) 70-87, and Buchheit, *Sendung* 151-172, who stresses that this was in part the result of Octavian's propaganda against Antony and his eastern allies.

hinted at by Thucydides and led him to coin the word προσ-
ξυνοικέω, "to live closely together." If it is historical, the
association of the Phocians with the Elymians doubtless was
rather close, although they seem to have kept a certain distance.
As Greeks whose ancestors at least had been participants in the
Trojan War, the Phocians had some reason to view the Sicanians
and whoever lived with them as people who could not be
trusted entirely. The foreigners whom the Phocians had come
to know better than any others had been the Trojans. This
may well have suggested to them the identification of the
Sicilian natives with Trojans. Thucydides' notice indicates that
elements from the eastern Mediterranean arrived in the Sicilian northwest before the Phocians, and reminiscences of their
cultural activity are evident in the archaeological finds and in
their cult. Such a population could aptly be called "Trojan";
they were, in a way, barbarians, although they were not totally
identical with barbarians. To some extent, they must have appeared more Greek than barbarians elsewhere. As many
scholars have recognized, the term Trojan sums up this state
of affairs best.

More probably, the Greeks of Selinus played an important
part in Trojanizing their neighbors in the northwest. Selinus,
which was founded around the middle of the seventh century
by colonists from Megara Hyblaea near Syracuse, was the
most westerly of all Greek cities in Sicily and therefore may
have been particularly intent on Grecizing her environment.
In the case of the Elymians this was hardly necessary because
the latter, as is shown by the archaeological evidence, had been
eager to accept Greek artistic traditions even before the
founding of Selinus. The many Greek sherds found at Segesta,
the architecture of the archaic sanctuary and the "temple," and
the honors bestowed on Philip of Croton signal the continuing
Hellenization of Segesta under the influence of Selinus. The
intermittent strife and warfare between the two cities could
not obscure the fact that the ties between them were unusually

close and even included the exchange of *conubium*.[95] The Trojanization of Segesta by the Selinuntines was the result of this intensive cultural contact rather than of the periodic hostility between the two cities. It is one of history's ironies that Segesta, on grounds of her Hellenization, could successfully call on Athenian help against Selinus.

It seems likely that the ethnic elements that arrived from the east in the Segesta-Eryx region were some Phoenicians. Aside from considerations already mentioned this would be entirely consistent with the Phoenicians' influential role in Sicily from the middle of the eleventh century to the eighth, i.e. before the Greek colonization of the island.[96] It would also explain, better than anything else, the close association of the Phoenicians and the Elymians after the arrival of the Greeks, which is attested by Thucydides (6.2.6):

> But when the Hellenes began to arrive by the sea in large numbers, the Phoenicians left most of their settlements and concentrated on the towns of Motya, Soloeis, and Panormus where they lived together close to the Elymians, partly because they trusted in their alliance with the Elymians, and partly because from there the voyage from Sicily to Carthage is shortest.

We may assume, then, that some Phoenicians in the Sicilian northwest had fused with the native Sicanians into a new people whose culture, except for much of the Eryx cult, was neither Phoenician nor completely Hellenized. Its Phoenician component, however, had provided the cultural impetus that led to a predilection for Mycenaeanizing and, later, Greek traditions and thus to the considerable cultural superiority of the Elymians over the Sicanians. In contrast to the rest of

[95] Thuc. 6.6.2; cf. Dunbabin, *The Western Greeks* 335.
[96] Cf. notes 28 and 72. A. M. Bisi, *Sicilia Archeologica* 1 (1968), rightly points out that there is no trace of a Phoenician *facies* at Eryx, but there remains the remarkable chronological coincidence between the Phoenicians' appearance in the west and the first "Elymian" pottery.

western Sicily where native, incised pottery is found in far greater quantities than painted, the Segestans followed the Mycenaean and Greek preference for painted pottery, and the incised specimens are few by comparison.

It would have been without precedent if the Greeks of Selinus, or Sicily in general, had admitted that Phoenicians rather than Greeks or people related to the Greeks had arrived in Sicily before them and established a culture which, while not matching the Greek one, still was far superior to that of the native Sicanians. Hence, for the reasons we briefly discussed above, they could aptly be called Trojans. At the same time, the landing of the Phocians may well have been invented to reflect the Elymians' unusual receptiveness to Greek culture. Selinus called on Syracuse as an ally and Thucydides used the Syracusan Antiochus as his source for Sicilian history before the Athenian intervention. It stands to reason that the Elymians did everything to encourage the notion of their Trojan descent because it corresponded to their desire to be recognized by the Greeks and to share in their culture.

In the fourth century B.C., as is shown by a reference in the geographer Pseudo-Scylax,[97] the Trojan descent of the Elymians was no longer emphasized. As a result, Trojans and Elymians are listed as separate peoples. By that time, the connection between Trojans and Elymians, while it cannot have fallen into complete oblivion, was no longer played up for political and cultural reasons. Later, in spite of the ardent "re-Trojanization" of the Elymians in Roman times, the indigenous Sicanian component of this people was not forgotten as is evident from Dionysius (1.52.1): "They (the Trojans) had settled in the land of the Sicanians, for the latter had given them land out of friendship." Even Vergil writes: Teucri mixtique Sicani (*Aen.* 5.293).

In sum, the most likely explanation for the Trojan legend in Sicily is that it was the result of a variety of factors. Prom-

[97] Pseudo-Scylax 13 in *GGM* 1.21.

inent among these were the peculiar ethnic and cultural situation in the Sicilian northwest, an ambiguous attitude of hostility mixed with friendliness on the part of the Elymians' Greek neighbors which corresponds perfectly to the inherently ambiguous way in which the Greeks, depending on the circumstances, viewed the Trojans, and finally, deliberate political and cultural manipulation. By means of the Trojan legend some places in the western Mediterranean were trying to demonstrate that they wanted to belong to the Greek κοινή, while elsewhere the legend would result from the identification by the Greeks of native βάρβαροι with the Trojans. In Sicily both factors, in all their varieties, were at work and, most importantly, although no real Trojan ever set his foot on Sicilian soil, there was an ethnic and cultural foundation on which the claim to Trojan descent could be based. And since the claim of the Elymians to Trojan ancestry thus was uncommonly well supported, had been generally accepted by his time and was—not in our sense scientifically, but imaginatively—true, Thucydides could and had to present the Trojan landing in Sicily as the ἀλήθεια. Lastly, it was because of this unique constellation of contributory causes that the Trojan legend in the northwest of Sicily was incomparably stronger and more persistent than Trojan foundation legends anywhere else. The legend finally became so well established that the Trojan foundation of Eryx and Segesta in some versions takes place even before the fall of Troy.[98] In strength and persistence, only the Trojan legend in Latium compares with the Sicilian one, although for different reasons.

[98] Lycophron's story (951-977) of the daughters of Phoinodamas takes place at the time of Laomedon. Similarly, Dionysius relates (1.52) that the ancestors of Aegestus had lived in Sicily since Laomedon's time before Aegestus returned to Troy to assist Priam against the Achaeans. Thereafter Aegestus, joined by Elymus and Aeneas, sails back to Sicily. This legend of a pre-Trojan War settlement of Trojans in Sicily may ultimately have led to Hellanicus' dating the arrival of the Elymians to before the Trojan War.

CHAPTER III

SICILY, ETRURIA, AND

ROME

IN THE Roman literary tradition, the Trojan legend of Rome is closely interwoven with the legend of Aeneas' arrival in Latium and the founding of Rome by one of his descendants. Roman authors did not make any distinction between the Aeneas legend and the Trojan legend. The same is not true of the Greek traditions of the founding of Rome. Our earliest source for Aeneas' arrival in Italy is Hellanicus, who relates that Aeneas went there from the land of the Molossians either with Odysseus or after Odysseus, and founded Rome.[1] The meeting of Odysseus and Aeneas in Italy is also attested by later writers. Odysseus preceded Aeneas even in Latium, and Hellanicus seems to have been the first to bring Aeneas to Latium beside Odysseus. This sequence of events, which we can establish from the literary sources, is confirmed by archaeological finds which antedate the literary tradition. We will see shortly that the Aeneas theme, in all its manifestations, was popular among the Etruscans as is attested by the numerous finds especially of Attic black-figure vases and by three Etruscan terracotta statuettes. The earliest of these artifacts, to which also belongs the scarab (Fig. 44) we discussed earlier, date from ca. 525 to 520 B.C. A famous representation of Odysseus preceded by more than a century these repre-

---

[1] *FGH* 4 F 84, quoted by Dionysius 1.72.2; cf. Chapter I, p. 38. The text reads: Αἰνείαν φησὶν ἐκ Μολοττῶν εἰς Ἰταλίαν ἐλθόντα μετ' Ὀδυσσέως (μετ' Ὀδυσσέα) οἰκιστὴν γενέσθαι τῆς πόλεως. The question of which reading should be preferred has given rise to much debate although the problem has been unnecessarily compounded by the erroneous relation of the phrase μετ' Ὀδυσσέως to the founding of Rome. The principal discussions are Jacoby's commentary *ad.loc.*; Schur, *Klio* 17 (1921) 137-152; Boyancé, *REA* 45 (1943) 282-290, and Phillips, *JHS* 73 (1953) 57-58.

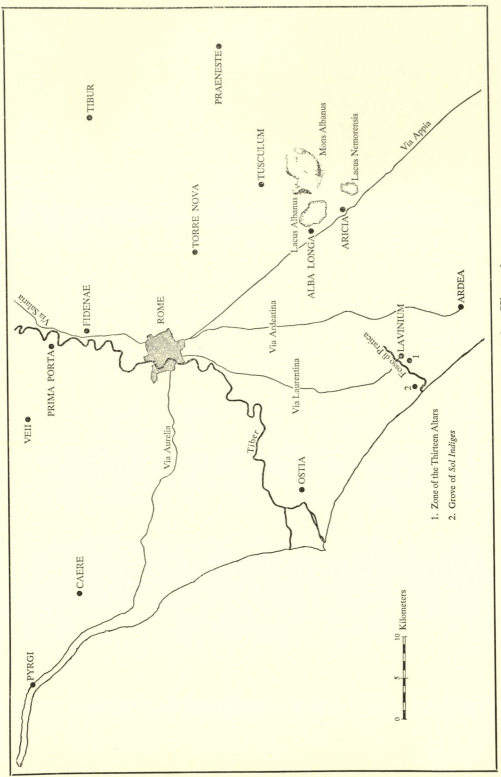

2. Map of Ancient Latium (after Kiepert)

1. Zone of the Thirteen Altars

2. Grove of *Sol Indiges*

sentations of Aeneas on Italian soil. This is the krater of Aristonothos, which was made in Cerveteri, the ancient Caere, around the middle of the seventh century.[2] Its front shows the blinding of Polyphemus (Fig. 84). True to the description in the *Odyssey* (9.371-372) Polyphemus has sunk backwards, and blood spatters on his face and neck (9.388, 397). His tormentors on tiptoe are guided on the far left by Odysseus, who with his left leg pushes himself away from the wall of the cave and thus generates the thrust of the shaft. The number of his companions, four, corresponds to their number in the *Odyssey*.

Before Hellanicus brought Aeneas to Rome, which is only a reflection in literature of the tradition of Aeneas in Etruscan art and the Etruscan influence on Rome, a Greek version had been current according to which some captive Trojan women, led by Rhome, burnt the ships of their Greek masters and thus forced them to stay in Latium and to found Rome. Hellanicus temporarily tried to reconcile the Trojan and the Aeneas tradition with somewhat awkward results: the Trojan Rhome burns the ships, and the Trojan Aeneas has no choice but to found Rome. In the greater part of the fifth century, however, the Aeneas legend was eclipsed by the Trojan legend centering around Rhome. So far as it appears from the extant sources, Aeneas was not related to Rhome or connected with her in any other way by Greek historians until the third century B.C., which merely reflects the revival of the Aeneas legend by the Romans at that time. The implications of this eclipse of Aeneas for almost two centuries will be seen shortly.[3] We should be aware that after the expulsion of the Etruscans Aeneas is associated neither with Rome nor with Latium, and it is only around 300 B.C. that he appears in association

[2] All details about the krater, including a bibliography, can be found in the excellent article by B. Schweitzer, *MDAI(R)* 62 (1955) 78-106.

[3] See Chapter IV, pp. 187-188. A detailed summary of the various versions of the Rhome legend is given by F. Krampf, *Die Quellen der römischen Gründungssage* (Berlin 1915) 15-20.

with Rome and, for the first time, the Latins. This two-century-long silence, which is not accidental, again militates against the assumption that Aeneas was fervently accepted in Rome in the fifth century. But regardless of whether we are dealing with the Trojan or the Aeneas legend in Italy, both are of a later date than the Trojan legend in Sicily. We have to investigate, therefore, in what ways the Sicilian Trojan legend may have influenced the Etruscan or Roman legends.

Stesichorus

It has often been contended that the Sicilian poet Stesichorus of Himera connected the Trojan legend of the Elymians with Aeneas and even sang of Aeneas' landing in Italy. Our evidence is the *Tabula Iliaca* in the Capitoline Museum in Rome (Fig. 85), which combines representations from the *Iliad*, the *Aithiopis*, the *Little Iliad*, and, above all, the *"Iliupersis* according to Stesichorus" (*IG* 14.1284).[4] The Iliadic scenes, as we saw earlier, reflect the traditional characterization of Aeneas as a great warrior (Fig. 32).[5] Of the two representations of the Trojan which purport to be based on Stesichorus' *Iliupersis*, one is the familiar motif of the hero carrying his father, while he is leading Ascanius. Anchises holds the *cista sacra* with the household gods as he passes through the Scaean Gate (Figs. 29, 86a). A woman, probably Creusa, is seen standing on the left, and Hermes, who is said by Servius (*Aen.* 1.170) to have built a ship for Aeneas in Naevius' *Bellum Punicum*, leads the group toward the shore. The second scene at the lower right of the Stesichorean part

---

[4] The well-documented and up-to-date discussion of Sadurska, *Les tables iliaques* 24-37, lists most of the relevant bibliographical references. Besides Sadurska, the detailed discussion by U. Mancuso, *RAL* 14 (1909) 662-731, should always be consulted. The date proposed by Sadurska—last quarter of the first century B.C.—is far better supported by iconographic parallels and historical criteria than Mancuso's assumption that the *Tabula* dates from the time of Claudius.

[5] See Chapter I, p. 33.

106

of the *Tabula* continues this first representation. Aeneas, Ascanius, and Anchises, accompanied by the trumpet-bearing Misenus (Figs. 85, 86 a and b) embark on a ship, and an inscription makes clear what Anchises is carrying: τὰ ἱερά, the sacred objects. Most importantly, the destination of the group is spelled out: they sail εἰς τὴν Ἑσπερίαν, to "Hesperia."

It is generally admitted that the pictorial representation does not literally reflect whatever Stesichorus may have written about Aeneas, although it can hardly be doubted that the inscription Ἰλίου Πέρσις κατὰ Στησίχορον applies also to the scene with Aeneas' departure. But regardless of whether the *Tabula Iliaca* was a demonstration object for school children or, more probably, adorned the home of an erudite Augustan connoisseur, some details, especially of the representations with Aeneas, are bound to have been influenced by the spirit of the early Principate when the interest of the Julian family and the Roman people in general in the ancestral Aeneas legend had reached an unprecedented peak. This is why the scene of Aeneas' departure from the gates of Troy is placed in the very center of the Stesichorean part of the *Tabula*.[6] Moreover, the conspicuous importance the *cista* is given in both scenes conforms to the Italian-Roman tradition, whereas Stesichorus, being a Greek, is unlikely to have emphasized or even mentioned this detail in his poem.[7]

The objections that have been raised against Stesichorus' knowing of Aeneas' voyage to "Hesperia" are not valid. It is disturbing that Dionysius mentions some forty-six authors, some of whom are utterly obscure, as having written about Aeneas' travels, and Stesichorus is not among them although his fame in antiquity is attested by several authors. On the other hand, why should a rather obscure artist claim Stesi-

---

[6] So K. Weitzmann, *Ancient Book Illumination* (Cambridge, Mass., 1959) 48-49, and Lippold, *RE* 4A (1932) 1893-1894.

[7] See Chapter I, pp. 59-60.

chorus' *Iliupersis* as the source for his work without having some basis in fact?[8]

If we recognize the testimony of the *Tabula Iliaca* as valid, all this means is that in the sixth century B.C.[9] somebody in Sicily knew that Aeneas had left the Troad and sailed west. The silence surrounding Stesichorus' account in our sources indicates that this detail must have played a very subordinate role in a poem which writers such as Longinus (13.3) and Dio Chrysostom (2.33) judged to be worthy of Homer. The chief problem is the exact meaning of "Hesperia."

Stesichorus himself did not use this term. It is not found before Hellenistic times, and its original meaning seems to have been no more than the vague denotation "lands in the west,"[10] while it later came to be used primarily as a synonym for Italy and Spain. Stesichorus' indication nonetheless has been taken as referring specifically to Campania or Sicily, or both.

The Campanian theory[11] is based on the presence of Mi-

---

[8] So Boyancé, *REA* 45 (1943) 282, answering the arguments of Perret, *Origines* 110-115.

[9] Stesichorus may have been born as early as the third quarter of the seventh century, but he is reliably known to have been a contemporary of Phalaris, the tyrant of Syracuse, whose floruit must be placed between 570 and 554 B.C. Schmid-Stählin, *Geschichte der griechischen Litteratur* 1 (Munich 1929) 469-475, give a comprehensive discussion and endorse this early chronology. The contention of U. von Wilamowitz-Moellendorff, *Sappho und Simonides* (Berlin 1913) 233-242, that two poets by the name of Stesichorus existed has been accepted by several scholars, such as Schur, *Klio* 17 (1921) 150, and Hoffmann, *Rom und die griechische Welt im vierten Jahrhundert* 111. They therefore ascribe the *Iliupersis* to Stesichorus II, who supposedly lived in the early decades of the fifth century. See, however, S. Ferrarino, *Athenaeum* n.s. 15 (1937) 229-251.

[10] "Hesperia" occurs for the first time in Apollonius Rhodius' *Argonautica* 3.311 and is explained by the scholiast: Ἑσπερίην δ' αὐτὴν εἶπεν ἐπεὶ πρὸς δυσμὰς κεῖται. For a detailed discussion of the pertinent passages see Boas, *Arrival* 35-37.

[11] Proposed, e.g., by W. Christ, *SBAW* (1905) 106-107; G. de Sanctis, *Storia dei Romani* 1² (Florence 1956) 194, and Sadurska, *Les tables iliaques* 34. The lateness of the Aeneas legend in Campania was already recognized by H. Nissen, *NJP* 91 (1865) 375; cf. Perret, *Origines* 302-322.

senus, the eponymous hero of the Campanian promontory in the *Tabula*. Misenus, however, does not appear as Aeneas' companion before Varro and even was associated with Odysseus before then. Even Lycophron (737), who knows of Aeneas' arrival in Italy, numbers him as one of Odysseus' companions. Since Misenus is one of the important minor characters in the *Aeneid* and since his representation on the *Tabula*, where he stands on a promontory and carries a trumpet, is in perfect keeping with the main characteristics of his depiction in the epic (*Aen.* 3.239-240; 6.164ff.), it is reasonable to conclude that the popularity of Vergil's epic accounted for Misenus' being included in a scene of the *Tabula Iliaca*.[12] For while the departure of Aeneas certainly was mentioned by Stesichorus, some details of the *Tabula* also were inspired by the *Aeneid*.

The suggestion that Stesichorus, a Sicilian poet, connected Aeneas with the Elymians in the Sicilian northwest is tempting, but rests on rather questionable assumptions. Malten, in keeping with his hypothesis that the Trojans in Sicily were the descendants of Aeneas or, at any rate, an ethnic group from the Troad, thought that Stesichorus' account actually reflected this presumed historical reality.[13] But, as we have seen, one has to distinguish between the "Trojan" Elymians on the one hand, and Aeneas on the other. Another scholar attributed to Stesichorus both the identification of the Elymians with the Trojans, and the identification of the Sicilian northwest with the destination of Aeneas' voyage.[14] If the Trojan tradition in Sicily, however, were indeed the purely literary invention of one writer, the persistence of this legend and the absolute silence, broken only by a sculptor of the first century A.D.,

---

[12] So J. Hubaux, *AC* 2 (1933) 162; cf. earlier, F. Cauer, *Berliner Studien* 1 (1884) 465. Cauer went too far, however, in assuming that Stesichorus had brought Aeneas to Rome.

[13] *ARW* 29 (1931) 46-48; cf. Schur, *Klio* 17 (1921) 151.

[14] E. Wikén, *Die Kunde der Hellenen von dem Lande und den Völkern der Apenninenhalbinsel bis 300 v. Chr.* (Diss. Lund 1937) 66, elaborated recently by Schmoll, *Sprache* 7 (1961) 107-108.

about Stesichorus' remarkable achievement both are inexplicable. For most legends that are merely the fictitious products of fertile minds and have no historical kernel are rather short-lived or lead a meager existence, as is shown, for instance, by the Aeneas legend in Arcadia.[15] The lack of references to Stesichorus' Aeneas in other authors does not rule out the possibility that the poet may have mentioned his landing in Sicily and even at Eryx. The very late association, however, of Aeneas and the Elymi in our extant literary sources is a strong argument against this possibility, and the burden of proof rests with those scholars who argue from no evidence in favor of Stesichorus' connecting the Elymians and Aeneas.

Another argument that has frequently been advanced is that, by sheer process of elimination, "Hesperia" has to be identical with Sicily. Mancuso gave this theory a slightly different twist:[16] in the first century A.D., he asserted—and the same applies to the last decades of the first century B.C.—official dogma held that Aeneas had landed in Latium. Therefore a more specific word than "Hesperia" would certainly have been used in the *Tabula* had Stesichorus sung of Aeneas' landing there. In Mancuso's view, the choice of this vague term thus seemed to indicate that Stesichorus had mentioned Sicily as Aeneas' destination. The sculptor, of course, could not say so, since it conflicted with the official version of the Aeneas legend. Thus he fortuitously chose the term "Hesperia," which his clientele was bound to take in its narrowest meaning.

We have to take into account, however, that the official version by that time was Vergil's. It is precisely Vergil who in his epic assigns to Sicily an importance which appears to have gone beyond precedent. While Aeneas' landing in Sicily in Book Three of the *Aeneid* still is not much different from

---

[15] This was clearly recognized by Malten 58; cf. Cauer (note 12, above) 476-477.

[16] *RAL* 14 (1909) 721 n. 5.

the tradition reflected by Dionysius and Livy, many scholars have seen something awkward in his return to Sicily after the Dido episode. The following explanation is similar to many that have been offered:[17]

> It is difficult to suppose that so awkward a combination as this can have entered into the original plan of the *Aeneid*. As things now stand it might occur to the reader that the fifth *Aeneid* would naturally have followed the third, as the sixth might naturally have followed the fourth. Vergil had not, probably, at the time of death, harmonized the Sicilian and Carthaginian episodes in a manner satisfactory to himself.

The function of Book Five in the *Aeneid* is far more purpose-ful.[18] Nettleship himself seemed to realize this when he noted that Vergil made Sicily "the centre of the story of Aeneas."[19] There is no indication, however, that this was the case in Stesichorus' time. If Stesichorus had known of Aeneas' land-ing in Sicily or Italy, there is no reason why the sculptor of the *Tabula* could not have said so, except that he may have wanted to use a poetic rather than a prosaic term.

As a result, it ultimately is impossible to ascertain what Stesichorus actually wrote about the geographic destination of Aeneas' travels. A plausible explanation may nonetheless be suggested. In the early Greek literary tradition, exactly where Aeneas was going to establish his rule had been left somewhat indeterminate. Homer seems to imply that Aeneas was to remain in the Troad; Arctinus has him settle on Mt. Ida, and—even as late as the fifth century—so does Sophocles. Hellanicus, in his *Troika*, wrote of Aeneas' reaching Pallene in the Chalcidice,[20] where the representation of his flight is

[17] H. Nettleship in Conington-Nettleship, *The Works of Vergil* 2 (Hildes-heim 1963) lix.

[18] See W. Wimmel, *Gnomon* 33 (1961) 47-54, and my article, "*Aeneid* V and the *Aeneid*," *AJP* 89 (1968) 157-185.

[19] *Op.cit.* lviii.

[20] *FGH* 4 F 31; see Jacoby's remarks *ad loc.*

also found on the tetradrachms, which date from before 525
B.C., of the nearby city of Aineia (Fig. 87). It is not clear
whether Hellanicus at first considered Pallene the terminal
point of Aeneas' travels and later, at a more advanced age,
made up his mind to send him to Italy with Odysseus. This
latter version was followed by his pupil Damastes of Sigeum,
while a much later writer, Simmias of Rhodes, who lived
around 300 B.C., knew only of Aeneas' accompanying Andromache as Neoptolemus' captive to Epirus.[21] All the other
notices about Aeneas' travels come from later writers, and the
earliness of their sources cannot be ascertained. Yet it is reasonable to assume that the goal of Aeneas' travels was pushed farther and farther west with increasing decisiveness as time went
on. In Hellanicus' initial indecision or, at any rate, the lack of
clarity of his *Troika* fragment, and in the fact that subsequent
writers would have Aeneas travel less far west than Hellanicus
had done, we may see the context into which Stesichorus'
notice has to be placed. Probably the poet made his statement
purposely vague and intended it to mean that Aeneas was
setting sail for an unspecified place somewhere in the west.
Nothing but the very vagueness of this reference in Stesichorus' poem is likely to account for its failure to attract any
attention for centuries. The example of the *Tabula Iliaca*
shows that in later times it was possible to read into it whatever one preferred. According to de Longpérier, whose views
have been accepted by many others, the purpose of the *Tabula
Iliaca* was less to illustrate the arrival of the Trojans in Italy
than to illustrate the myth which established the divine
descent of the *Gens Iulia*.[22] Naturally the Julians were interested to find as early an authority as possible for the westward
travel of their ancestor, and the vagueness of Stesichorus'

[21] Damastes: *FGH* 5 F 3. Simmias: Schol. Eurip., *Androm.* 14; cf. Chapter I, note 84.

[22] A. de Longpérier, "Fragment inédit de Table Iliaque," *RPh* 1 (1845)
440.

notice could easily be adapted for such a purpose. The isola-
tion of the monument shows that this interpretation was not
widely accepted. The *Tabula*, therefore, provides no indication that Aeneas was connected with the Trojan Elymians before Roman times, let alone that an Aeneas cult flourished
in Sicily among the Elymians.[23]

Sicily and Etruria

The earliest evidence for the Aeneas legend on Italian soil
is the archaeological finds that have come to light in Etruria.
Before we discuss them more fully, it remains to investigate
whether the Trojan legend is likely to have reached Etruria
from Sicily, given that the Trojan legend in the Sicilian
northwest was current by the time of the Greek colonization
of the island. If such an influence took place, the Etruscan
Aeneas legend would be a later and more developed manifestation of the Trojan legend in Sicily. There are primarily
three possible points of contact between the Sicilian northwest
and Etruria.

First, it is well known that the Etruscan alphabet belongs to
the west Greek group. More specifically, there are many
affinities with inscriptions from central Greece. It has, therefore, been suggested that the origin of this particular alphabet
group, which includes those of Phocis, Locris, Elis, and
Etruria, has to be sought in the intellectual center, Delphi.[24]
This would give us a connection, however tenuous, between
the Phocians in Sicily and Etruria. Thucydides states that the
Phocians came to Sicily soon after the Trojan War and that
they landed in Libya first. The historical validity of this notice
presents a problem as does the somewhat imprecise chronology, although the period of the Phocian *nostos*, prolonged by

---

[23] As is assumed by Alföldi, *Early Rome* 287; the heroon of Aeneas in
Segesta, which is mentioned by Dionysius (1.53.1), was doubtless built in
Roman times.

[24] See F. Sommer, *IF* 42 (1924) 95-96; cf., earlier, Müller-Deecke, *Die
Etrusker* 2 (Stuttgart 1877) 526-532.

their stay in Libya, would coincide with the early date for an Etruscan migration, which has been suggested by some of the proponents of an at least partially eastern descent of this people.[25] According to Herodotus (1.94.6), the Etruscans also landed elsewhere first before settling in Italy.

There are several instances that testify to the close association between Delphi, the home of the Phocians, and Etruscan cities. The account that Tarquin sent his sons and Brutus to Delphi (Livy 1.56.5) may be legendary, but the people of Agylla-Caere, where the Tarquins fled after their expulsion from Rome (Livy 1.60.2), sent an embassy to Delphi to expiate their slaughter of the Phocaean captives.[26] Strabo (5.1.7; 5.2.3) relates that the Caeretans also built a treasury at Delphi as did the Etruscan city of Spina. In the light of these connections with Delphi, the Apollo sanctuary at Portonaccio has been called "Delphizing," especially if one accepts the reconstruction of its acroterial group as the fight of Heracles and Apollo over the Ceryneian hind, analogous to the pedimental scene of the Apollo temple at Delphi.[27] Before Veii can be taken, the Romans have to send envoys to Delphi (Livy 5.15.3). The historicity of this embassy has found general acceptance. This Etruscan awareness of Delphi, however, does not enable us to conclude that they were also aware of the Trojan legend of the Sicilian Phocians. Moreover, the "Trojan" and the "Delphic" interpretation of the Veii acroteria are mutually exclusive.

Some contact between Etruria and the Sicilian northwest, however, doubtless took place. A manifestation of this is the little bronze statuette (Fig. 88) of an Etruscoid warrior in the Trapani Museum, which was found at Eryx. It dates from the

[25] See, e.g., F. Schachermeyr, *Etruskische Frühgeschichte* (Berlin 1929) 191-201; R. Carpenter, *Folktale, Fiction, and Saga in the Homeric Epics* (Berkeley and Los Angeles 1962) 63-67; Carratelli, *PP* 17 (1962) 5-14.

[26] Herodotus 1.167. The family tomb of the Tarquins may have been in Caere; see *CIL* 11.3626 and 3627.

[27] See below, pp. 134-135.

seventh century, when Etruscan ships roamed the Tyrrhenian Sea and were likely to have made trade contacts with the Elymian part of Sicily. But the shoulders of one Etruscan warrior are too small for bearing the proof of close cultural interchange between the two regions of the kind that would suggest to the Etruscans the adoption of the Trojan legend from Sicily.

A second and more complex problem is the cult of Venus Frutis at Lavinium.[28] Our source is the *vetustissimus auctor annalium* (Pliny, *N.H.* 13.84), the first Roman annalist, Cassius Hemina, who lived around the middle of the second century B.C., and is quoted by Solinus 2.14 as follows:

> And let us not pass over in silence that Aeneas, in the second summer after the fall of Troy, was driven to the Italian shores, as Hemina relates, with no more than six hundred companions and pitched a camp in the territory of Laurentum. When he was dedicating the statue, which he had brought with him from Sicily, to his mother Venus, who is called Frutis, he received the Palladium from Diomedes . . .
>
> (Nec omissum sit, Aenean aestate ab Ilio capto secunda Italicis litoribus adpulsum, ut Hemina tradit, sociis non amplius sescentis in agro Laurenti posuisse castra. ubi dum simulacrum, quod secum ex Sicilia advexerat, dedicat Veneri matri, quae Frutis dicitur, a Diomede Palladium suscepit . . .)

The other source for Venus Frutis is a notice in Festus (80.18 Lindsay): *Frutinal templum Veneris Fruti[s]*.

Frutis has most commonly been interpreted as an Etruscan transliteration of the Greek word Aphrodite.[29] The place of

---

[28] The most comprehensive discussion is Schilling, *Vénus* 75-89; cf. Koch, *RE* 8A (1955) 845-946, and Perret, *Origines* 545-549.

[29] See, for instance, M. Hammarström, *Glotta* 11 (1921) 216-217. A survey of scholarly theories is listed by S. Ferri, *SCO* 9 (1960) 167-169, but Ferri's equation of Frutis with "Phrygian" does not bear closer scrutiny.

Aphrodite, however, was already held by the goddess Turan in the Etruscan pantheon although the two deities are not exactly the same. Robert Schilling, to whom we owe the most lucid discussion of the Venus cult in Italy, therefore concluded that Frutis had to be a special kind of Aphrodite. Since two of the Solinus manuscripts read *Ericis* instead of *Frutis* and since Servius (*Aen.* 1.720) relates that Aeneas brought the Sicilian Venus with him to Latium, Schilling and others assume that the Trojan Erycina was directly transferred from Sicily to Lavinium, where the Venus cult is attested as early as the fifth century B.C. Lavinium, in Roman times the seat of the Penates and even of an Aeneas cult,[30] would indeed be an eminently suitable place for a Trojan Venus.

The validity of this conclusion is marred by serious difficulties. The phrase *ut Hemina tradit* may well refer only to the first sentence or, even more specifically, only to the phrase *sociis non amplius sescentis.*[31] Solinus' method of using his source makes it impossible to ascertain whether and to what extent both sentences reflect Hemina's opinion. Another difficulty is that the second sentence presupposes that the Trojan Palladium became the Roman one, but this Roman-inspired version does not seem to have originated before the time of Varro[32] when it also appeared on Caesar's denarius (Fig.

[30] See Chapter IV.

[31] So P. Chavannes, *De Palladii raptu* (Diss. Berlin 1891) 71 n. 2, followed by Perret, *Origines* 549; cf. P. K. Gross, *Die Unterpfänder der römischen Herrschaft* (Berlin 1935) 77 and n. 36.

[32] So G. Wissowa, *Hermes* 22 (1887) 43, followed by Perret, *Origines* 546 (with reference to Serv., *Aen.* 2.166). Contra, M. Vollgraff, *BAB(Lettres)* 1938, 34-56, whose argument that the identification must have been current by the time of Callimachus is inadequately supported; cf. Gross 70ff. Bömer, *Rom und Troia* 61-62, differentiates between this identification and the version that Aeneas saved the Palladium, which is not attested before the first century B.C. A recently found Palladium, whose head is Attic, of the late sixth century, is considered to have come to Rome in late Republican or imperial times; see E. Paribeni, *BA* 49 (1964) 193-198, and A. W. van Buren, *AJA* 69 (1965) 359-360 with pl. 87.

2a). If the entire sentence therefore is attributed to Cassius Hemina, this might show that some later, spurious elements entered into the tradition of his writings. This seriously impairs his reliability as a historical source.

Nor is the linguistic interpretation of Frutis as an Etruscan or Latin deformation of "Aphrodite" compelling. She may as well have been a native Latin goddess: the genitive *Fruti*[s] and the noun formation *Frutinal* suggest this strongly.[33] If Frutis meant "Aphrodite," we would have the curious instance of "Venus Aphrodite." As in the case of the Eryx goddess, the Frutis cult may have had several strata, i.e. an indigenous one followed by a Greek and a Roman one, although the goddess' native name was not changed. The Roman name was merely added; we thus have a Venus Frutis just as we have Venus Erycina. This superimposition of various cult strata was a rather common phenomenon in the history of the Venus cult, and the Lavinian cult would be no exception. The Greek origin of the cult of the Dioscuri at Lavinium raises the possibility of Greek influences on the cult of Frutis. There is no certain evidence, however, that Aphrodite corresponded exactly to the Etruscan Turan,[34] and thus Aphrodite-Frutis may have served to complement Turan in many respects other than the Trojan one. Finally, it cannot be proved that it was some Trojan-minded Etruscans who imported Aphrodite to Lavinium so that she might complement their Turan; the discovery of a dedicatory inscription to Castor and Pollux at Lavinium[35] suggests that Aphrodite may have reached Lavinium either *after* the end of the Etruscan domination or independent of Etruscan influences. Aphrodite

[33] For the details see Koch, *RE* 8A (1955) 845; cf. Wissowa, *RuK*² 290 n. 2 and G. Radke, *Die Götter Altitaliens* (Münster 1965) 134-135.

[34] Cf. F. Messerschmidt, *SMSR* 5 (1929) 21ff.; M. Pallottino, *Etruscologia*⁵ (Milan 1963) 242, and R. Bloch, *The Etruscans* (London 1960) 153-154. Turan means "ruler," "mistress," and the goddess seems to have had a wider variety of functions than Aphrodite.

[35] See Chapter IV, pp. 151-152.

then may not even have complemented Turan, but, at La-vinium, have been entirely unrelated to her.

The two artifacts which Schilling adduces in support for his case for a Trojan Venus Frutis are by no means conclusive. One is an Etruscan mirror, which is so badly preserved that the scene represented on it is incapable of interpretation.[36] Granted that the inscriptions on it have been deciphered cor-rectly, Aeneas appears on this mirror in connection with Minerva, and not Turan. On a second mirror there is a some-what simplified representation of Aphrodite's rescue of Aeneas from Diomedes (Fig. 89), although no legends identify the figures. This episode also occurs on several vases found in Etruria,[37] but the mirror and the vases reflect no more than the popularity of the Aeneas myth in Etruria without pro-viding any clues about Venus Frutis. Moreover, although the Etruscan influence on Latium was considerable, it would be wrong to consider the cults of Latium merely as a Latin manifestation of Etruscan cults. Even if we had conclusive evidence that the Etruscans emphasized Aeneas' association with Aphrodite, such evidence would be of only limited value for the study of the cult of Venus Frutis at Lavinium.

In sum, the explanation that Frutis was the name of a native Latin goddess whose cult was superseded by that of Venus and, possibly, by that of Aphrodite, appears to be the most plausible one. By the time of Cassius Hemina, it was almost impossible to disassociate the Venus cult in Latium and the Aeneas legend, especially since the Erycina cult had been introduced in Rome a few decades earlier and developed strong Aeneadic overtones. Therefore, even if both sentences are ascribed to Hemina, the value of his statement as evidence

[36] Schilling, *Vénus* 80. The mirror is described in Gerhard, *Etruskische Spiegel* 5.103 no. 85a, with the comments by Helbig in *Bullettino dell'Isti-tuto* (1882) 132-133: "I graffitti sono quasi irreconoscibili sotto le ebollizi-oni dell'ossido."

[37] See below, pp. 127-128. A fuller description of the mirror can be found in Gerhard 5.149-150 with pl. 112.1.

for an earlier period still is open to doubt. The quotation of Hemina by Solinus simply presents too many difficulties to permit us to use it as evidence for a close cultic nexus between Sicily and Etruria or Sicily and Lavinium.

A third possible point of contact between Sicily and the Roman region is the trade and political relations between Sicily and early Rome. These relations were formalized perhaps as early as 509 B.C., but most probably around 470 B.C. in the First Treaty between Carthage and Rome.[38] One section of the treaty granted to the Romans and Carthaginians exactly the same rights for commerce in that part of Sicily which was under Carthaginian domination (Polybius 3.22.10). The conditions governing Roman trade in that area therefore were less stringent, for instance, than the conditions imposed on her trade in Libya and Sardinia. The reason may well have been that the Carthaginians wanted to arouse the interest of non-Greek merchants in the Carthaginian part of Sicily and to give a more privileged treatment to them than to their Greek colleagues. Otherwise, the Carthaginians would have run the risk that the Romans might have traded almost exclusively with the Greeks in the east of Sicily.[39] About the dimensions of the Roman trade with the Sicilian west little can be ascertained, although the indications are that traffic between the two areas was not very intense.[40] There is a strong possibility that the Romans at that time may have learned of and come in contact with the Erycina cult, although this is still far from proving or even making it plausible that they

[38] Polybius 3.22-23. The massive bibliography on the treaty has been compiled by R. Werner, *Der Beginn der römischen Republik* (Munich 1963) 304 n. 1 (two and a half pages in small print). I have followed the date suggested by Werner (p. 340); cf. P. Pédech, *La méthode historique de Polybe* (Paris 1964) 385-387, who dates it to 509, and A. J. Toynbee, *Hannibal's Legacy* 1 (London 1963) 528, who dates it to ca. 500 B.C.

[39] So E. Kornemann, *Römische Weltgeschichte* 1³ (Stuttgart 1954) 96-97, and E. A. Scharf, *Der Ausgang des Tarentinischen Krieges als Wendepunkt in der Stellung Roms zu Karthago* (Rostock 1929) 55.

[40] See J. H. Thiel, *A History of Roman Sea Power before the Second Punic War* (Amsterdam 1954) 6.

were in any way motivated to introduce the Trojan legend from Eryx to Latium at that time.

The same conclusion applies to all three points of contact between Sicily and Etruria or Rome. Given the present state of our knowledge, they furnish no secure basis for demonstrating that Eryx was a stage in the transmission of the Trojan legend to Italy.

Other possibilities have been suggested. Malten noted that the cult of the Eryx goddess must have been famous all over Sicily. He then went on to posit that Aeneas reached Rome via Syracuse.[41] In his view, the fact that a series of towns along the Italian coast from the southern tip of the peninsula to Campania were named after companions of Aeneas indicated the progress of the Aeneas legend toward Rome. Again, however, we must differentiate between the Aeneas legend and the Trojan legend. Although it is not quite as late as the Aeneas legend in the Sicilian northwest, the Aeneas legend in Magna Graecia and Campania is of a late date, as are the place names; the latter were evidently invented to constitute a belated analogy to the earlier Odysseus legend.[42] The trade and other contacts between Syracuse and Etruria and Latium have been unduly belittled, although they demonstrably existed even before the Greek colonization of Sicily,[43] but still prove nothing about the spreading of the legend. To cancel out, however, Syracuse as a way station of the Trojan legend of Segesta on the grounds that Syracuse was a Doric foundation is to take too narrowly political a view of the connotations of the Trojan legend at that time.[44] While Syracuse would cer-

---

[41]*ARW* 29 (1931) 50; cf. Büchner, *RE* 8A (1958) 1444.

[42] Bömer, *Rom und Troia* 35-36, with detailed documentation; cf. Phillips, *JHS* 73 (1953) 53.

[43] The pertinent archaeological material has been discussed by Hugh Hencken, *AJA* 62 (1958) 259-272.

[44] Among others, E. Ciaceri, *Studi Storici* 4 (1895) 502-506, argued that the Doric Heracles was designed to obliterate ("offuscava") the Aeneas legend in Sicily, thus reflecting the hegemony of Syracuse; cf. id., *Culti e*

tainly not be inclined to adopt the Trojan legend, she may well have tolerated it and thus at least passively have contributed to its spread. For a similar reason, the argument that some Etruscan cities adopted Aeneas as their founder hero out of enmity toward the Greeks, and especially toward Odysseus, is not compelling.[45] We saw earlier that Aeneas had quite a few friends among the Greeks, more, at any rate, than was good for his reputation. Moreover, he was similar to Odysseus in many respects.

Nor is there any other fully satisfactory explanation for the sudden appearance of the Aeneas myth in Etruria at the end of the sixth century B.C. One criterion, however, which has been rather overlooked in discussions of Aeneas in Etruria, deserves some emphasis. We must not assume that the period from which the earliest evidence dates is tantamount to the date at which the legend actually was accepted in Etruria. It may have been in existence there considerably earlier, although a sudden and strong interest in it seems to have arisen around 525 B.C. The suggestion that the Phocaeans, who were driven away by the united Etruscans and Carthaginians in 540 B.C., transmitted the legend to Etruria[46] cannot be totally rejected, nor can it be corroborated by any literary or archaeological data; it has to remain, as so much that pertains to matters Etruscan and Trojan, purely conjectural. Before then, we perhaps have an indication of the Etruscan awareness of the Trojan legend in a scene on an oinochoe of the late seventh century from Tragliatella near Caere. It shows two men on horseback apparently emerging from a Labyrinthine figure which is labelled TRUIA. It is doubtful, however, that this

---

miti 318-320. *Contra*, Perret, *Origines* 88 and the numismatic evidence presented in Chapter II note 92.

[45] This explanation for the introduction of Aeneas in Etruria has been offered most recently by Schauenburg, *Gymnasium* 17 (1960) 189.

[46] So Bömer, *Rom und Troia* 36-39. *Contra*, Schauenburg 188-189, who identifies the date of the earliest finds with the period of the introduction of the legend.

name refers to old Troy itself and it may mean no more than "fortified place."[47]

Inevitably the occurrence of the Aeneas legend in Etruria has revived speculations about the origin of the Etruscans, although none of the conclusions that have been reached are justifiable on the basis of the evidence, archaeological, cultic, and literary, which is available at present.[48] Whatever the reasons for Aeneas' popularity in Etruria may have been, little can be gained from proposing a narrowly ethnographic interpretation of his legend. It is more fruitful to analyze the artistic and other evidence with the purpose of finding out under what aspects Aeneas was known in Etruria and under what circumstances his legend was transmitted to Rome.

Aeneas in Etruria

The earliest proof of the popularity of the Aeneas legend in Etruria is the vase paintings showing Aeneas' departure with Anchises from Troy. There are altogether fifty-eight known vases with this motif, which have been collected and discussed by K. Schauenburg.[49] Fifty-two are of the black-figure type and date from the last quarter of the sixth century, and its last decade in particular. Five are red-figure vases, and the final specimen is the Etruscan red-figure amphora which has been discussed earlier (Fig. 45). The occurrence of this sub-

[47] The oinochoe has been published most comprehensively by G. Q. Giglioli, *SE* 3 (1929) 111-160 with pls. 23-27. I have followed the interpretations of J. L. Heller, *CJ* 42 (1946-1947) 123-139, and Ogilvie, *Livy* 37. Alföldi, *Early Rome* 282, considers the vase a document for the Etruscans' belief in Trojan descent but overlooks, e.g., Steph. Byz. s.v. Τροία, where the name is glossed as χάραξ ("palisaded camp").

[48] The most tempting argument in favor of the equation Trojans = Etruscans is that it would solve several problems simultaneously; for a summary see Carpenter (note 25, above) 63-67. Carpenter, however, is fully aware of the limits of this method, and other explanations, for instance, of the Roman tradition of a Trojan landing in Latium can be suggested; see Chapter IV.

[49] *Gymnasium* 67 (1960) 176-190; cf. Brommer, *Vasenlisten*[2] 273-274.

ject on vases thus is restricted to the period from 525 B.C. to 470 B.C.

The provenience of twenty-seven vases is known, and probably has some significance. Seventeen are from Etruria, while four are from southern Italy, and three of these four are from Nola, which was under Etruscan domination at that time. Five are from Sicily, where three were found in Gela, one in Agrigento, and one in Syracuse; it should be noted that none were found in the Sicilian northwest nor in Himera, Stesichorus' home. Another vase never was exported from Athens. Since most of the vases whose provenience is not known belong to rather early collections of European museums, they may well have come from Etruria although no proof is possible. On the basis of this evidence Schauenburg has concluded that Athenian vase painters, out of due consideration for their Etruscan customers, chose Aeneas' departure from Troy as one of their favorite motifs.

The Sicilian provenience of five of these vases should not be stressed. The Sicilians doubtless had heard of Aeneas and were quite familiar with the Trojan cycle, as is suggested by the numerous representations of scenes from the Trojan cycle which have been found in Sicily. The vases picturing Aeneas should not be separated from this context. Besides, a look at the Sicilian *CVA* catalogues shows that other motifs, such as Amazonomachies, Gigantomachies, and the exploits of Heracles and Theseus were much more in demand. Therefore we must consider the conclusion reached by Professor Giacomo Caputo on whose compilation of the Sicilian evidence Schauenburg relied:[50]

The vases with the representations of Aeneas, who always leaves Troy with Anchises, depend on the same kind of epic (*Iliupersis*) and were not chosen with reference to Sicily, whose market they reached without preconceived

[50] *BA* 31 (1937-1938) 272.

design, without political intentions, and without any sentiment of patriotic pride (regarding Aeneas) which, inci-
dentally, had no reason to thrive in Camarina and Gela.

Given that most of the Aeneas-Anchises vases were exported to Etruria, it is not surprising that a few should have
been sold on the way. If the paintings were indeed modeled
on the *Iliupersis*, it probably was not the *Iliupersis* of Stesichorus. For it has rightly been noted[51] that Stesichorus stressed
Aeneas' escape from the burning city amid the battle that
was raging around him as is shown on the Capitoline *Tabula
Iliaca* (Fig. 85). When a painter wanted to indicate that the
setting of his painting was the thick of battle he usually added,
as is known from numerous examples, one pair or two of
fighting men. A black-figure hydria, which formerly was in
Munich, is typical in this respect (Fig. 90).[52] Aeneas, Anchises, and the diminutive Ascanius are surrounded by warriors. To their immediate left, an archer with his characteristic pointed cap precedes them, while two hoplites with their
shields flank the group on both sides. Two women are visible
on the far right. Anchises' head is turned back, and his watchful gaze rests on the pursuer and the women, who are about
to be separated from the men. One of them probably is
Creusa. A red-figure example, which bears out the same point,
is a cup by the Pythocles painter in the Vatican (Fig. 91).[53]
A hoplite again is shown in full pursuit of Aeneas and the
backward-looking Anchises. An archer in Phrygian attire tries
to ward him off, and another warrior, followed by a woman,
leads the way. On both vases the Trojans are heavily armed
and this underlines the martial aspect of their escape from
their city.

Such battle scenes are missing from the Aeneas vases that

[51] By H. Luckenbach, *Jahrb. Klass. Phil. Suppl.* 11 (1880) 629-630, and
Schneider, *Der troische Sagenkreis* 175-176.
[52] Munich 1717; Beazley, *ABV* 362 no. 36.
[53] *Museo Etrusco Gregoriano* 2 (Rome 1842) pl. 85.2; Beazley, *ARV*² 36.

came to light in Sicily. Only the lekythos from Agrigento shows a bearded archer following the Trojan, and he probably does so with friendly intent.[54] A black-figure lekythos from Gela shows Aeneas and Anchises flanked by Creusa and Aphrodite (Fig. 92), and a similar composition is found on a lekythos from the Villa Pace al Piombo in Camarina (Fig. 93). Anchises also is represented with his head turned on a black-figure amphora from Gela (Fig. 94), but since no pursuers are visible, this gesture must be interpreted as his looking back at the burning city rather than looking out for a pursuing enemy.[55]

If we did not have the votive statuettes from Veii (Fig. 111) neither the predominance of the Aeneas-Anchises motif on vases in Etruria nor the predilection for the scene of his escape would be particularly noteworthy. A look at Beazley's index shows that the majority of Attic black-figure finds come from Etruria. As we saw earlier, what distinguished Aeneas most from the less fortunate Trojan heroes was his survival, which is epitomized by the moment of his departure, and it would be unjustified to see in this particular representation any symbolic or allegorical meaning which is not inherent in it.

More importantly, the vases have to be placed in their proper artistic context. Aeneas was known in Etruria not only as the man who escaped the sack of Troy, but his representations in Etruria mirror the many-sided characteristics he had in the literary tradition. Etruria also is the provenience of the greater part of the vases with the warrior Aeneas. They may be listed here as follows:

[54] Benndorf, *Vasenbilder* 103 with pl. 51.2.

[55] So Schneider (note 51, above) 176. The lekythos from Gela now is in the Museo Nazionale in Syracuse, inv. 19882; published by C. H. E. Haspels, *Attic Black-figured Lekythoi* (Paris 1936) 216 no. 10, and Caputo, *BA* 31 (1937-1938) 267-268 with figs. 1 and 2. Also in Syracuse is the Gelan amphora, inv. 23512; *CVA* Siracusa 1 III H, pl. 4.4; Beazley, *ABV* 604; Caputo 268-269 with fig. 3. Caputo also published the Camarina lekythos on pp. 269-271 with figs. 4 and 5.

1) Black-figure amphora in Munich (Fig. 95).[56] During the battle over the body of Achilles, Aeneas appears as the Trojans' foremost fighter, thus living up to Poseidon's prophecy in *Iliad* 20. While Ajax in the center carries away the body of Achilles, Aeneas on the left fights against Neoptolemus, and Paris and Menelaos battle each other on the right.

2) A Chalcidian amphora, now lost. Paris has just killed Achilles, and Aeneas protects him against the onrushing Ajax (Fig. 96).[57]

3) Black-figure amphora in Munich (Fig. 97).[58] Hector, aided by Aeneas and Deiphobus, fights over Troilus' corpse with Achilles, who is encouraged by Athena and Hermes. As in many representations of the Troilus episode Hector is the protagonist, and Aeneas is second to him.

4) Black-figure amphora in Florence (Fig. 98).[59] This again is a representation of the Troilus episode in Etruria, where it perhaps is best known from the painting in the Tomb of the Bulls. Hector, Aeneas, and Agenor move against Achilles, who has butchered Troilus at the altar.

5) Pontic black-figure amphora in Copenhagen (Fig. 99).[60] Aeneas goes into battle as described in *Iliad* 20. The Trojan hero does not waver and stands his ground, while the death of Achilles is already foreshadowed: Paris, clad as an archer as he is so often (Fig. 96), points an arrow at the Greek hero from behind. The parallelism between the representations on the front and back sides of this amphora is striking and cer-

[56] Munich 1415; *CVA* Munich 1 (Deutschland 3) pl. 45.2. From Vulci.
[57] The vase was published by A. Rumpf, *Chalkidische Vasen* (Berlin 1927) pl. 12, and Pfuhl, *Malerei und Zeichnung der Griechen* 3.38 and fig. 163. From Vulci.
[58] Munich 1426. Beazley, *ABV* 95 no. 1; E. Buschor, *Griechische Vasen* (Munich 1940) 107 with fig. 123. From Vulci.
[59] Florence 70993. Published by H. Thiersch, *Tyrrhenische Amphoren* (Leipzig 1899) 45 no. 24; L. A. Milani, *Il R. Museo Archaeologico di Firenze* 2 (Florence 1912) pl. 40.1; Heidenreich, *MdI* 4 (1951) pl. 24.1.
[60] National Museum, inv. 14066. See the detailed discussion by Hampe-Simon, *Griechische Sagen* 45-51 with pls. 18-19. From Vulci.

tainly intentional. The other scene (Fig. 100) shows Achilles' fierce onrush against Hector, who has sunk to his knees in the center of the composition and is attacked from behind by Athena. In both paintings, the human victim is in the center, the victorious hero, on the left, and the interfering divinity—Apollo guided Paris' arrow—on the right. The painter already has made Poseidon's prophecy come true: the real, surviving hero is the unyielding Aeneas, whereas Achilles, who seemingly is victorious in *Iliad* 20, has sunk on one knee and will soon be hit by Apollo's arrow. This representation, which borders on hero worship, reflects the high esteem in which Aeneas was held in Etruria; it is not the work of a Greek painter.

6) Corinthian aryballos in Vienna (Fig. 101).[61] On this black-figure vase Aeneas fights against an unidentified opponent. Both are dressed as hoplites and accompanied by two horsemen.

7) Red-figure kylix-krater by the Tyszkiewicz Painter in Boston (Fig. 102). The painting shows the combat of Aeneas and Diomedes. The composition does not differ from the representations of this episode discussed in Chapter I (Figs. 9-11).[62] The painter, Oltos, again did not literally follow the text of *Iliad* 5, because Athena encourages Diomedes in the same way as Aphrodite comes to Aeneas' rescue. As on the cup by the Kleophrades Painter (Fig. 9), Diomedes wounds Aeneas with a spear and not a boulder.

8) A red-figure cup by Oltos in Berlin also shows Aeneas pitted against Diomedes, but the occasion is the battle over

[61] Kunsthistorisches Museum, Antikensammlung inv. IV-3473; see K. Masner, *Die Sammlung antiker Vasen und Terrakotten im österreichischen Museum* (Vienna 1892) 5 no. 55; illustration in *Annali dell'Istituto* 38 (1866) pl. Q, and in S. Reinach, *Répertoire des vases peints grecs et etrusques* 1 (Paris 1899) 318 no. 1. From Cerveteri.

[62] See Chapter I, pp. 14-16. The vase is in the Museum of Fine Arts, inv. 97.368; Beazley, *ARV*² 290 no. 1; Caskey-Beazley, *Catalogue Boston* 2.13-19, with pl. 36. From Vulci.

the slain Patroclus (Fig. 103).[63] The immediate opponent of Aeneas, who stands to the left of Patroclus and is accompanied by Hippasus, is Ajax (cf. Fig. 12). The representation is very conventional and only the name inscriptions make an identification possible.

9) Also by Oltos is a cup in the Thorvaldsen Museum in Copenhagen (Fig. 104) with the combat of Aeneas and Diomedes. The painter again chose to represent its crucial moment, i.e. Aphrodite's intervention. True to *Iliad* 5 Diomedes attacks her without being awed. The remainder of another figure, perhaps Athena, is visible on the left, and an archer also comes to the rescue of Aeneas. Most probably he is Pandarus whom Aeneas encouraged to shoot an arrow at Diomedes (*Iliad* 5. 166-178).[64] Two older men watch the combat from the right.

10) The same motif is found on a black-figure vase in Würzburg which was made in Etruria (Fig. 105).[65] Aeneas has sunk to his knees and Aphrodite, who is winged, spreads a mantle over him to take him out of Diomedes' sight. Diomedes has drawn his sword and attacks the Trojan. The composition is rounded out by two more hoplites and two archers, as well as a dog and a bird.

11) Black-figure hydria in the Vatican. Aeneas has come to the aid of Hector who has sunk to the ground in his fight against Ajax. Two unidentified combatants are shown to the left of this group[66] (Figs. 106 a and b).

Representations are not lacking of Aeneas in his role as

[63] Berlin F 2264; Beazley, *ARV*² 60 no. 64; Johansen, *Iliad* 198-200 with fig. 81. From Vulci.

[64] Cf. Chapter I, pp. 36-37. Thorvaldsen Museum inv. 100; Beazley, *ARV*² 60 no. 67; F. P. Johnson, *Art Bulletin* 19 (1937) 546 with fig. 8.

[65] Beazley, *EVP* 17-18 and 49; E. Langlotz, *Griechische Vasen in Würzburg* (Munich 1932) 142-143 no. 799, with pl. 232; R. Bronson, *ArchClass* 18 (1966) 28-34. From Vulci.

[66] S. Albizzati, *Vasi antichi dipinti del Vaticano* (Rome 1925) 44-45 no. 125, with pl. 12; Payne, *Necrocorinthia* 325 no. 1396; Johansen, *Iliad* 68 with fig. 13. From Cerveteri.

Paris' accomplice during their expedition to Sparta. The splendid oinochoe in Paris with this scene has already been mentioned (Fig. 36), as has the skyphos by Macron in Boston (Fig. 37). The same motif appears in the painting, also by Macron, on a cup in Berlin (Fig. 107).[67] Paris, in the garb of a traveler, leads Helen away on the left. Aeneas, whose dress is identical with Paris', in the center of the composition is shown turning away Timandra who, according to Hesiod, was one of Helen's sisters. To their right, Euopis tries to appease Helen's father Tyndareus and Tyndareus' brother Icarius.

On a red-figure cup from Nola the scenes of Helen's morning toilet and the Trojans' arrival are combined (Fig. 108).[68] Aphrodite and a winged Eros aid Helen, while Menelaos receives Paris and the identically dressed Aeneas. Aeneas and his divine mother once more are represented in the same painting.

We noted earlier that Aeneas in this expedition appears in a role which is the complete opposite of his $\epsilon\dot{v}\sigma\dot{\epsilon}\beta\epsilon\iota\alpha$ or piety. It is worth noting, therefore, that this motif, just as that of Aeneas and Anchises, persisted in Etruscan art. The sculptures on three funerary urns in Volterra represent the moment of Helen's arrival aboard Paris' ship. On the first urn (Fig. 109), the pilot of the ship with his Phrygian cap is shown on the far left. Paris is seated and attentively watches the arrival of Helen, who appears to be dragged by two of Paris' henchmen. The center of the composition is held by Aeneas. He is every bit Paris' accomplice: confidently he has placed his right hand on Paris' shoulder while his left carefully rests on the grip of his sword. He watches Helen as intensely as does Paris. A second funerary urn repeats this compositional scheme and so

[67] Berlin F 2291. Beazley, *ARV*[2] 459 no. 4; Ghali-Kahil, *Enlèvements* 53 no. 12, with pl. 3.3.

[68] Berlin F 2536. Beazley, *ARV*[2] 1287 no. 1; Ghali-Kahil 61-62 no. 15, with pl. 9.1-2.

does a third, although the composition in these is much calmer.[69]

The theme of Troilus' ambush also recurred on funerary urns. On one specimen from Volterra (Fig. 110), Troilus is placed in the center of the composition on his rearing horse, and he tries to push away Achilles, who is drawing his sword and being aided by an unidentified companion.[70] On the right three Trojans are approaching, evidently the same trio of Hector, Aeneas, and Agenor, which frequently appears on the vases with this subject. This episode in Aeneas' life, therefore, was as little forgotten in later Etruscan art as was his expedition to Sparta.

It is remarkable that the vase paintings from Etruria with Aeneas' flight outnumber the vases with Aeneas as a warrior and Paris' accomplice by only twenty to fifteen. The percentage of vases with the two latter motifs thus is considerably higher in Etruria than their over-all percentage. The continuity of subject of Aeneas βουληφόρος as evidenced by the urns shows that the Etruscans' awareness of Aeneas as a mighty warrior or Paris' helper was by no means submerged in their interest in his escape, which at any rate is the more distinctive Aeneas theme. The Etruscan black-figure amphora (Fig. 105) and the Pontic amphora (Fig. 99) show that the interest in Aeneas as fighter was as strong as that in Aeneas as founder of a city; both these vases and the Munich amphora with the *doliolum* (Fig. 45) are products of Etruscans. The picture of Aeneas, therefore, which emerges from the Etruscan finds, is true to the composite character he had in the literary tradition.

This is one of the reasons which make it difficult to believe that the Romans in the fifth century recognized in Aeneas a

[69] Volterra, Guarnacci Museum, inv. 254, 255, and 430; E. Brunn, *I rilievi delle urne etrusche* 1 (Rome 1870) 23 nos. 17.2, 17.2a, 18.3, with pls. 17.2 and 18.3; Ghali-Kahil 275 nos. 233 (pl. 97.2) to 235.

[70] Guarnacci Museum, inv. 376; Brunn no. 51.8.

symbol of their religious aspirations and thus adopted him as their ancestor at this early time.[71] On account of the Munich amphora (Fig. 45) and the scarab (Fig. 44), on both of which the *sacra* of Troy are shown, we may assume, with some justification, that some south Etruscan cities, Vulci in particular, considered Aeneas as a founder-hero. The other vases with his flight testify to his popularity, although this particular representation is hardly dominant and cannot be used as evidence for cultic ancestor worship.

When Aeneas appeared in Italy, therefore, he belonged to the Etruscans. Most of the vases date from the last two decades of the sixth century when Rome was under the political domination of the Etruscans. The beginning of the end of this domination was the expulsion of Tarquinius. It did not abruptly terminate the Etruscan influences at Rome. Rather, a gradual decline of the political fortunes of the Etruscans at Rome set in, and this protracted struggle lasted until the 450's when the contact with Etruscan art, which had continued to flourish until the same decade, also was suddenly broken.[72] Although we have seen repeatedly that it would be wrong to take too narrowly political a view of the use of legends at this early a time and a Doric city like Syracuse may not have closed its gates to the Trojan legend, the Romans are not likely to have actively adopted a founding hero who was closely identified with the Etruscans, just as Syracuse did not adopt the Trojan legend of her political antagonist Segesta. There can be no doubt that Aeneas was known in Rome, but he was known there as the hero of the Etruscans. In view of their prolonged struggle with the Etruscans, it is implausible to assume that the Romans warmly espoused the cause of the Etruscan Aeneas at the very beginning of the *libera res*

[71] Cf. Chapter I, p. 11.

[72] Scullard, *The Etruscan Cities and Rome* 243-266, provides a sound summary of the scholarly discussions concerning the Etruscan rule at Rome and its end; cf. A. D. Momigliano, *JRS* 53 (1963) 95-121, and the various papers in *EFH* 13 (1967).

publica. There was a marked tendency at that time to turn to Greek traditions in cult, art, and law to counterbalance the still prevailing Etruscan influence. One such measure was the introduction of the Greek cult of the Dioscuri into Rome in 484 B.C. by the patricians. Their temple was made a programmatic part of the new Forum which was deliberately created as the civic center of the new Republic. The suggestion of one scholar,[73] therefore, that the Greek twins may have been introduced intentionally to contrast with the Trojan Aeneas, the hero of Etruscan legends, deserves serious consideration. The polemical antithesis between the Trojan pair of Aeneas and Anchises, and the Dioscuri reappeared in the 40's B.C. when Caesar and Octavian made the most of their Trojan descent by placing the Trojans on their coins (Figs. 2a and 40b). Sulpicius Rufus, a friend of Cicero's, in turn issued a coin which showed Brutus' head on the obverse, and on the reverse, Castor and Pollux as warriors, each armed with a spear and dagger.[74]

Aside from this historical framework, which suggests the improbability of a Roman takeover of Aeneas in the early fifth century, there is the complete absence of any pertinent archaeological finds in Rome. No artifacts have yet been found at the site of Rome which would attest the official recognition of Aeneas there, let alone his popularity. The recent excavations by Gjerstad have shown that the black- and red-figure material found in Rome, especially in the Forum

[73] Carratelli, *PP* 17 (1962) 16-23. A recently found votive tablet shows that the cult of the Dioscuri had been imported from Tarentum to Lavinium by the early fifth century B.C.; see Chapter IV, p. 151. If it reached Rome via Lavinium and Tusculum, it therefore must still be considered Greek in character. For the early Roman Forum and its political implications see the lucid remarks by Frank Brown, *EFH* 13 (1967) 57-60. The archaeological evidence about the Regia (Brown 47ff.) and the Comitium (E. Sjöqvist in *Studies D. M. Robinson* 1 [St. Louis 1951] 400-411) shows that un-Etruscan tendencies were not restricted to the plebs.

[74] *BMC Rep.* 1.566 no. 4205, with pl. 55.15; Sydenham no. 1082, with pl. 28.

and the Sant'Omobono area, is far from scanty and that overseas trade, especially with Attica, was an important factor
in the economy of the archaic city.[75] The material is of course
far from being as plentiful as the Etruscan finds, but one could
reasonably expect some trace of Aeneas in Rome if he had
indeed been cherished there at this early time. Still, if a vase
with Aeneas from the early fifth century or earlier were found
in Rome, it would be likely to testify to the persisting Etruscan
influence rather than his popular acceptance by the Romans.

The Etruscan evidence which definitely has cultic character
consists of the votive statuettes from Veii of a young, beard-
less warrior, who is distinguished by his huge shield and carries an older, bearded man (Fig. 111). There can be little
doubt about the identification of the pair as Aeneas and
Anchises. The statuettes are commonly dated to the middle
of or the early fifth century.[76] Bendinelli's suggestion that
Cephisodotus' group of Eirene and Ploutos (Fig. 112) has to
be the *terminus post quem* is not compelling; even if the
Etruscan sculptor was superior to his Greek contemporaries
in rendering the pathos of an interlocked group, he is unlikely
to have influenced Cephisodotus or vice versa.[77] The statuettes

[75] See E. Gjerstad, *Mélanges Piganiol* 2 (Paris 1966) 791-794, where he
summarizes the more detailed discussion in his *Early Rome* 4 (Lund 1966).
Fragments of 451 Greek vases from the period from 575 to 450 B.C. were
found in Rome, among them 195 Attic vases dating from 530 to 500 B.C.,
and 145 Attic vases from 500 to 450 B.C. Cf. the earlier summary by E.
Paribeni, *BCAR* 76 (1956-1958) 3-21 with pls. 1-18, where fragments of
238 vases are listed and described.

[76] The statuettes have been the subject of considerable discussion. The
most important contributions are Giglioli, *BMIR* 12 (1941) 8-15 with pls.
1-2; A. Fuhrmann, *AA* (1941) 422; G. Bendinelli, *RFIC* 76 (1948) 88-97
with pl. 1; Alföldi, *Urahnen* 16-17; Bömer, *Rom und Troia* 14-15; Bloch,
The Origins of Rome 45-47. J. Gagé, *Huit recherches sur les origines
italiques et romaines* (Paris 1950) 73 n. 5, quotes Professor Santangelo,
the excavator, as favoring a fourth century date for the statuettes, but this
opinion has never been defended in writing.

[77] Bendinelli 91-94, esp. 93: "Non si potrebbe quindi assegnare ad artista
etrusco la creazione del gruppo statuario Enea-Anchise, almeno di non
voler assegnare ad un artista etrusco l'onore di precursore ed anticipatore

have been said to have been modeled on a larger statuary group, and fragments of such a group have been said to exist in an unnamed private collection.[78] Both these contentions, however, have not been substantiated to any extent and, as of this date, cannot be used in support of further conclusions.

Similarly, we must be careful not to arrive at any hasty conclusions about the mythological episode that was represented by the famous acroterial statues which adorned the roof of the temple of Portonaccio in the southwest of the Veian plateau and which date from the end of the sixth century. The splendid Apollo (Fig. 113), made by an Etruscan artist, belonged to that group as did statues of Hermes, of Heracles with a doe (Fig. 114), and of a female figure who carries a child (Fig. 115) and is commonly referred to as κουροτρόφος although παιδοφόρος is perhaps a more fitting term.[79] Pallottino thus reconstructed the acroterial group—analogously to the pediment of the Apollo temple at Delphi in which Heracles and Apollo fight over the sacred tripod—as Heracles and Apollo's dispute over the Ceryneian hind, with the *kourotrophos* Latona looking on. This tentative reconstruction can further be supported by the representation on an amphora from Vulci on which a tripod is visible beneath the doe, and by the evident similarity of many vase paintings with the Ceryneian episode to those showing the struggle over the

---

di Cefisodoto." However, the similarity (not noticed by Bendinelli) between the helmet of the Veii Aeneas and the (restored) helmet of Aeneas in the Parthenon metope (Fig. 41a) is rather striking; cf. C. Picard, *RA* 6th ser. 21 (1944) 154.

[78] Schauenburg, *Gymnasium* 67 (1960) 177 n. 10, with reference to H. and I. Jucker, *Kunst und Leben der Etrusker* (Cologne 1956) 127 no. 324; Alföldi, *Early Rome* 287, with reference to Jucker 139 no. 359. Such a statue is not mentioned by Jucker in either place.

[79] The principal publications on the acroteria are M. Pallottino, *ArchClass* 2 (1950) 122-178; M. Santangelo, *BA* 38 (1952) 147-172; E. Stefani, *NSA* n.s. 7 (1946) 38-59.

tripod.[80] The main difficulty with this suggested interpretation is the twofold representation, which has no literary or artistic precedent, of Apollo as a warrior and as a child in the same acroterial group. Pallottino was fully aware of this and therefore stated modestly that "any attempt to interpret the statue, and consequently the mythological episode that is represented, still remains hypothetical today."[81]

Silvio Ferri's "Trojan" reconstruction, however, of the acroteria is even more hypothetical. After another scholar had already identified the *kourotrophos* as Creusa, who carries one of her children in a very similar way on the Aineia coin (Fig. 87), Ferri proposed the following arrangement for the acroteria (Fig. 116): Hermes, Creusa, and Aeneas proceed from left to right, from the east (Troy) to the west (Hesperia). On the far right is Apollo who, after Hermes has led the group to the ships as he does on the *Tabula Iliaca* (Figs. 29, 86a), will guide them to Hesperia with his numerous oracles.[82] On the *Tabula*, however, Creusa does not carry a child and seems to remain behind (Fig. 29), although this aspect of her representation may well have been inspired by the *Aeneid*.

Ferri's reconstruction is based on rather labored technical and visual arguments concerning the bases of the statues.[83]

---

[80] The amphora, which seems to have been lost, is listed by F. G. Welcker, *Alte Denkmäler* 3 (Göttingen 1851) 269 n. 1. For the other vases, see E. Gerhard, *Auserlesene griechische Vasenbilder hauptsächlich etruskischen Fundorts* 2 (Berlin 1843) 51-54 with pls. 89-91; cf. G. Q. Giglioli, *NSA* 16 (1919) 20-28. The principal ancient source is Apollodorus 2.5.3; cf. Pindar, *Olymp.* 3.28ff.; Euripides, *HF* 375ff.; D.S. 4.13.1; Hyginus, *Fab.* 30.

[81] *ArchClass* 2 (1950) 129. Not convincing is the attempt of D. Rebuffat-Emmanuel, *Latomus* 20 (1961) 469-484, to demonstrate that the temple was dedicated primarily to Artemis and that Artemis, although she is not represented, has the moral preeminence in the acroterial group. Besides, acroteria need not be related to the deity of the temple; see below.

[82] *ArchClass* 6 (1954) 118-120 with pl. 28; followed by Alföldi, *Urahnen* 17 and *Early Rome* 287; *contra*, Schauenburg, *Gymnasium* 67 (1960) 177. Fuhrmann, *AA* (1941) 428, was the first to interpret the statue as Creusa.

[83] He relies on Stefani's (note 79, above) description and arrangement, which are in need of correction, of the statue bases; see Santangelo, (note 79, above) 171 n. 15.

Their gist is to demonstrate that "the 'static' posture of Heracles does not conform with that of the other acroteria and that thus he must be assigned elsewhere."[84] A look, however, at the Heracles fragment shows that this is not so; its dynamism quite obviously was meant to constitute the visual and conceptual equivalent of the impetuously striding Apollo one of whose arms is stretched out in vehement action. Most importantly, there is no trace of an acroterial statue representing Aeneas and Anchises. It seems wiser to base a reconstruction on the sculptures which have been found and demonstrably belong to the Portonaccio temple, than to use a nonexistent acroterion as the linchpin of a rather bold hypothesis.

Even if an acroterial group with Aeneas graced the temple at Portonaccio, this still would be no indication of the existence of a cult of Aeneas in Etruria. The subject matter of acroterial decorations usually has no direct bearing on the nature of the deity to which the temple is dedicated.[85] Likewise, votive statuettes often do not represent the patron deity of a given sanctuary, and the ex-votos of Aeneas and Anchises therefore provide no indication that the cult at Veii centered around Aeneas.[86] The votive inscriptions do not mention his name, while dedications to Minerva and Ceres are prominent. These artifacts, however, testify to the continuing popularity of the Aeneas legend in south Etruria at the very time the Romans struggled to rid themselves of Etruscan influences. With his eyes on the Augustan age, one scholar pronounced the stat-

[84] Ferri 118.

[85] So, rightly, Pallottino, *SE* 26 (1958) 338. Cf. the argument concerning the acroteria of the Asclepius temple at Epidaurus, which is discussed by J. F. Crome, *Die Skulpturen des Asklepiostempels von Epidauros* (Berlin 1951).

[86] Momigliano, *RSI* 70 (1958) 130, rightly observes that "the cultic value of statues found in temples varies from case to case." Similarly, Pallottino, *loc.cit.* The votive inscriptions have been discussed by Rebuffat-Emmanuel (note 81, above).

uettes to be symbols of piety,[87] but more striking is the deliberate emphasis on Aeneas as a warrior, who is anxious to protect his father behind the massive shield: "He is still catching his breath from a true combat."[88]

There is no indication that the Romans adopted or "evoked" Aeneas from the Veientines, whom they had barely managed to dislodge from the Janiculum after 484 B.C., after the fall of Veii in 396 B.C. The most important deity of Veii in the eyes of the Romans was Juno, and the Romans therefore decided to spirit her away to Rome by *evocatio*.[89] As the patroness of the enemy, she remained so suspect to the Romans that she was granted a temple only *extra pomerium*. Although we do not know what Etruscan goddess she exactly corresponded to, there is no known relation between her and the Trojan artifacts from Veii, nor does Livy associate her directly with the Trojan theme of the siege and fall of Veii.

The familiarity with Trojan history that was current at Veii left its mark on Roman literature. It is likely to have inspired the intensive parallelism which is found in Livy's account (5.1-25) between the siege of Veii and the siege of Troy[90] and, in this instance, provided a real, historical starting point for one of the Hellenizing adaptations in Roman historiography. It should be noted that it is the Romans who are cast in the role of the victorious Greeks, whereas the Trojan Veientines are their conquered enemies. This indicates that in the first part of the fourth century the Romans had not yet come to consider themselves as Trojans. Vergil was most keenly aware of this inversion, which is paralleled by the

[87] Bendinelli (note 76, above) 94-95, who thinks the statues were replicas of a Pietas-Eusebeia group; see, however, the just strictures of Alföldi, *Urahnen* 44 n. 95.

[88] J. Gagé, *MEFR* 73 (1961) 76.

[89] The significance of this episode is well discussed by Ogilvie, *Livy* 673-675, and U. Basanoff, *Evocatio* (Paris 1947) 42-46.

[90] See especially 5.4.11; cf. Ogilvie, *Livy* 626ff.; J. Hubaux, *Rome et Véies* (Paris 1958) passim and esp. 199-201.

events in the second half of the *Aeneid*. One of these is Mezentius' death at the hands of Aeneas, a story which is generally considered to have been inspired by the historical events at Veii. This assumption, on the part of Vergil's Trojans, of the role of their former conquerors, the Greeks, has often been interpreted in almost moral terms as Vergil's implied and tragically ironic criticism of the bloody mission of Aeneas.[91] The reasons for this incongruity, however, are basically historical. Rome conquered Veii, a "Trojan" city, but later on Rome herself was to adopt the same Trojan myth. The "inconsistency" in the epic reflects a fact in Roman history and history need not be consistent. There was a good historical reason for likening Aeneas' opponents to vanquished Trojans. In so doing, Vergil recognized and paid homage to the Etruscan origin of Rome's Trojan heritage, and his epic and the selection of its hero may have been intended, at least in part, as a gesture of reconciliation with the Etruscans.[92]

Veii was far from being destroyed completely. This can be inferred from Livy's account (5.49.8), and some inscriptions have confirmed that the cults of Minerva and Ceres flourished at least until the beginning of the third century B.C.[93] After 396 B.C., however, we have no evidence that would attest Aeneas' recognition there, let alone in Rome, in the early fourth century. We must keep in mind, of course, that our knowledge about cults in the fifth and fourth centuries B.C. is accidental and scanty, and future discoveries may change the picture. For the time being, however, we must base our conclusions on the evidence that is actually available. It

[91] Most recently, by W. R. Nethercut, *G & R* n.s. 15 (1968) 82-95; the best exploratory study is still W. S. Anderson, "Vergil's Second *Iliad*," *TAPA* 88 (1957) 17-30.

[92] For the details of this suggestive interpretation see R. Enking, "P. Vergilius Maro Vates Etruscus," *MDAI(R)* 66 (1959) 65-96, esp. 94-95.

[93] See M. Santangelo, *RAL* n.s. 8 (1948) 454-464, and *Latomus* 8 (1949) 37-45.

does not indicate that Aeneas had a cult in Veii or that he was adopted in Rome from Veii after Veii's fall.

The following picture, then, presents itself from the literary sources and the archaeological finds. Aeneas was popular in Etruria, especially in Vulci from where we have artifacts which suggest his role as a founder-hero. While it is uncertain whether condottieri from Vulci ever occupied Rome,[94] Hellanicus' notice that Aeneas founded Rome may well reflect the claim of some elements in Rome with Etruscan sympathies.[95] They thus juxtaposed the foundation of the city by the Trojan with the indigenous Latin tradition of an Alban foundation; and the Roman historians, starting with Fabius Pictor, of course tried their best to reconcile these two traditions later.

The end of the Etruscan influence in Rome in the 450's also set a temporary end to the attempts to make Aeneas the immediate founder of the city. Perhaps the year 484 B.C. was the crucial year in this process. It is the year the Romans began the skirmishes against the Veientines in the course of which, i.e. certainly by the 450's, they drove them from that hill beyond the Tiber which the Etruscans used to call Aineia (D.H.1.73.3), whereas the Romans renamed it Janiculum after a Latin deity. In the same year the cult of the Greek Castores was introduced into Rome, perhaps in polemical antithesis to Aeneas and Anchises, and their temple was made a part of the newly emerging Forum. At any rate, so long as the Etruscans remained Rome's formidable opponents in Italy, the Romans were not inclined to associate the Etruscan Aeneas with the foundation of their own city. This accounts for his eclipse in the Greek accounts of Rome's foundation until the early third century B.C. True to their penchant for providing Greek ancestry for any known city or nation, the

[94] A painting in the François Tomb in Vulci points to Vulci's claim to have imposed a king on Rome; Scullard (note 72, above) 256-258 offers a good summary of this complex question.

[95] For this view, and that presented in the next sentence, cf. the remarks of P. Grimal in *Lexicon der Alten Welt* (Zurich 1965) 49.

Greeks continued to link Rome to the Trojans in the interval. But it is the Trojan woman Rhome, and not Aeneas, who again is the center of the legend as is shown, for instance, by Aristotle's account.[96] The time would come after the Etruscan power had been broken for good, when Rome found compelling reasons for reviving the legend of Aeneas as her founder. Even then this legend was not popular in the sense that it belonged to the people; the task to make it so fell to Vergil and Augustus.

[96] Quoted by D. H. 1.72.3-4. For the tradition of Rhome see also Alföldi, *Urahnen* 9-13, and C. J. Classen, *Historia* 12 (1963) 447-448, 452; cf. note 3.

CHAPTER IV

LAVINIUM AND ROME

Aeneas at Lavinium

THE PART played by Lavinium in the development of the Trojan tradition of Rome, one scholar has aptly observed, "is one of the most obscure problems in Roman tradition."[1] The question that concerns us here is to how early a time we can trace Aeneas' association with Lavinium. Hellanicus' notice that Aeneas founded Rome reflects, as we have seen, the Etruscan influence at Rome and it predates Aeneas' connection with Lavinium: the latter is only a secondary development.[2] All the sources for it are late and either Roman or reflecting Roman tradition. Aeneas is first associated with Lavinium in the *Alexandra* of Lycophron (1250-1260), who, in his cryptic way, alludes to the miracle of the sow and the thirty piglets and to the prodigy of the tables. It cannot be shown in any way that Lycophron used Timaeus as his source here; even if he did, Timaeus' version dates from the early decades of the third century and reflects a current but not necessarily old tradition.[3] Fabius Pictor, the first Roman historian, made no mention of Lavinium but connected the prodigy of the sow with Ascanius' foundation of Alba after thirty years (*FGH* 840 F 2), and we will dwell on this rivalry between Alba and Lavinium shortly. The most emphatic statement about Lavinium as the first Trojan foundation on Italian soil comes from Varro (*L. L.* 5.144): *oppidum quod primum conditum in Latio stirpis Romanae, Lavinium; nam ibi di Penates nostri.* Although Varro was not exactly scrupulous about associating any number of places with the

[1] Ogilvie, *Livy* 39.

[2] Cf. Boas, *Arrival* 17; Perret, *Origines* 344; de Sanctis (Chapter III n. 11) 196 n. 1; Castagnoli, *ArchClass* 19 (1967) 247 n. 43.

[3] Cf. Chapter I n. 83; Jacoby, *FGH* IIIb *Noten*, p. 332 n. 317.

Trojans or Rome's *familiae Troianae*, references to Aeneas' foundation of Lavinium are also found in other authors, Dionysius in particular.[4] Vergil begins the proem to his epic with an obvious reference to this tradition (*Lavinaque venit litora*; *Aen.* 1.2-3), but when the destination of Aeneas' wanderings is named for the first time in the epic itself, it turns out to be the Tiber (2.781-782). Accordingly, Aeneas lands virtually in Rome, at the mouth of the Tiber, and the prodigies that had been associated with Lavinium come to pass there (*Aen.* 7.116-134; 8.80-85).

The *vates Etruscus* could associate Aeneas almost directly with the beginnings of Rome, but the Romans after the 450's B.C. could not. Rome gave up her claim to have been founded by Aeneas because of chronological exigencies which, in turn, reflect a concession to the Latin tradition of Rome's foundation. After the foundation of Rome had been fixed at somewhere in the eighth century, Aeneas could not be considered her founder since the fall of Troy was reckoned to have taken place in the twelfth or thirteenth century. The list of Alban kings therefore came to occupy the interval. This later foundation of Rome signifies the triumph of the indigenous Latin tradition: Rome is founded by the Latins from Alba, and the Trojan Aeneas is only the remote ancestor. The relegation of Aeneas to the background is accounted for by his Etruscan associations.

Scarce as they are, the notices of the Greek historians of the fourth century permit us to catch a glimpse of the conflict between the Etruscan/Trojan and the Latin tradition. The Sicilian Alcimus, whose testimony probably dates to the 340's, wrote that Aeneas and Tyrrhenia had a son Romulus, whose daughter Alba gave birth to Rhomus, the founder of Rome.[5] Tyrrhenia of course is the daughter of Tyrrhenus,

[4] D.H. 1.55-60, esp. 1.59.3; 5.12.3; 8.49.6; Cato frgs. 8-12 (Peter); Strabo 5.229; Plut., *Cor.* 29; Val. Max. 1.8.8; *Origo Gent. Rom.* 12.4.

[5] *FGH* 560 F 4=*FGH* 840 F 12=Fest. 326 L.; cf. Jacoby's commentary

the Etruscan ancestor. If Rome had been founded by Romulus, it would be an Etruscan foundation, and therefore Romulus is awkwardly duplicated by Rhomus whose Latin/Alban credentials are more impeccable. Any Etruscan reminiscence, however, disappeared by the time of another Sicilian historian, Callias, who wrote around the end of the fourth century. He returned to the story of the Trojan woman Rhome, who now marries Latinus, the king of the Aborigines, and their sons Rhomus, Rhomylus (and Telegonus) found the city named after Rhome (*FGH* 564 F 5a). From then on, the version of Rome's foundation by Romulus and, at times, Remus, prevails, and it reflects an indigenous Roman tradition which originated in the fourth century at the latest.[6] When the legend of the ancestor Aeneas was revived, therefore, he could not any longer be presented as the founder of Rome but by necessity had to found another city. This city happens to be Lavinium. We saw that there are no literary sources which would attest Aeneas' connection with that city before the end of the fourth century B.C.[7] when Rome, after overcoming the Latins, directed her attention to Magna Graecia and revived the story of her Trojan descent as a means to seek closer ties with the Greek world. Thus we must turn to cult and archaeology to see whether they provide any indication of Aeneas' association with Lavinium before then. Before we do so, a brief comment is necessary on the role of Lavinium in the Roman literary and historiographical tradition.

This role is characterized by the constant competition, analogies, and parallels, of which only a few can be cited here, with the role of Alba. Vergil's Jupiter proclaims that Lavin-

---

ad loc. Classen, *Historia* 12 (1963) 449, rightly stresses that as Sicilians, Alcimus and Callias can be expected to have been well acquainted with the Italic west and its legends.

[6] See Classen, *op. laud.* 456-457, followed by Gabba, *EFH* 13 (1967) 143-144.

[7] There is no need to emend, with Kiessling, Aristotle's *Latinium* to *Lavinium* (D.H. 1.72.3); see, e.g. Rosenberg, *RE* 1A (1920) 1077.

ium will be *sedes regni* for thirty years, Alba, for three hundred (*Aen*. 1.267-274).[8] Both Alba and Lavinium are called the homes of the Penates, Rome's ancestral gods, and of Vesta.[9] Twice Alba tried, without success, to transfer the Penates of Lavinium to Alba.[10] The Greek mythographer Conon, who lived in the late first century B.C., preserved a version according to which Aeneas settled in Alba, and not Lavinium (*FGH* 26 F 1). The story that Latinus disappeared after the battle against Mezentius and became *Iuppiter Latiaris* on the Alban mountain is paralleled by the story of Aeneas' disappearance after fighting Mezentius and his enjoying worship as *Iuppiter Indiges* by the Numicus in Lavinium;[11] we shall return to this story shortly. In Naevius and Ennius, Aeneas may have married the daughter of the king of Alba, and not Lavinia.[12]

Alba, in contrast to Lavinium, had been a politically powerful city and indeed had gained preeminence among the Latin cities.[13] Being a Latin was identified with Alban descent: *cum omnes Latini ab Alba oriundi sint* (Livy 1.52.2), and the Latins are defined as *populi Albenses* (Pliny, *N.H.* 3.5.69). This preeminence of Alba was reflected in Rome: ". . . there is no trace of prominent *familiae Lavinates* in Rome, but only of *Albanae*. Among the Roman aristocracy the Alban origin possessed more prestige. Not only was the first king of Rome

[8] Cf. also Livy 1.6.3; Cato frg. 13. For a comprehensive discussion see W. Ehlers, *MH* 6 (1949) 166-175, and Alföldi, *Early Rome* 246-250.

[9] Alba Longa: Livy 1.20.3; D.H. 2.65.1; Ovid, *Fasti* 3.11; Lucan 5.400. Lavinium: D.H. 2.52.3; 5.12.3; 8.49.6; Varro, *L.L.* 5.144; Plut., *Cor.* 29.2; Val. Max. 1.8.8; Serv., *Aen.* 7.661; *Origo Gent. Rom.* 13.7. Both: Lucan 7.394, followed as it were by Wissowa, *RuK*[2] 164.

[10] D.H. 1.67.1-2. Cf. Tilly, *Vergil's Latium* 63 n. 5, and A. Bernardi, *Athenaeum* n.s. 42 (1964) 245. Serv. auct., *Aen.* 3.12, tells of an analogous Roman attempt.

[11] Latinus: Festus 212 L.; Schol. Bob. in Cic., *Planc.* p. 154 (Stangl). Aeneas: Livy 1.2.6; Serv. auct., *Aen.* 12.794; Festus 94 L.

[12] See F. Leo, *Geschichte der römischen Literatur* 1 (Leipzig 1913) 167 on the basis of Ennius, *Ann.* frg. 33 Vahlen (=frg. 31 Warmington).

[13] See Cato in *Origo Gent. Rom.* 12.5; D.H. 3.31.4; Livy 1.52.2; Festus 276 L.; cf. Philipp, *RE* 12 (1925) 949 and Alföldi, *Early Rome* 243-245.

connected with Alba but also the origins of such institutions as the Roman dictatorship and the Vestal virgins."[14]

Compared to this, the Lavinian tradition is entirely secondary. In many respects, it is modeled upon Alba's and reflects the attempt to establish Lavinium as the Trojan counterpart of the Latin center Alba. In the literary and historiographical tradition, this attempt did not meet with much success. It has been assumed, therefore, that "the leadership of Lavinium was suppressed by Roman historiography to permit the rule of Rome to follow immediately after the rule of Alba. We must therefore pursue the traces of the preeminence of Lavinium in byways where they were not deliberately wiped out."[15]

But why would the influential Roman historians—Fabius, Cato, Varro, and Livy, to name only a few—who did their best to promote Rome's claim to Trojan descent, want to defeat their purpose by suppressing the Lavinian tradition on which this claim came to be based? The Trojan tradition of Lavinium was meant to be strengthened by the close cultic association between Rome and Lavinium after 338 B.C. and Livy, for one, tried to read it back into regal times as is shown by his account of the death of Titus Tatius at Lavinium.[16] All this suggests is that once Rome had abandoned, in the first half of the fifth century, the notion of her foundation by Aeneas and her connection with Trojan descent had ceased being actively promoted by anyone in Rome, the Latin foundation myth gained the upper hand. It became so well established that it easily maintained its preeminence over the later, Lavinian tradition which provided a somewhat more remote link between Aeneas and Rome. The tradition of Lavinium's founding by Aeneas originated in the second half

[14] Alföldi, *Early Rome* 250.

[15] Alföldi, *loc.cit.*

[16] Livy 1.14.1-3; also, D.H. 2.52.3; Varro, *L.L.* 5.152; Plut., *Rom.* 23.1-4; Solinus 1.21; Zonaras 6.4. But see Ogilvie, *Livy, ad loc.*

of the fourth century for several reasons that we will shortly discuss. It was promoted in cult and by Roman historians who tried to support Lavinium's claims by disputing those of Alba. The tradition of the Alban and Latin association with Rome was indigenous, popular, older, and stronger, and it easily survived the challenge of the Trojan Lavinium whose promotion was largely the result of political and diplomatic considerations. We will see that once this revival of the Aeneas legend had fulfilled its immediate purpose in the fourth and third centuries, Rome's claim to Trojan descent suffered an eclipse almost two centuries long until it was revived by Caesar (Figs. 2 a and b), the proud member of an Alban family (Suet., *Iul.* 6.1). It would not have fallen into oblivion if it had been a living and popular legend.

We therefore must turn to the cults of Lavinium to see whether Aeneas played any role in them. The most significant ritual in Roman times, i.e. after 338 B.C., was the obligation of the Roman consuls, the dictator, the praetors, and the generals about to depart to the provinces to sacrifice to the Penates and Vesta at Lavinium, both at the beginning and end of their term of office.[17] There are specific examples to illustrate this well-known practice. In 137 B.C., for instance, the proconsul Gaius Hostilius failed to sacrifice at Lavinium before leaving for his province in Spain, and this omission was said to have caused his bad luck there (Val. Max. 1.6.7). Cicero's contemporary Scaurus was prosecuted because he neglected to carry out the rites at Lavinium properly: *crimini dabat sacra publica populi Romani deum Penatium quae Lavini fierent opera eius minus recte casta fieri* (Asconius, *Scaur.* 21 Stangl). Of the emperor Marcus Aurelius it is said that after his return from the war against the Marcomanni *Romam ut venit triumphavit et inde Lavinium profectus est* (Hist. Aug., *M. Ant.* 27.4). The bulk of the inscriptions

[17] Serv. auct., *Aen.* 2.296; 3.12; 8.664; Macrob. 3.4.11; cf. Weinstock, *RE* 19 (1937) 430.

found at Lavinium (*CIL* 14.2065-2085) in fact date from the second century A.D., and the cult survived into the time of Julian (*CIL* 14.2065).

The Penates worshiped were those of Rome and also of the Latins: *sacra principia p(opuli) R(omani) Quirit(ium) nominisque Latini.*[18] The basis of the annual sacrifices was a *foedus* concluded between Rome and Lavinium in 338 B.C. Livy (8.11.15) presents it merely as the renewal of the legendary *foedus* between Aeneas and Latinus (D.H. 1.59.1; Verg., *Aen.* 12.161ff.), and the Roman writers generally tried to project the custom of the yearly sacrifice to the Penates at Lavinium into Rome's mythological past. The origin of the rites was attributed to Romulus,[19] to Numa (Lucan 7.396), and to Ascanius (Schol. Ver., *Aen.* 1.259), and the *foedus* was similarly thought of as having been renewed by Romulus after the murder of Titus Tatius at Lavinium (Livy 1.14.1-3; Plut., *Rom.* 23). All these versions date from the late Republic or the early Empire. They are attempts to project the antiquity of the Lavinian rites into the earliest possible times of Rome although they may ultimately date, as does the story of Titus Tatius, to the third century B.C.[20]

The version that the annual sacrifices were made to the Penates, Vesta, *and Aeneas* may be of an even later date. It is found only in the Veronese scholia to the *Aeneid* (1.259):[21] *Aeneae Indigeti (Ascanius) templum dicavit ad quod pontifices quotannis cum consulibus (ire solent sacrificaturi).* The Penates and Vesta were not linked to the Trojan legend to start with: they are far older in Latium than the arrival of

---

[18] *CIL.* 10.297=Dessau 5004; see Wissowa, *Hermes* 50 (1915) 29-31.

[19] Varro, *L.L.* 5.152; Livy 1.14.1-3; Strabo 5.230; Plut., *Rom.* 23.3.

[20] See Ogilvie, *Livy* 72, and Glaser, *RE* 4A (1931) 2473.

[21] It would be too facile to explain this notice away as a misunderstanding on the part of the scholiast, although the extent of his education and learning does not inspire great confidence; see Georgii (Chapter I, n. 3) 20. Castagnoli, *ArchClass* 19 (1967) 244 n. 31, is the latest writer to discount its historical value.

the legend of Aeneas.[22] It is evident, however, that the Lavinian Penates were Trojanized and connected with Aeneas, and thus came to be considered the ancestral gods of Rome. When and how did the Penates of Lavinium become the Penates to which the Roman magistrates sacrificed?

A common answer to these questions has been that the rites reflect the former political preeminence of Lavinium. By analogy to Alba and the cult of *Iuppiter Latiaris* the Romans are supposed to have assumed the care for the established cults of Lavinium. We saw, however, that the political preeminence of Alba is directly attested, whereas that of Lavinium is not. This was recognized, for instance, by one authority to whom we owe a lucid discussion of the problem.[23] He concludes that the Romans paid homage to Aeneas' Penates at Lavinium because Lavinium must have been a city of some political significance, otherwise the legend of Aeneas could not have become located at Lavinium in ancient times. This is, unfortunately, a circular argument which proves nothing about an early association of Aeneas with Lavinium. More recently, Professor Alföldi has tried to support this theory of a primeval political primacy of Lavinium by claiming that Aeneas, due to Etruscan influence, was considered the Latin ancestor by the late seventh century B.C. and that a federal cult at Lavinium centered around him—the very cult that the Romans took over in 338 B.C.[24] For several reasons, this is a problematic assumption; let us first return to that aspect of it which is best documented by the ancient literary sources, i.e. the cults of Lavinium prior to 338 B.C.

Strabo (5.232) mentions a temple of Aphrodite "that is common to all the Latins," and goes on to say that priests from Ardea had the care of it. This was doubtless the temple

---

[22] So, rightly, Weinstock *RE* 19 (1937) 440, and Alföldi, *Early Rome* 258; cf. Bömer, *Rom und Troia* 90ff. *Contra*, Latte, *RRG* 295 n. 5.

[23] Weinstock 428-440.

[24] *Early Rome* 246-287; *Urahnen* 19ff.

of Venus Frutis. We saw earlier that there is no evidence that she was connected with the Trojan myth before Roman times,[25] and even then the notices about her cult are meager and she does not seem to have been Trojanized as heavily as the cult of the Penates. There also was a famous cult of Juno at Lavinium. Because the Kalendae were sacred there, she was Juno *Kalendaris*, but her cult has no connection with Lavinium's Trojan tradition.

The cult, however, that was connected with it was that of *Indiges* or *pater Indiges* or *Iuppiter Indiges*. This deity was worshiped in a grove by the Numicus and later was identified with Aeneas. Livy, as we have seen, calls Aeneas *Iuppiter Indiges* (1.2.6), even if hesitantly, and the first demonstrable occurrence of the title *Aeneas Indiges* is found in Varro.[26] Scholars are agreed that the identification of Aeneas with *Indiges* is a secondary development.[27] Who was *Indiges* and to what time can his identification with Aeneas be dated?

The origin of the *deus Indiges* concept has been a matter of dispute for some time, although most authorities agree that *Indiges* is a divine ancestor. According to a tradition that goes back to Hesiod (*Theog.* 1011-1016) and dates at least to the sixth century B.C.,[28] the ancestor of the Latins was Latinus. He was the son of Odysseus and Circe, daughter of Sol; we have here a combination of a native, Latin tradition with that of Odysseus which, as we saw earlier,[29] antedates that of Aeneas' arrival in Latium. Aeneas' exploits, the battle against Mezentius in particular, were therefore modeled on those of

[25] Chapter III, pp. 115-119.

[26] *ARD* 15 frg. 12 (Agahd) in *Jahrb. Klass. Philol. Suppl.* 24 (1898) 191-192; cf. Vergil, *Aen.* 12.794; Mart. Capella 6.637; *Origo Gent. Rom.* 14.4. Recent excavations have shown that the sanctuary is located at the mouth of the Fosso di Pratica; see Castagnoli, *ArchClass* 19 (1967) 235-245.

[27] See, most recently, W. Eisenhut, *Der Kleine Pauly* 2 (1967) 1394-1395, who also lists the bibliography on the *Indiges* question.

[28] So Wilamowitz, *Hermes* 34 (1899) 611; cf. my articles in *Latomus* 26 (1967) 627-628, and *Latomus* 28 (1969).

[29] Chapter III, pp. 103-105.

Latinus: Latinus had been *Iuppiter Latiaris* and Aeneas became *Iuppiter Indiges*. Equally relevant is Pliny's notice that the grove by the Numicus was sacred to *Sol Indiges* (*N.H.* 3.5.56), Latinus' father. To counter this indigenous, earlier tradition of the deity of the shrine, Anchises, the father of Aeneas, was proffered to establish an equally venerable Trojan claim (D.H. 1.64.5). This rivalry between the tradition of the Trojan and Latin ancestors at Lavinium is but a part of the general rivalry between the Latin and the Trojan traditions about the origins of Rome which we discussed earlier and whose beginnings are traceable to the latter part of the fourth century. The theory that Aeneas was identified with the Latin *Indiges* much earlier, i.e. by the sixth century, depends on nonliterary evidence, which we now must discuss briefly.

The main points of this hypothesis are that the rise of Aeneas as the ancestor of the Latins took place beginning with the late seventh century B.C., which was "the consequence of the overwhelming Etruscan influence encroaching upon the life of this people."[30] Further, Aeneas had a federal cult at Lavinium, which had its roots in the Etruscan cult of Aeneas as an ancestor and which the Romans merely took over in 338 B.C.

The constant conflict in our sources between the Latin and the Trojan tradition of Rome militates against the assumption that Aeneas was fervently accepted or even considered as the Latin ancestor in the sixth century. If Aeneas had been the father of the Latins this rivalry would have been pointless. Moreover, there is as yet no evidence that Aeneas had a cult in Etruria.[31] Even if he did, this does not mean that a Latin city, such as Lavinium, would have made this cult her own. Although the Etruscan influence on Latium was considerable,

---

[30] Alföldi, *Early Rome* 254-255; 250-287, and *Urahnen*, passim. C. Koch, *Gestirnverehrung im alten Italien* (Frankfurt 1933) 100-113, posited the existence of a Latin cult of their ancestor Aeneas before 338 B.C. without, however, attributing its origins to the Etruscans.

[31] Cf. Chapter III, p. 136.

it would be wrong to use it for explaining each and every cultural and cultic phenomenon in Latin territory.[32] As for Lavinium specifically, the only hint of an Etruscan connection is found in Livy's statement that Tarquinius Collatinus, in the late sixth century, retired there to live in exile (2.2.10). Livy's notice, however, is hardly conclusive.[33] On the other hand, the markedly Latin character of the inhabitants of Lavinium has often been noted. For instance, the magistrates of Lavinium were called "praetors," which indicates that it was one of the earliest Latin foundations, although it was younger than Alba.[34] Lavinium belonged to the Latin League and supplied one of the two dictators, Spurius Vecilius, in 493 B.C. when the League concluded the *foedus Cassianum* with Rome.[35]

Lavinium's independence from Etruscan cults is attested by the find of a votive inscription to the Dioscuri, which dates from the turn of the sixth century. Bloch's admirable summary may be quoted in full:[36]

The text, which is very short, is a dedication as follows:

Castorei Podlouqueique qurois. The morphological anomalies are considerable. It is hard to account for the form *Podlouquei*, meaning 'to Pollux.' On the one hand, the letter-combination 'dl' existed neither in Latin nor in the Italic languages; on the other hand, the labio-velar which ends the name 'Pollux' is very strange. *Qurois* is no less puzzling. It is a unique case, applying purely and simply to the Greek *kouroi*. The Latin inscription is modeled upon

[32] This has been emphasized, most recently, by G. Radke, *Gymnasium* 73 (1966) 350. Cf. our discussion of Venus Frutis in Chapter III, pp. 117-118.

[33] See Ogilvie, *Livy, ad loc.*

[34] A. Rosenberg, *Der Staat der alten Italiker* (Berlin 1913) 72; for the archaeological finds relating to Lavinium's period of habitation see Tilly, *Vergil's Latium* 61-63, and Bömer, *Rom und Troia* 91-93.

[35] D.H. 3.34.3. If one denies, with Alföldi (*Early Rome* 112ff.), the historicity of the *foedus*, this Lavinian dictator would be an invention.

[36] *The Origins of Rome* 144-145; see also F. Castagnoli, *SMSR* 30 (1959) 109-116; Weinstock, *JRS* 50 (1960) 112-114; Degrassi, *ILLRP* 1271a.

a Greek dedication. As it stands, the dedication shows no Etruscan influence whatever. At Lavinium the two heroes were worshiped with their purely Greek characteristics almost from the time of their introduction to Rome.

Nor does the artistic evidence point to any overwhelming Etruscan influence. The most significant finds that have come to light at Pratica di Mare, the site of the ancient Lavinium, are from an ancient sanctuary. The part that has been excavated to date comprises a row of thirteen archaic altars (Fig. 117), made of local tufa stone, and fragments of more have been found although the exact number of these additional altars cannot be determined.[37] Their basic design is rectangular, and their dimensions vary from ca. 2.40 to 3.80 meters in length, and ca. 1.90 to 2.40 meters in width. Adjacent to the thirteenth altar were found the remains of a sacred building which was in use briefly from the second half of the sixth century to the first half of the fifth. The altars date from the second half of the sixth century, which is the date of the oldest (the thirteenth; Fig. 118), to the second century. The later altars are rightly considered to be restorations of earlier ones, as is shown by the example of the most recent altar, the eighth, under which the older altar, also dating from the sixth century, has been found. Their architecture is that of the common Greek "stepped altar,"[38] with a wide staircase across the front and flanked by antae. Like all Greek altars the

[37] The most authoritative discussion of the altars is F. Castagnoli, "Sulla tipologia degli altari di Lavinio," *BCAR* 77 (1959-1960 [1962]) 145-172. See also the remarks by Lucy T. Shoe, *Etruscan and Republican Roman Mouldings. MAAR* 27 (1965) 100-103, whose relative chronology of the altars is correct, although her absolute date for the later altars has to be revised in the light of the stratigraphic finds which became fully available only after her study was completed. My account of the Lavinian site and cult complex is based in part on a visit to Pratica di Mare and discussions with the excavators in August 1967, although my views should not be regarded as reflecting theirs. A full publication of the excavations cannot be expected until more of the sanctuary has been explored.

[38] For this type see H. Hoffmann, *AJA* 57 (1953) 189-195.

Lavinian ones look to the east. The alignment of altars in a row also has more Greek than Italic precedents.[39] So far as the type of altar is concerned then, Castagnoli, the excavator, has clearly emphasized that it can be considered[40]

> a document of the powerful degree of influence exerted by Greek civilization on archaic Italy. The Lavinian examples in particular are of noteworthy interest as testimony of a direct influence of Greek models on sixth century Latium, without the need of Etruscan mediation, analogous to what is shown in the very same Lavinium (which in these relations could therefore have had a prominent position) by the inscription of Castor and Pollux.

The profiles of the altars are different from the more solid tectonic forms found on Greek altars, and are characterized by two projecting and opposed mouldings. Many Italic altars and funerary cippi are shaped similarly, including an altar at the Etruscan Portonaccio and two altars at the Sant'Omobono area in Rome. The inspiration for this kind of shape seems to have come from the Doric capital and appealed to the Italic preference for a mobility of forms and direct contrasts. Decisive and exclusive Etruscan influence is not discernible; and instead of speaking of a determining Etruscan influence, one does more justice to the archaeological facts by speaking of a common contribution of Etruria, Latium, and part of Campania.[41] The altars exemplify the nature of the relations between Lavinium and Etruria: there must have been some cultural interchange, but Etruscan traditions did not dominate Lavinium, and Lavinium derived much inspiration directly from the Greeks. The evidence of the altars is confirmed by that of the votive statuettes, of which only a small part have

[39] See Castagnoli 155 and 159 for detailed documentation. The closest parallel is a row of seven altars at Paestum; see P. C. Sestieri, *Paestum*[2] (1953) 43, and B. Neutsch, *AA* (1956) 379 with fig. 115 no. 10.

[40] Castagnoli 155.

[41] Castagnoli 172.

yet been published.[42] Some votive heads find their closest parallels in Etrusco-Latin art, whereas others exhibit marked Greek influence, which persisted into the fourth and even third century.

The only positive identification of deities revered at the sanctuary comes from two dedicatory inscriptions. The earlier is that of Castor and Pollux, which was found by the eighth altar. The second, with Ceres' name, dates from the third century and was found at the site before formal excavations had started.[43] Confirmation of the worship of Venus Frutis at this particular sanctuary is still lacking. At any rate, the available evidence enables us to conclude that Lavinium, from the sixth century on, had an impressive sanctuary. The Dioscuri had been worshiped there since the turn of the sixth century, and their cult reached Rome shortly thereafter. After 338 B.C. the cult of Lavinium came to center around the Penates of Rome. These facts must be taken into account in any explanation of Lavinium's connection with Rome's Trojan legend.

It is of central importance here that according to a considerable part of our tradition, the Penates were the same as the Dioscuri.[44] Iconographically, this conflation is attested by the denarii issued by Manius Fonteius in 103 B.C.[45] One type (Fig. 119) shows the heads of the Dioscuri on the obverse, and a galley with oars on the reverse; this is an allusion to the protective power of the Dioscuri at sea. The same details

[42] By B. M. Thomasson, *Opusc. Rom.* 3 (1961) 123-138. One of the heads (no. 20), although it is of course much smaller, is very similar to that of the Ludovisi "Juno" (Fig. 166).

[43] Published by M. Guarducci, *ArchClass* 3 (1951) 99-103; for discussions since then, see Thomasson 133 n. 2. Castagnoli (note 36, above) surmised that the sanctuary may have been that of Venus Frutis.

[44] Cass. Hemina frg. 6 (Peter)=Serv., *Aen.* 1.378; Varro in Macrob. 3.4.7 and Serv., *Aen.* 3.12; cf. D.H. 1.68-69; see R. B. Lloyd, *AJP* 77 (1956) 38-46; N. Masquelier, *Latomus* 25 (1966) 88-98; Weinstock, *JRS* 50 (1960) 112-113, and *RE* 19 (1937) 452-455.

[45] *BMC Coins Rep.* 1.192-195 nos. 1204-1230, with pl. 30.17-18; Sydenham nos. 566, 566a, 566b. I cannot agree with C. Peyre, *MEFR* 74 (1962) 433-462, esp. 459, that this identification did not take place prior to 103 B.C.

are found on another denarius (Fig. 120) except that the two heads are defined by the legend PP (PENATES PUBLICI). Penates and Dioscuri were publicly associated with each other in Rome in the temple of the Penates on the Velia. The Penates were represented there as two seated youths holding spears (D.H. 1.68.2), and this representation corresponds to the iconography of the Penates in their shrine in the Aeneas relief of the Ara Pacis (Fig. 8). We do not have any record of its building, but the Velia shrine is first mentioned by Varro (*L. L.* 5.54) in the list of the Argei of the second half of the third century B.C. The actual foundation of the temple must have been earlier; Platner-Ashby, for instance, date it "a little earlier than the First Punic War."[46] We cannot be certain that the deities were conflated at this temple at that time, but they were at Lavinium. How did this fusion come about?

For this, Professor Weinstock has given a plausible explanation.[47] He notes that in the main centers of their cult, Sparta and Tarentum, the Dioscuri used to receive two amphorae. As for Lavinium, Timaeus wrote in the early third century he had learned from local informants that κέραμος Τρωικός, 'a Trojan earthen jar,' or, collectively, 'Trojan earthenware or pottery' was among the holy objects in the Lavinian sanctuary (*FGH* 566 F 59). In turn, at Rome the Penates were worshiped, besides the temple on the Velia, in the temple of Vesta, in whose inner part, the *penus*, their *sacra* were kept. During the Gallic invasion in 390 B.C., Livy (5.40.7-8) reports, the *sacra* were placed in *doliola*, earthen jars; and according to Plutarch (*Cam.* 20.8) there were two jars. Livy's main concern was to tell the aetiological myth of the place known as Doliola, which he presumes was so called from the burial of sacred objects in jars, but it is probable that

---

46 *Topographical Dictionary* 388; cf. Lloyd (note 44, above) 42-44.
47 *JRS* 50 (1960) 113-114. The suggestion that κέραμος is collective singular is my own.

1 5 5

the place called Doliola and the sacred *doliola* have no connection. We can conclude that the *doliola* in fact were themselves among the *sacra* to be saved.[48] Their common symbols,
then, facilitated the identification of Penates and Dioscuri.

Whether the Penates originally were in fact the Dioscuri is
open to question. If this was the case, their conflation must
have been current by the 470's, which is the date of the
Etruscan amphora on which Creusa is shown carrying a
doliolum (Fig. 45).[49] Such an early date at least is not attested by the literary sources, which of course are very scant
for cults of that period, nor is it of central importance for our
investigation. But it is this identification which enabled the
Romans to continue, after 338 B.C., the cult of the Dioscuri at
Lavinium as that of the Penates. Livy gives as the reason for
the privileged treatment of Lavinium that Lavinium had not
defected from Rome (8.11.15). The cause probably was the
common bond between Lavinium and Rome in the form of
the cult of the Dioscuri. It had reached Rome from Lavinium
in the early fifth century and therefore an *evocatio*, even in its
new form as the cult of the Penates, would have been absurd.
Lavinium had a major sanctuary where the Dioscuri had been
worshiped, and Rome's willingness to take care of this cult may
well have been, to some extent, a genuine act of *pietas* toward
an old and important shrine that was connected with the
principia of the Roman Republic.

The important point, however, in the Roman reorganization of the Lavinian cult after 338 B.C. is the Trojanization of
Lavinium's Penates and their identification with Rome's own.
For this we have two literary testimonies from the period
immediately after this reorganization. One is Timaeus' statement, based on Lavinian informants, that "Trojan" earthenware was among the sacred objects of the sanctuary. By

---

[48] So Ogilvie, *Livy* 723-724, thus obviating, e.g., Pugliese Carratelli's
objections to Weinstock's solution (*PP* 17 [1962] 21-22).
[49] See P. J. Riis, *EFH* 13 (1967) 72.

analogy to the "Trojan" altars on which Aeneas was said to have sacrificed at Lavinium (D.H. 1.55.2), this phrase does not mean that the pottery had in fact come from Troy or was characteristically Trojan in an artistic sense. Like the altars, it is best understood as something pre-existing which later came to be associated with Aeneas and the Trojans.

The other passage comes from Strabo and shows that the legend of Rome's ancestry had entered into the world of politics. Immediately before his description of Lavinium and Ardea he says this about the people from Antium (5.3.5):

> They used to have ships and to join the Tyrrheni in their acts of piracy, even though they were already subjects of the Romans at that time. For this reason, Alexander sent in complaints in earlier times. Later on, it is for the same reason that Demetrius, when he sent back to the Romans the pirates he had captured, said that although he was doing the Romans the favor of sending back the captives because of the kinship between the Romans and Greeks (διὰ τὴν πρὸς τοὺς Ἕλληνας συγγένειαν) he did not think it was right that bands of pirates should be sent out by the very men who were in command of Italy . . .

The date is 290 B.C. It has been thought that the appeal to the "kinship between Romans and Greeks" is an allusion to the Romans' descent from Odysseus.[50] The specific reason Demetrius gives for his action suggests a different interpretation:

> and who built in their Forum a temple in honor of the Dioscuri and worshiped them, whom all call Saviors, and yet at the same time sent to Greece people who would plunder the native land of the Dioscuri. And the Romans stopped this practice.

Timaeus' statement shows that the Penates were identified

[50] Most recently by Kienast, *Hermes* 93 (1965) 482 n. 3.

with the Dioscuri at that time. Demetrius' emphasis on "the kinship between Romans and Greeks" by virtue of the Dioscuri therefore can be considered as referring to the use of the Trojan legend by Rome. This interpretation is supported by a passage from Plutarch's *Life of Flamininus*, who in 194 B.C. dedicated his arms to the Dioscuri and in the dedicatory inscription explicitly called himself a descendant of Aeneas (*Flam.* 12.6). The dedication was made at Delphi in a spirit of fraternal harmony between Romans and Greeks.

In addition to the Trojanization of the Penates of Lavinium, Aeneas was worshiped as a *Lar* in the vicinity of that city. The evidence is a dedicatory inscription on a small cippus from Tor Tignosa, which is about five miles inland from Lavinium and one third of a mile from the Numicus.[51] The inscription dates from the end of the fourth century or from the first half of the third, although as competent an epigrapher as Degrassi has dated it and three other inscriptions, which were found in the same spot, to the second half of the third century. At any rate, they doubtless date after 338 B.C.

The inscription reads: *Lare Aineia D(ono* or *onum)* which has been translated as "Dedication to Lar Aineias" although we are not certain of the case endings. A further problem is the exact meaning of *Lar*. According to some scholars, he is a deified ancestor,[52] and thus *Lar Aineias* and *Aeneas Indiges* would be related terms. Other scholars have argued more plausibly that Lares were originally gods of the field,[53] and even demons of fertility.[54] Without trying to synthesize these opinions, we can say, in any event, that they would not be mutually exclusive for the *Lar Aineias* at Tor Tignosa. His

[51] Details in M. Guarducci, *BMCR* 19 (1956-1958 [1959]) 3-13, who also published the other three cippi in *BCAR* 72 (1946-1948) 3-10; Weinstock, *JRS* 50 (1960) 114-118; Degrassi, *ILLRP* 10-12 and 1271.

[52] So E. Samter, *Familienfeste der Griechen und Römer* (Berlin 1901) 105ff., and Weinstock 116-117, with further bibliography.

[53] So e.g., Wissowa, *RuK²* 166-174, and Latte, *RRG* 90-94.

[54] E. Bickel, *RhM* 97 (1954) 7-8.

cult came there from Lavinium where *Aeneas Indiges* was worshiped in a grove by the Numicus probably since 338 B.C. or shortly thereafter. By the fourth century, as is suggested by the more than 1200 ex-votos that have been found so far in the zone of the thirteen altars, the deities at Lavinium were invoked primarily in their capacity as benevolent powers of healing and blessing. Some of the votive terracottas are of the type that has aptly been termed a manifestation of "therapeutic folly,"[55] i.e. in the form of parts of the male and female body. Given the provenience of anatomic terracottas or ex-votos in the shape of oxen or hoofs of oxen from all kinds of sanctuaries in central Italy, it is not possible generically to interpret them in terms of a return to "agricultural" magic religiosity and practices, nor does it follow that the Lavinian deity was a goddess of the earth or of fertility. The frequent occurrence, however, at Lavinium of small rectangular ex-votos in the form of weights for wool on the loom, and the find of the votive inscription to Ceres suggest that the deity, in the fourth and third centuries, indeed was intrinsically related to the needs of the country folk.

This is the archaeological and religious context into which the cippus of Aeneas and its three companion cippi of Parca Maurtia, Neuna, and Neuna Fata must be placed, even if they were not found at the site of the Lavinian sanctuary but at some distance from it. It suggests that the emphasis must be placed on the first and primary aspect of these goddesses, i.e. childbirth, a conclusion which already had been reached independently of the archaeological finds.[56] Like the deity of

---

[55] A. della Seta, *Museo di Villa Giulia* (Rome 1918) 166. For an excellent interpretation of ex-votos of this type see Q. Maule and H. R. W. Smith, *Votive Religion at Caere: Prolegomena. Univ. Cal. Studies Class Arch.* 4.1 (1959) 60-88. Cf. P. Decouflé, *La notion d'ex-voto anatomique chez les Etrusco-Romains* (Bruxelles-Berchem 1964).

[56] By S. Weinstock in *Festschrift für Andreas Rumpf* (Krefeld 1952) 151-160, and L. L. Tels-de Jong, *Sur quelques divinités romaines de la naissance et de la prophétie* (Amsterdam 1960) 72-85, 93-104.

the sanctuary, they answered a more private and, for lack of a better term, primitive need of the populace. Rather than being lofty deities of fate and destiny,[57] they were "anatomic" deities of childbirth, perhaps different manifestations of the sanctuary's divinity. In Aeneas' connection with them as a *Lar* we may discern the Romans' attempt to insure their ancestor at least a share of their popularity. In keeping with the early stages of the reactivation of the Aeneas legend by the Romans it was not an imposing attempt: Aeneas' cippus is only one third the size of the goddesses'.

Why did the Romans, in the last decades of the fourth century B.C., accept the notion of their descent from Aeneas and even incorporate it into the political and religious reorganization of the Lavinian cults in 338 B.C.? Several answers suggest themselves. First, with the gradual decline of the Etruscan political threat Rome was bound to become less averse to her connection with the founder hero who had belonged to the Etruscans but was also a Greek. At the same time, the protracted struggle against the Latins stands to have lessened the Romans' inclination to accept an exclusively Latin legend of origins. By reviving the legend of the Etruscan Aeneas, Rome signaled that she, in 338 B.C., had in fact taken the place which formerly belonged to Etruria: she had become the most powerful state in Italy, and Demetrius made due reference to that. Whereas the first occurrence of the Aeneas legend at Rome, as exemplified by Hellanicus and Damastes, reflects the Etruscan influence at Rome, its revival, starting in the later fourth century, is the expression of the Roman supremacy over Latium.[58] Only ten years before the end of the Latin wars, in 348 B.C., the Romans had adopted the Etruscan *saeculum* idea for the institution of their own *ludi saeculares*,

---

[57] As was posited by Guarducci (note 51, above) esp. 12-13, who saw in the association of Aeneas with these deities an anticipation of the role of *fatum* in the Aeneid, and a consecration of *sacra principia populi Romani*.

[58] This second point was already made by Hoffmann, *Rom und die griechische Welt* 123-126, followed by Momigliano, *JRS* 35 (1945) 104.

which in part were aimed at securing the submission of the Latins: *utique semper Latinus obtemperassit.*[59] The success of this measure was not apt to discourage the Romans from drawing on another Etruscan tradition to secure not only the political, but also the religious loyalty of the Latins.

Still, a direct connection of Rome with Aeneas was bound to evoke memories of the Etruscan domination of Rome. By virtue of the common Penates, therefore, Rome could credibly present herself as an indirect foundation of Aeneas via Lavinium.[60] A precedent for such a priority of Lavinium had been set by the arrival of the Dioscuri from Lavinium in Rome in the early fifth century. The Penates were now identified with the Dioscuri; it followed that the Penates also had reached Rome from Lavinium. Since they were the Trojan Penates, Aeneas of course had to found Lavinium first. The Latin and the Trojan foundation legends of Rome could thus be combined; pragmatic as the Romans were, they had no interest in suppressing the former, which was the more popular legend anyhow.

Rome's principal motivation in reviving the Aeneas legend was her orientation toward the Greeks in southern Italy and the Greek world in general after the end of the Latin wars. The descent from Aeneas was found to serve as a close political and cultural bond between Romans and Greeks. Rather than being a Latin, "barbarian," city, Rome aimed to show that she had a respectable pedigree and this is why she turned to the Homeric hero Aeneas rather than to the Trojan slave woman Rhome. The Romans placed the emphasis on the Greek aspect of the Trojan legend, and this use of the legend found its immediate reflection in Greek historiography. Before the latter part of the fourth century, the Greek historians had

---

[59] The phrase is from the acta of the Severan secular games (Pighi, *De ludis saecularibus* 156). Concerning the origin of the *ludi saeculares* I have followed the arguments of Lily Ross Taylor, *AJP* 55 (1934) 101-120; further details in *Latomus* 26 (1967) 625-626.

[60] Cf. T. Mommsen, *Römisches Staatsrecht* 3 (Leipzig 1887) 579 n. 3.

been less than unanimous about the nationality of Rome's founders. Antiochus of Syracuse, for instance, considered Rome a Sikel city (D.H. 1.73.4), and another tradition attributed its foundation to the Pelasgians (Plut., *Rom.* 1.1). After 338 B.C., however, the Greek/Trojan version is the only one to occur, and Heracleides of Pontus simply referred to Rome as a Greek city—πόλις Ἑλληνίς.[61] This Grecization of the Trojans is clearly preserved, for instance, in Dionysius' account of Aeneas' arrival in Latium. King Latinus sees the newly arrived Trojans "armed like Greeks" (1.57.3), and some divinity bids him in a dream "receive the Greeks into his land to dwell with his own subjects" (1.57.4). The description culminates in Aeneas' pronouncement: "We are natives of Troy, not the least famous city among the Greeks" (1.58.2). The artistic reflection of this is the "Greek" appearance of Aeneas on the Roman coins (Figs. 122-123). In the field of religion, the assimilation of one of the earliest Greek cults at Rome, that of Castor and Pollux, to the Aeneas legend also reflects the Roman endeavor to give this legend as many Greek components as possible.

Before we further discuss the development of this legend in Rome, a few comments need to be made on some artifacts that pertain to our discussion. We saw earlier that because Latinus was the native, Latin ancestor, he was vested with greater authority in Latium than Aeneas and was worshiped as a god, *Iuppiter Latiaris*. Aeneas' deification was subsequently modeled on Latinus'; at the same time the attempt was made to bring Aeneas into as close a relation as possible with Latinus. On the cover of the so-called cista Pasinati

[61] Apud Plut. *Cam.* 22.2. Perret's interpretation of the passage ("Aristote . . . et Héraclide de Pont nous font connaître que Rome passe pour une ville grecque, ce qui est exactment l'inverse d'une fondation troyenne"; *Origines* 410) reveals one of the chief erroneous assumptions on which his study is based, i.e. the failure to recognize the ambivalence of the claim to Trojan ancestry; see Chapter II, pp. 93ff. and Norden, *NJA* 7 (1901), 326-329.

(Fig. 121) Latinus appears in the dress of a god and is placed in the center of the composition. Aeneas stands on his left and receives the nuptial wreath that has been taken away from the slain Turnus, who is carried off by two soldiers and a *Dira* on the far left. To the left of Latinus are, from right to left, a most agitated queen Amata, who unsuccessfully tries to persuade Lavinia to follow her, while an unidentified female figure, perhaps Venus, stands between Lavinia and Latinus. The river god Tiber, flanked by a Silenus and the nymph Iuturna, dominates the lower part of the composition.

The cista has been considered a genuine work of the late third century B.C.,[62] but many details arouse serious doubts about its authenticity. To the objections concerning its artistic style and composition a few may be added which relate to its literary inspiration. The representation does not strictly depict a scene from the *Aeneid*, but it illustrates the event that would immediately follow upon the end of the epic. The oath scene, however, between Aeneas and Latinus appears to be modeled on *Aeneid* 12.161ff. where Latinus is characterized at the outset by *ingenti mole* (12.161). This was traditional enough, reflecting the greater authority of the Latin ancestor, but his gesture of raising the arm is unparalleled in ancient art and explained by the similarity with *Aeneid* 12.196:

suspiciens caelum, tenditque ad sidera dextram.

An even more pronounced indication of the influence of the *Aeneid* is the prominent part the Tiber is given within the composition. Naevius and Ennius certainly mentioned the Tiber, but the role he plays in the *Aeneid* is unparalleled in the literary tradition. We already saw that Vergil has Aeneas

---

[62] By Alföldi, *Early Rome* 257, after H. Brunn, *Annali dell' Istituto* 36 (1864) 356-376, had dated it to the fifth century B.C. That the latter date was untenable was recognized immediately by H. Nissen, *NJP* 91 (1865) 375-393, who, however, passed no judgment on the authenticity of the cista. C. Robert, *Archaeologische Hermeneutik* (Berlin 1919) 327-332, showed convincingly that it is a forgery.

land at the mouth of the Tiber rather than the Lavinian coast. The Tiber is one of the recurring and integrating motifs of the epic,[63] and there is a veritable *laus Tiberis* (*Aen.* 7.25-36). Of all the figures on the cover the Tiber, with his imposing sideburns, looks most like a fake.

The recognition of Latinus' greater authority may also be reflected in an oath scene that appears on the reverse of Roman gold staters which were struck during the Second Punic War (Fig. 122).[64] They show a bearded older warrior of imposing stature—*ingenti mole*—who is clad only in a loincloth. Opposite him stands a younger man in a cuirass with a mantle on his left arm. Both men point with their drawn swords to a pig held by a youth who is kneeling between them. If the identification of the younger man, who is armed in Greek fashion, with Aeneas, and of the older with Latinus is correct, Latinus is the more important of the two: whereas Aeneas leans on a short spear, Latinus holds a very tall spear, the sign of *imperium: hasta summa armorum et imperii est* (Festus 55 L.). In the last decade of the second century B.C., this scene recurs on a denarius of the moneyer Tiberius Veturius Barrus.[65] The representation repeats the earlier one, with one important exception: Aeneas' spear is as tall as Latinus' (Fig. 123). The Trojan ancestor now is considered equal to the Latin one.

A result of the competition between Latinus and Aeneas was the cult of *Aeneas Indiges* at Lavinium in Roman times.

[63] See, e.g., *Aen.* 2.781-782; 3.500-501; 5.82-83, 796-797; 6.87; 7 passim; 8.29-78, 331, 473, 540; 9.125; 10.199, 421, 833; 11.316, 393, 449; 12.35; discussed in detail by Buchheit, *Sendung* 178-187.

[64] *BMC Rep.* 2.131 nos. 75-77, with pl. 71.21-22. Sydenham nos. 69-70, with pl. 13; R. Thomsen, *Early Roman Coinage* 1 (Copenhagen 1957) 91-93. I have followed the interpretation of A. Alföldi, "Hasta—Summa Imperii," *AJA* 73 (1959) 20-22, who, however, did not draw any conclusions from the different representations of Aeneas. The identification proposed by him is strengthened by the fact that Aeneas on the *Ara Pacis* (fig. 8) held a *hasta* in his left hand; see Simon, *Ara Pacis Augustae* 23.

[65] *BMC Rep.* 2.281 nos. 550-554, with pl. 94.4; Sydenham nos. 527 and 527a, with pl. 18.

It was meant to be the counterpart to that of *Iuppiter Latiaris* and this accounts for its absence elsewhere. The official cult of Aeneas never reached Rome, but it may well have existed there as the private cult of one or more of Rome's numerous *familiae Troianae*, the noble families that prided themselves on Trojan descent.[66] In Rome, it may be added, a given clan could promote its peculiar rites and gods. Some of these became public under gentilicial care, and some remained private. Aeneas' cult seems to have belonged to the latter category because most of the references to his divinity are rather vague.[67] Servius (*Aen.* 6.777) relates that (*Romulus*) . . . *secundum Ennium referetur inter deos cum Aenea*, and it is Romulus and even Scipio, but not Aeneas, who appear in Horace's catalogues of mortals who were deified.[68] For the *deus Romulus* there is epigraphic evidence outside of imperial *elogia*.[69] By contrast, Aeneas' divinity was played up solely by the Julian family. The statues of both Romulus and Aeneas in the Forum of Augustus were juxtaposed with those of Caesar and Augustus to underline subtly the latter's claim to divine honors.[70] In the funeral procession of Augustus, Aeneas' *imago* was grouped with the *imagines* of Augustus'

---

[66] Besides the Julii, the Caecilii (Festus 44 L.), Aemilii (Fest. 23 L.), Memmii, Sergii, Cluentii (all mentioned by Serv., *Aen.* 5.117), and Iunii (D.H. 4.68.1) belonged to this group. Cf. Varro's (Serv., *Aen.* 5.704) and Hyginus' (Serv., *Aen.* 5.389) works *De familiis Troianis*; see Weinstock, *JRS* 50 (1960) 118 and *RE* 19 (1937) 446-447.

[67] E.g., Gellius 2.16.9; D.S. 7.5.2; Vergil, *Aen.* 1.259-260 and 3.158; see Conington-Nettleship on *Aen.* 3.158 ("superhuman glory, not apotheosis"). Cf. Livy's somewhat hesitant phrase *quemcumque eum dici iusque fasque est* (1.2.6).

[68] *C.* 1.12.33; 3.3.15; 4.8.24; *Ep.* 2.1.5. Scipio is mentioned in 4.8.18-20; see my remarks in *TAPA* 97 (1966) 228-229.

[69] *CIL* 11.5206 (Fulginiae); 5997 (Sestinum); 7.74 (Durocornovium); cf. the dedications to *Quirino* (Dessau 3150 [Amiternum]), and *Quirino Augusto* (*CIL* 12.2201 and 2202 [Gallia Narb.]).

[70] Gagé, *MEFR* 47 (1930) 138-156. Romulus' deification may also be the reason he is closely associated with Augustus in Jupiter's prophecy in *Aeneid* 1 and that of Anchises in *Aeneid* 6 (cf. Chapter V, pp. 225-226) as well as on the shield in *Aeneid* 8 where Romulus is first and Augustus is last.

ancestors, but not with those of the ancestors of the Roman people.[71] None of the numerous festivals and none of the public games commemorated him.[72] The most elaborate description of Aeneas' purification in the waves of the Numicus and of the ensuing apotheosis—Aeneas had to be subject to some metamorphosis—is found in Ovid (*M.* 14.596ff.), who then proceeds to call him *Indiges* (14.608). It is well known, however, that in the last books of the *Metamorphoses* Ovid seems to have been anxious to fall into line with imperial dogma; that the Julian family was indeed eager to propagate this story of Aeneas' deification is also shown by the famous *elogium* found in the Pompeian forum[73] near the statuary group of the Trojans (Fig. 6).

The only extant artistic reflection of Aeneas' apotheosis also dates from Julio-Claudian times, and is found on the Great Cameo of Paris (Fig. 124).[74] Hovering in its upper section is a figure with a Phrygian cap, who carries the globe in his hands and supports the deified Augustus. If the figure represented a god, he would have wings as, for instance, Aurora on the armor of the Prima Porta Augustus (Fig. 138), and thus he cannot but be a mortal who has been deified. The two primary interpretations the figure has received are Alexander the Great and Aeneas. The main objection to this sec-

[71] Dio 56.34.2; Tac. 4.9.3; for details see H. T. Rowell, *MAAR* 17 (1940) 139, and J. C. Richard, *MEFR* 78 (1960) 67-78.

[72] This was rightly emphasized by Schwegler, *Römische Geschichte* 1².309, whose remarks on the lack of the popularity of the Aeneas legend have lost none of their validity.

[73] *CIL* 1 p. 283 with Mommsen's commentary; A. Degrassi, *Inscr. Italiae* 13.3, Elogia no. 85. S. Borszák, *AAntHung* 1 (1951-1952) 209-211, has discussed the Ovidian passage perhaps somewhat too narrowly from the approach of the historian of religion, but the literary context must also be taken into consideration; cf. *TAPA* 98 (1967) 181-191. Cf. Arnobius' (*Ad Nat.* 1.36) sneer: "Those Indigetes who creep into the river, and pass their lives with frogs and little fishes."

[74] A summary of the studies of this gem is conveniently found in H. Möbius, *Festschrift F. Zucker* (Berlin 1954) 265-274. Of particular importance are the discussions of J. P. V. D. Balsdon, *JRS* 26 (1936) 152-160, and B. Schweitzer, *Klio* 34 (1942) 328-356.

ond interpretation has been that the *sphaira,* symbolizing the Roman claim to world domination, does not seem to be a fitting attribute of the Trojan ancestor. However, we saw earlier that it was precisely this aspect of Aeneas which was stressed in his Roman representations, notably the Belvedere Altar (Fig. 18).[75] The Romans' claim to world domination was directly related to their descent from the east and reached its greatest justification in the Roman conquest of the east, which became so important a theme in Augustan literature and art (*Aen.* 1.289-290):

hunc tu olim caelo spoliis Orientis onustum
accipies secura: vocabitur hic quoque votis.

On the Great Cameo of Paris, the divinity of Augustus literally is based on that of his ancestor: Aeneas carries Augustus. This is merely in keeping with the claim of the Julii to divine descent through Aeneas and Venus, whereas Augustus never tried to imply his own divinity by associating himself with Alexander. And it is Aeneas, identified throughout Vergil's epic with Augustus, to whom Anchises prophesies the future conquest of the world by Augustus (*Aen.* 6.794-796):

super et Garamantas et Indos
proferet imperium. iacet extra sidera tellus,
extra anni solisque vias . . .

This is the context in which the representation of Aeneas with the *sphaira* on the Great Cameo must be viewed.

The only popular representation of Aeneas which sometimes is said to have cultic significance is the occurrence of Aeneas/Anchises/Ascanius group on private funerary monuments in the first and second centuries A.D. They have been found as far away as Turkey, but the majority of them, seven,

---

[75] See Chapter I, pp. 24-25. For the view that the figure, because of the *sphaira,* has to be Alexander, see especially L. Curtius, *MDAI(R)* 49 (1934) 141. On Augustus' models for his own divinity see Taylor, *Divinity* 142-180.

come from the regions along the Rhine and Danube. Of particular interest is a group in Cologne (Fig. 125 a and b), which once more is modeled on the group in the Augustan Forum, the Pompeian copy of which (Fig. 6) we discussed earlier.[76] The martial aspects of Aeneas are emphasized even more than in most of his Roman representations: besides wearing armor and a sheathed sword he wears a helmet, and his curly hair wells out from under it. Anchises again is shown holding the *cista*, and Aeneas' terrific stride is shown by the bulge of his cloak (Fig. 125b). Considerably more sedate is a group found in Pannonia (Fig. 128).[77] Aeneas has grasped the baby-faced and cheerful-looking Ascanius around the wrist, while he presses the almost puppet-like Anchises against his left side. The surface of the statues is rather flat, and the whole

[76] Chapter I, pp. 8-9. The Cologne group was published by M. Ihm *BJ* 93 (1892) 66-75, with pls. 8 and 9; unfortunately, the head has been lost since. Ascanius was part of this group, as shown by a second such group found in Cologne, which repeats the first one in all details, except that Ascanius is preserved; see A. Brüning, *BJ* 108-109 (1902) 114, with pl. 2.3. Further reliefs are listed by Ihm 69 with fig. 2 (Vienna); Haug-Sixt, *Römische Inschriften und Bildwerke in Württemberg²* (Stuttgart 1914) 401-402 no. 544 (Stuttgart); G. G. King, *AJA* 37 (1933) 70 no. 2, with pl. 11.1 (Intercisa); L. Manino, *Bollettino della Soc. Piemontese di Archeologia e Belle Arti* 6-7 (1952-1953) 33-53 with fig. 2, and H. Dütschke, *Antike Bildwerke in Oberitalien* (Leipzig 1880) 35-36 no. 48 (altar from Torino). This altar is not listed by W. Altmann, *Die römischen Grabaltäre* (Berlin 1905), who thus concludes (276 n. 1) that Aeneas was not represented on Roman funerary altars. See also, M. Lawrence, *MAAR* 20 (1951) 152-153 with fig. 41 (from Yükseklik). See further the following note and for the Torre Nova sarcophagus and the Camuccini relief, Chapter I, pp. 25-26.

[77] Published, with an excellent commentary, by E. B. Thomas, *Acta Arch. Acad. Scientiarum Hungaricae* 6 (1955) 97-98 no. 7, with pl. 26.3. For the view that Aeneas' representation has religious significance see E. S. Strong, *Apotheosis and After Life* (London 1915) 201-202 (the wanderings of Aeneas, like those of Heracles, symbolize the trials and victories of the soul), followed by Gagé, *MEFR* 47 (1930) 153-154; Dütschke 36 (as Aeneas saves the *sacra* and his family, so the soul rescues its treasures and bears them into a better world); King 70: "But the flight of Aeneas from burning Troy and his recommencement of a new life across the water . . . carried with it the pledge which inheres in all prototypes, of the life of the world to come"; Manino 39 (Aeneas' representation hints at his descent to the underworld). *Contra*, for instance, Thomas 97.

sculpture is somewhat schematic, but this corresponded to the artistic tastes of the local population. The group thus illustrates the adaptation of Roman imperial art forms into the artistic tradition of the provincials.

These monuments cannot be considered to have been connected with a sepulchral cult of Aeneas. They should not be viewed in an isolated way, for the popularity of the Aeneas theme in these centuries was bound to find a few reflections in funerary art without developing cultic overtones. Moreover, many representations of funerary monuments neither are associated with funerary ritual nor have religious connotations. The she-wolf and the twins, for instance, is a subject which occurs far more often on these monuments and, like the representation of the imperial Aeneas group, was intended as an expression of the provincials' solidarity with Rome's masters and perhaps of their desire to ennoble their descendants.

The artistic, literary, and cultic evidence shows that the chief interest in Aeneas was taken by Rome's leading families. This fact is essential for an understanding of the adoption and development of the Aeneas legend in Rome.

The Aeneas Legend and the Cults of Venus Erycina in Rome

The Lavinian evidence suggests, as we have seen, that the adoption of Aeneas by Rome was the basis of the political and religious reorganization of the Lavinian cults of the Penates/Dioscuri and *Indiges*. Another, "very remarkable tradition,"[78] fits this picture. Dionysius relates that a son of Aeneas, named Romus, founded the cities of Capua, Anchisa, Aenea, and Rome. It is not known to whom Dionysius was indebted for this tradition, although it must have originated

---

[78] So Niese, *HZ* 69 (1888) 490, on D.H. 1.73.3 (=FGH 840 F 40a); cf. the *Etymol. Magn.* s.v. "Καπύη" and " Ῥώμη," and Schur, *Klio* 17 (1921) 143-146.

long before 216 B.C. when Capua defected from Rome. For good reasons it has therefore been dated to the late fourth century. Once more it shows that legend was used politically to establish closer ties with the Greeks in southern Italy.

This notice, and those of Timaeus and Strabo, indicate that the Romans' consciousness of their "Trojan" ancestry must already have been rather well established in 281 B.C., when king Pyrrhus of Epirus crossed over to Magna Graecia at the urgent request of the Tarentines (Pausanias 1.12.1):

> For they were already engaged in a war with the Romans, but could not hold out against them by themselves. They had shown their good will to Pyrrhus previously, because they had sent a fleet to help him in his war with Corcyra. The most forceful arguments, however, of the Tarentine ambassadors were their accounts of Italy, how its prosperity matched that of all of Greece, and their plea that it was counter to divine law to dismiss his friends, when they had come to supplicate him. When the ambassadors urged these considerations, Pyrrhus remembered the sack of Troy, and he had the same hopes for his success in the war, as he, a descendant of Achilles, was waging war against a colony of the Trojans. So the proposal pleased him, and since he never lost time once he had made up his mind, he immediately proceeded to man warships . . .

This was hardly the hour when the Trojan legend was imposed on the Romans, let alone created. Perret himself was aware that the passage expressed more than he was willing to admit:[79]

> Pyrrhus suddenly recalled, as if this had already been an old, uniform, and indisputable tradition, the tradition relating to the Trojan origins of the Romans.

[79] *Origines* 479: "Pyrrhus s'est brusquement souvenu, comme d'une tradition déjà ancienne, uniforme et indiscutable, de la tradition romaine relative à l'origine troyenne des Romains."

170

The incident, if reliably reported, indicates only that the Trojan origin of Rome was already believed at the time of Pyrrhus.[80] That Pyrrhus' motivation was political is evident from Dio's version (frg. 40.2):[81]

> Pyrrhus, the king of Epirus, had a rather high opinion of his powers because foreign nations thought he was a match for the Romans. And he believed it would be opportune to help the fugitives who had taken refuge with him, especially as they were Greeks, and at the same time to surprise the Romans with some plausible pretext before he should suffer injury at their hands.

And Pyrrhus took his propaganda rather seriously: the silver didrachms he issued in southern Italy and Sicily bear Thetis and Achilles' shield on the reverse (Fig. 126a), while on the obverse is shown the youthful head of Achilles, which is only an idealized portrait of Pyrrhus himself (Fig. 126b). At the same time he issued coins with the anti-barbarian Athena Promachos (Fig. 127).[82]

It was in keeping with the ambiguities inherent in the claim to Trojan descent that the Trojan legend could be applied in a hostile way to the Romans. Pyrrhus used it as the rallying cry of the Greeks against the *barbaroi*, and the political overtones overshadowed the original cultural distinction. The use, however, to which the Romans put the Aeneas legend at Lavinium as well as the Capuan episode suggest that it was the Romans who started capitalizing on the Trojan legend for political purposes. Demetrius' reply and the Capuan tradition show most clearly that this was done to seek closer ties with

---

[80] Bickerman, *CW* 37 (1943-1944) 84.

[81] ὅτι Πύρρος ὁ βασιλεὺς τῆς Ἠπείρου τό τε φρόνημα πολλῷ μεῖζον ἔσχεν ἅτε καὶ ὑπὸ τῶν ἀλλοφύλων ἀντίπαλος τοῖς Ῥωμαίοις εἶναι νομιζόμενος, καὶ ἐν τύχῃ οἱ ἡγήσατο ἔσεσθαι τοῖς δὲ πρὸς αὐτὸν καταφυγοῦσιν, ἄλλως τε καὶ Ἕλλησιν οὖσιν, ἐπικουρῆσαι καὶ ἐκείνους σὺν προφάσει τινὶ εὐπρεπεῖ προκαταλαβεῖν, πρίν τι δεινὸν ὑπ' αὐτῶν παθεῖν.

[82] *BMC Thessaly* 111 nos. 7-8, with pl. 20.11; 112 nos. 9-19, with pl. 20.12; see Kienast, *RE* 24 (1963) 110-111.

the Greek world. This is borne out by that example of a political and religious reorganization which is even better documented than Rome's *foedus* with Lavinium: Eryx and Segesta in Sicily. The organization of the chrysophoric community centering around the Erycina cult as well as the coinage after 241 B.C. indicate that Rome, by using the legend politically, tried to appeal to the Greeks and tie them to Rome as allies so as to counter the Carthaginian influence on the island.[83] Pyrrhus had tried to play on the contrast between the Trojan legend of the Sicilian northwest and the Heracles legend of the Doric colonies and even celebrated a great festival in honor of Heracles at Eryx (Plut., *Pyrrh.* 23.7-12). The Romans, however, made it a point to appeal to *all* Greeks in Sicily, and both Heracles and the Trojan ancestors (Fig. 49) appear on the coins of Segesta immediately after the First Punic War.

Given the systematic activation of the Aeneas legend by the Romans, Pyrrhus' pronouncement was merely a reaction to it. Far from seeing in the Romans the kinsmen of the Greeks, the Epirote king exploited the ambivalence of the claim to Trojan ancestry by emphasizing that the Trojans were the barbarian enemies of the Hellenes. Pyrrhus only responded to Roman initiative. Nor does anything suggest that the Greek historiographers were trying to impose the legend of Trojan descent on Rome. The fragments of Timaeus, for instance, who witnessed the emergence of the Trojan legend in Rome, bear the imprint of a fascinated observer rather than of a

---

[83] Cf. Chapter II, p. 64; details in Kienast, *Hermes* 93 (1965) 478-489. On the subsequent instances of the political use of the legend as a means of interfering in Greek politics (Illyria, Acarnania, Ilion, etc.) see Norden, *NJA* 7 (1901) 256-257; M. Holleaux, *Rome, la Grèce et les monarchies héllénistiques au IIIe siècle avant Jésus-Christ (273-205)* (Paris 1921) 7 n. 3 and 53-60; J. Colin, *Rome et la Grèce de 200 à 146 avant Jésus-Christ* (Paris 1905) 36-39, 160-165; E. Manni, *PP* 11 (1956) 179-190. I have not been able to see the dissertation of H. Kirchner, *Die Bedeutung der Fremdkulte in der römischen Ostpolitik* (Bonn 1956), who also stresses (pp. 13ff.) that the initiative at Segesta and Eryx and elsewhere rested with the Romans.

propagandist who is trying to make Trojan descent attractive to the Romans.[84]

As a Sicilian, however, Timaeus was keenly aware of the implications of the conflict between Rome and Carthage, and thus he synchronized their foundation dates. Rome, the new power, clashed with Carthage in Sicily, and the impact on Rome's Trojan legend was profound.

In 263 B.C., the inhabitants of Segesta voluntarily took sides with the Romans after killing the Carthaginian garrison. They gave as a reason for their action their and the Romans' common descent from Aeneas.[85] The "Trojan" heritage of the Sicilian northwest must have made their claim more than credible, although Aeneas now is mentioned for the first time. The coins with Aeneas and Anchises (Fig. 49) show that this tradition dates to the First Punic War. At the same time, the assumption that the Greeks, in this instance and others, seized the initiative in making the Trojan legend a political theme[86] cannot be maintained without serious qualifications. For the action of the Segestans clearly presupposes the realization that the Romans attached great importance to their Trojan descent and were quite willing to see it exploited politically. As we have just seen, the subsequent manipulation of the legend in Sicily by means of the organization of the Eryx cult reveals the Roman initiative even more strongly.

The Erycina had been a Carthage-oriented goddess; the annual rites of καταγώγια and ἀναγώγια linked her to the "Punic" Sicca Veneria. All this changed after the First Punic War. Like the island, the goddess was won over from the

---

[84] For a sensible and brief discussion of the relevant fragments see T. S. Brown, *Timaeus of Tauromenium*. Univ. Cal. Public. Hist. 55 (1958) 33-34; cf. the remarks by A. Momigliano, *RSI* 71 (1959) 549-556, and the notices of Callias and Alcimus (pp. 142-143, above).

[85] Zonaras 8.9.12: Ἔγεσταν ἑκουσίως ἔλαβον. διὰ γὰρ τὴν πρὸς Ῥωμαίους οἰκείωσιν οἱ ἐν αὐτῇ ἀπὸ τοῦ Αἰνείου λέγοντες γεγονέναι προσεχώρησαν αὐτοῖς, τοὺς Καρχηδονίους φονεύσαντες. Cf. Cic., *Verr.* 4.72; D.S. 23.5.

[86] So Perret, *Origines* 502, followed by Bömer, *Rom und Troia* 45; for the opposite view, see the works cited in note 83.

173

Carthaginians to the Roman side. Schilling has summarized this brilliantly:[87]

> Finally, of a cosmopolitan goddess, the Romans made a national one. We have stressed the diversity of the religious "stratification" of the Eryx goddess, the different layers—Sicanian, Phoenician, Greek, Punic. At the arrival of the Romans, the oriental character dominated her, underscored as it was by the institution of the sacred courtesans. . . . Perhaps it is here that one must admire most the imaginative boldness of the Romans. Far from feeling embarrassed by the "Punic monopoly" of the Eryx goddess, they admirably exploited the Trojan environment in the land of the Elymians to reverse the situation. By virtue of the Trojan legend, they were able to claim Venus Erycina as *their* goddess.

The new character of the goddess was projected even into earlier times; Aelian (*N.A.* 10.50) relates that a sacrilege committed against her was the reason for the Carthaginian defeat at Himera and Hamilcar's cruel death in 480 B.C.

The anti-Carthaginian tendency of the goddess was well remembered in 217 B.C., when Q. Fabius Maximus, in an hour of dire national danger, decided, after consulting the Sibylline books, to vow a temple to Venus Erycina (Livy 22.9.7-11). In 215 B.C., the dedication took place in the most solemn manner possible: the dictator himself presided over the ceremony. It has rightly been noted that the date of the dedication of the temple, the choice of its location, and the rites connected with her cult all point to the fact that the Romans accorded to Venus Erycina the status not of a foreign goddess, but of a national one.[88]

Several details deserve special consideration. The anniversary of the temple dedication was celebrated on April 23, the feast of the *Vinalia Priora*, during which an offering of wine

---

[87] *Vénus* 244. For the Punic features of the cult see Chapter II, pp. 71-72.
[88] Schilling 243.

was made to Jupiter. At least by the time of Augustus, the origin of these libations was believed to have been a solemn oath sworn by Aeneas before his duel with Mezentius:

hostica Tyrrheno vota est vindemnia regi:
Iuppiter, e Latio palmite musta feres!
(Ovid, *Fasti* 4.893-894)

Similarly, the fact that the temple of Mens was dedicated in the same year and that it was separated from the temple of the Capitoline Venus by only *canali uno* (Livy 23.31.9) has been considered as more than a coincidence.[89] Did Aeneas' traditional reputation as the "mind" of the Trojans establish a link between the two cults of the "Trojan" Venus Erycina and Mens?

Other explanations have been offered.[90] After the disaster at Lake Trasimene of Flaminius, whose political behavior was considered eccentric by the ruling classes at least, an appeal to Mens may have suggested itself. The most evident link between the two temples is the men who dedicated them: Titus Otacilius, the commander of the fleet in Sicilian Lilybaeum, performed the rites for Mens. In the year preceding that of the dedication of the temples, the Carthaginians had tried to take that stronghold (Livy 21.49ff.), and this could well be considered an attempt to reoccupy Eryx, which had been their principal base of operations during the First Punic War. It therefore must have been quite an important concern for the Roman state religion to have the goddess of Mt. Eryx within the walls of Rome, without any "Trojan" considerations being implicit in her transfer. The meaning of cultic events may simply have been that the Sicilian commander secured for the Italian one the blessing of Mens, while the Italian one, Fabius Cunctator, assured Otacilius in Sicily of the favor of Erycina. The Sicilian goddess otherwise would have been likely to revert to her former association with the Carthagin-

---

[89] By Schilling 251-252.   [90] See Koch, *Religio* 84-85.

ians. Sicily was on the verge of defecting from Rome and a close tie between the island and Rome was called for.

This still does not explain why the goddess Mens was chosen. Perhaps this was done out of regard for Cunctator, whose level-headedness was his chief asset. If this was the case, the possibility that genealogical considerations were involved can hardly be denied, especially since another Fabius, Q. Fabius Gurges, had dedicated the first Roman Venus temple, that of Venus Obsequens, on April 23, 295 B.C. The tenacity of Fabius' efforts (Livy 22.9.7, 9; 23.30.13), however, suggests that he saw in this cult a better means for strengthening his *auctoritas* than in any political office, and this rather than genealogical concern accounts for his interest in it.[91] Consequently, the Trojan explanation for the reason why Mens was chosen to complement Venus Erycina deserves serious consideration. We saw earlier that Aeneas' traditional claim to fame had been his sagacity.[92] Moreover, the utilization of the Trojan legend had been instrumental in the Roman organization of the chrysophoric community of seventeen Sicilian cities with Eryx as the center. The Eryx goddess and Aeneas must have been closely associated since that time.

That the reasons for the transfer of the Erycina were connected with the Trojan legend is further suggested by the Romans' successful attempt to bring the Magna Mater from Pessinus/Pergamum to Rome a few years later, in 204 B.C. They appealed to Attalus for permission to do so because of their Trojan descent.[93] Not only was her temple built inside the *pomerium*, but on the summit of the Palatine, virtually in

[91] So T. Köves, *Historia* 12 (1963) 342-344; Koch 85 also denies that Fabius was motivated by genealogical considerations.

[92] See Chapter I, pp. 36-41.

[93] The numerous sources are listed by E. Schmidt, *Kultübertragungen* (Giessen 1909) 1 n. 1. Most scholars stress the Trojan overtones of the importation of this cult: e.g., H. Graillot, *Le culte de Cybèle mère des dieux à Rome et dans l'empire romain* (Paris 1912) 43-44; S. Aurigemma, *BCAR* 21 (1909) 31-65; A. Bartoli, *Mem. Pont. Acc. Arch.* 3rd ser. 6 (1947) 229-239; P. Romanelli, *MAL* 46 (1963) 221-222, who reports on

the heart of the city. This highly unusual and intentional step cannot be explained merely by the general quickening of religious fervor and sentiment that was prompted by the Second Punic War. It indicates that the Romans attributed to Magna Mater almost ancestral character; she was, after all, the great goddess from Mt. Ida near Troy. She was received in Rome by the *vir optimus* P. Cornelius Scipio Nasica. When, in 190 B.C., his cousins L. Cornelius Scipio and P. Cornelius Scipio Africanus went to Asia Minor, one of their first actions was to go to Troy and greet her inhabitants as kinsmen of the Roman people (Livy 37.37.3): *et Iliensibus in omni rerum verborumque honore ab se oriundos Romanos praeferentibus et Romanis laetis origine sua.* The transfer of the Erycina, then, seems to have encouraged the *evocatio* of the Asian goddess from Troy.

Another example of the mobilization of the Trojan ideology against Carthage is the Marcian oracle. It is reported by Livy, and even its most severe critics[94] admit that its general tenor, if not its exact formulation, goes back to the time of the Second Punic War (Livy 25.12.5-6):

> amnem, Troiugena, fuge Cannam, ne te alienigenae cogant in campo Diomedis conserere manus. Sed neque credes tu mihi, donec compleris sanguine campum, multaque milia occisa tua deferet amnis in pontum magnum ex terra frugifera . . .

Compare the beginning of the hexameter version of the Marcian oracle:

> Amnem, Troiugena, fatalem defuge Cannam,
> ne te alienigenae campo cogant Diomedis
> conseruisse manus hostes . . .
>
> (Baehrens, *PLM* 6.294)

---

the excavation of the temple on the Palatine (201-330). *Contra,* Bömer (note 117, below).

[94] E.g., E. Baehrens, in the Teubner text of *Poetae Latini Minores* 6.21, who dates the hexameter version to 76 B.C.

Diels' interpretation that the Romans as *Troiugenae* are of a different race than the *alienigenae* Greeks and thus are pictured as their enemies has been accepted unquestioningly.[95] Baehrens, however, sensed that this implication was not really in the text, and thus substituted *Argivigenae* for *alienigenae*. We saw earlier, however, that the Trojans nowhere are presented as the political enemies of the Greeks, and that the example set by Pyrrhus is an exception to this general rule. The prophecy thus expresses exactly the opposite of what Diehls thought it did: since the battle of Cannae is referred to, the *alienigenae hostes* can only be the Carthaginians. Against them fight the Trojan Romans, who are associated with the Greeks (*campo Diomedis*). This was precisely the use to which the Trojan legend was put in Sicily, Asia Minor, and the Greek world in general: to make the Greeks aware of their kinship with the Romans and of their common obligation to fight against that enemy of the Greek world, Carthage. The phraseology used in connection with the transfer of the Magna Mater is the same and thus supports the view that she was brought to Rome for anti-Carthaginian, Trojan reasons (Livy 29.10.5):

> . . . quandoque *hostis alienigena* terrae Italiae bellum intulisset, eum pelli Italia vincique posse, si mater Idaea a Pessinunte Romam advecta foret.

Beyond any doubt *hostis alienigena* here refers to the Carthaginians.

In 181 B.C. a temple of Venus Erycina was built outside the pomerium near the Porta Collina.[96] Its dedication was complemented by that of a temple to Pietas. The question whether Trojan considerations again accounted for this link

---

[95] *Sibyllinische Blätter* (Berlin 1890) 43 n. 2, followed, e.g., by Norden, *NJA* 7 (1901) 326, and Perret, *Origines* 454-458.

[96] For the details and relevant bibliography see Schilling, *Vénus* 254-262, and Koch, *RE* 8A (1955) 855-856; cf. Wissowa, *RuK*² 331.

has been the subject of some debate. Schilling, who rightly rejects Wissowa's attempt to explain the choice of Pietas by the fact that the son of the man who vowed the temple made good his father's vow and dedicated it, notes that the connection between these two temples seems to have been less strong than that between those of Venus Erycina *in Capitolio* and Mens. The later temples have in common only the date of their dedication. Schilling's main argument, however, is that the exotic features of the Porta Collina temple militate against a possible intentional association with the Pietas temple. The second Erycina sanctuary preserved the oriental features of the Sicilian cult much more than the thoroughly Romanized cult on the Capitol had done. On the anniversary of the dedication, the statue of the goddess was carried in a procession amid a sea of roses and other flowers. Her cult soon eclipsed that of her matronly predecessor on the Capitol. Ovid, therefore, writing in the *Fasti* under April 23, the dedication date of both Venus temples, chooses to describe the colorful spectacle at the Porta Collina and makes due mention of the particular kind of faithful the Sicilian Venus attracted (*Fasti* 4.865-870):

> numina vulgares Veneris celebrate puellae!
>   multa professarum quaestibus apta Venus.
> poscite ture dato formam populique favorem,
>   poscite blanditias dignaque verba ioco,
> cumque sua dominae date grata sisymbria myrto
>   tectaque composita iuncea vincla rosa!

The Sicilian influence of *hieroduleia* is reflected here, and in the Praenestine Fasti April 23 was known simply as *dies meretricum*.[97] The prayers addressed to the goddess had mostly

---

[97] *CIL* 1².316. Other shadowy characters used the portico of the temple as their favorite hangout; *CIL* 6.2274, e.g., mentions one Stiminius Heracla, *sortilegus ab Venere Erucina*.

erotic overtones. *Iuvenes* and *puellae* went to beseech her to deliver them from an unfeeling heart (Ovid, *R.A.* 553-554):

> illic et iuvenes votis oblivia poscunt
> et si qua est duro capta puella viro.

The very architecture of the temple explains its link with the temple of Pietas. The shrine probably stood on the west side of the Via Salaria,[98] and since the gardens of Sallust extended as far as the Via Salaria the temple of Venus Erycina is likely to have been called in imperial times *Templum Veneris Hortorum Sallustianorum*. This name is attested by several inscriptions[99] and recurs on a sketch that was made probably by Onofrio Panvinio, on the basis of a description by the Renaissance architect Pirro Ligorio, who lived in the sixteenth century (text fig. 3).[100] The drawing shows one half of a round building surrounded by a colonnade and is accompanied by some annotations with the measurements of the columns and capitals. The sketch also corresponds in all details to the description given by Flaminio Vacca,[101] who excavated in the Horti Sallustiani near the Porta Salaria:

[98] R. Lanciani, *Forma Urbis Romae* (Milan 1893-1901), pl. 3, followed by Nash, *MDAI(R)* 66 (1959) 111 fig. 1, placed the temple at the corner of the Via Sicilia and the Via Lucania, whereas Platner-Ashby, *Topographical Dictionary* 551, and M. Santangelo, *Mem. Pont. Acc. Arch.* 3rd ser. 5 (1946) 138, prefer a location near the present Via Belisario. Cf. G. Lugli, *I monumenti antichi di Roma e suburbio* 3 (Rome 1938) 33-336:

[99] *CIL* 6.122 (found *in situ*); 32451, 32468.

[100] *Cod. Vat. Lat.* 3439 f. 28. R. Lanciani, *BCAR* 16 (1888) 5, had this comment on the authorship of the drawing: "L'icnografia [sic] di mano del Ligorio è accompagnata dagli appunti che seguono, presi sul posto, da Onofrio Panvinio," and in *MEFR* 11 (1891) 168, he ascribed the authorship of *Cod. Vat. Lat.* 3439 without any qualifications to Ligorio. C. Hülsen, *MDAI(R)* 4 (1889) 271-272, pointed out that the drawing was by Panvinio and was based on Ligorio's description of the temple of Venus Hortorum Sallustianorum in *Cod. Parisinus* 309. See further the discussions by Pace, *Sicilia antica* 3.636-644 with fig. 168, and Nash, *MDAI(R)* 66 (1959) 132-137 with figs. 4 and 5.

[101] *Memorie scritte da Flaminio Vacca nel 1594* no. 58, in C. Fea, *Miscellanea filologica critica e antiquaria* 1 (1790) 78-79: "Cavandovi, trovò una fabrica di forma ovata, con portico attorno ornato di colonne gialle, lunghe

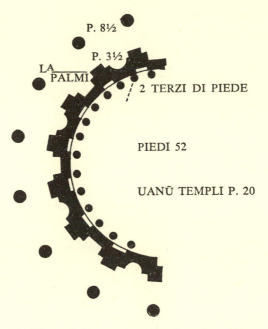

3. Plan of Venus temple. Drawing after
Codex Vat. Lat. 3439 f. 28

a great oval structure with a portico around it, which was adorned with yellow columns, fluted and eighteen palms long, with capitals, and Corinthian bases; and this building had four entrances with stairs that descended to a pavement, made out of small stones and pleasantly subdivided, and at each entrance there were two columns of oriental alabaster so transparent that the sun passed through them without impediment.

palmi dieciotto, scannelate, con capitelli, e basi corintie. Detto aveva quattro entrate con scale, che scendevano in esso al pavimento fatto di mischi con belli scompartimenti, ed a ciascuna di dette entrate vi erano due colonne di alabastro orientale si trasparente, che il sole vi passava senza impedimento." Vacca continues that the Cardinal di Montepulciano dismantled the columns for use in his chapel in S. Pietro di Montorio, while one of the alabaster columns was to be shipped to the king of Portugal, "ma quando furono in alto mare, l'impetuosa Fortuna, trovandosele in suo dominio, ne fece un presente al mare."

The identification of this building with the temple of Venus was first proposed by Lanciani, whereas Hülsen objected that it was merely a lavishly decorated pavilion, connected with fountains or, even more probably, it was a bath.[102] Hülsen completed the plan (text fig. 4) and contended that the layout was not suitable for a temple, but showed a marked similarity to the plan of a building on the Marble Map of Rome. This building, located near the Porticus Divorum, also had four entrances and stairs in its interior just as Vacca had written of the building in the Horti Sallustiani. However, Hülsen continued, the Marble Map showed that the former building was a *lavacrum*, a bath, and not a temple.

A newly discovered fragment of the *Forma Urbis* disposes of Hülsen's argument. The marble original of the segment with the round building, which Hülsen used as a parallel for that in the Horti Sallustiani, has been lost, but a drawing has been preserved in the same Vatican Codex in which the drawing based on Ligorio's description was found (Fig. 132).[103] The authenticity of the drawing of the Marble Plan fragment is beyond question, and the same therefore can be said of the sketch attributed to Ligorio (text fig. 3). Until recently, the inscription VACH, which identifies the building, was taken as referring to the Lavacrum Agrippinae, or Agrippae, which necessitated changing the reading from VACH to VACR.[104] The recently found fragment, however, contains the beginning of the inscription, which *in toto* now reads: MInerVACH (Fig. 133).[105] The round building, which is so similar to that in

[102] Lanciani, *BCAR* 16 (1888) 3-11; Hülsen (note 100, above) 270-274. His plan on p. 273 is our text fig. 3.

[103] *Cod. Vat. Lat.* 3439 f. 13; reproduced by I. P. Bellori, *Fragmenta vestigii veteris Romae* (Rome 1673), pl. 5.

[104] Lavacrum Agrippinae: Bellori 23; lavacrum Agrippae (mentioned by Hist. Aug., *Hadr.* 19.10): E. Sjöqvist, *Act. Inst. Rom. Suec.* 12, *Opusc. Arch.* 4 (1946) 99-115.

[105] G. Carettoni, L. Cozza, *et al., La Pianta Marmorea di Roma Antica* (Rome 1959) 97-102 with pl. 31.

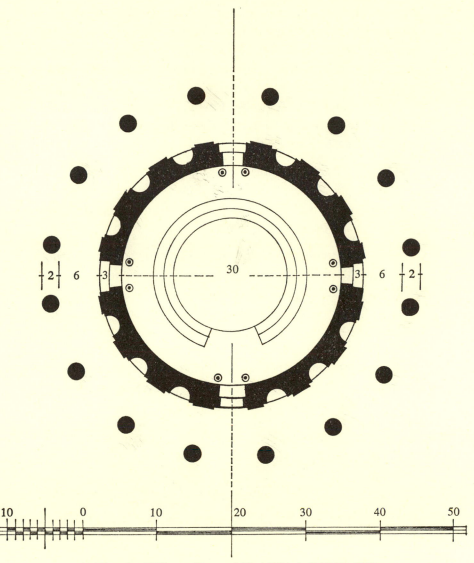

4. Plan by Hülsen. From *MDAI(R)* 4 (1889) 273

the Gardens of Sallust, thus turns out to be the temple of
Minerva Chalcidica.

The Gardens of Sallust were horribly devastated during
the sack of Rome by the Goths in 410 A.D. Nonetheless, two

closely related sculptures which doubtless belonged to a temple, the Ludovisi and Boston Thrones, were found in close proximity to the spot where Vacca discovered the round building. This is a further indication that this building was a temple.[106]

The Venus temple at the Porta Collina, therefore, was round. The same has been said about the temple at Eryx, for Strabo relates:[107]

There is a reproduction of this goddess in Rome, I mean the temple before the Colline Gate, which is called the temple of Venus Erycina. It is remarkable for its shrine and the surrounding colonnade.

The interpretation of the passage hinges on the word ἀφίδρυμα. It originally means "copy," "reproduction," especially of a statue, and used in a wider sense, also came to mean "shrine, temple." Strabo always is careful to say ἀφίδρυμα τοῦ ἱεροῦ, "reproduction of a temple," when one shrine in fact was the copy of another.[108] This is not the case here. All the Strabonic passage means is that in Rome, the Eryx goddess was worshiped at her temple near the Porta Collina under much the same appearance as in Sicily. Therefore we cannot conclude that the round temple in Rome was an imitation of the Eryx shrine, nor does the Considius coin (Fig. 54a) support this assumption.[109]

---

[106] So, rightly, Nash, *MDAI(R)* 66 (1959) 137. See the Appendix for a discussion of these two finds and a colossal head of Aphrodite, which was also found in the Horti Sallustiani.

[107] 6.2.6: ἀφίδρυμα δ' ἐστὶ καὶ ἐν Ῥώμῃ τῆς θεοῦ ταύτης τὸ πρὸ τῆς πύλης τῆς Κολλίνης ἱερὸν Ἀφροδίτης Ἐρυκίνης λεγόμενον, ἔχον καὶ νεὼν καὶ στοὰν περικειμένην ἀξιόλογον.

[108] E.g., 8.4.4; 16.4.4.

[109] Although this is believed to be the case by Pace, *Sicilia antica* 3.642-644 with note 6, where he asks for "la necessaria ingenuità prospettica." The architectural representation on this coin is not entirely unequivocal, but I accept the arguments of Cultrera, *NSA* n.s. 11 (1935) 327 (cf. Chapter II, p. 71), and S. Mirone, *RIN* 31 (1918) 189-198—an article apparently not known to either Cultrera or Pace—that the temple is at least tetrastyle.

While the Romans copied the features of the Sicilian cult as much as was permissible in the years after the *senatus consultum de Bacchanalibus*, they deliberately refused to copy the architecture of the Sicilian shrine also. The choice of a round temple and the dedication of a temple to Pietas on the same day are not due to accident. The oldest round temple in Rome had been that of Vesta. There were kept the Penates which by the late fourth century had become identified with those of Aeneas. The architecture of the new Erycina temple and Pietas as the goddess of the second shrine were chosen to complement, by reference to Aeneas, and offset the aspects of the new Venus cult, the institution of which seems to have been the subject of some discussion. The Erycina temple was vowed by a member of the *gens* Porcia in the year of Cato's censorship. The suggestion[110] that Cato was responsible for having the temple built *extra pomerium* is more than plausible; the decision to turn the still unspecified temple, which Glabrio had vowed, into a shrine of Pietas may well have originated also with this staunch defender of Roman morals.

The Erycina cult at the Porta Collina was a compromise which would be unthinkable without the antecedents of the Capitoline Erycina cult and the cult of Magna Mater. The latter was kept tightly under control and led an isolated and obscure existence until the time of Augustus. The spirit of this cult, however, was not to be denied entirely and the establishment of a somewhat freer Erycina cult outside the *pomerium* was a concession to it. In the light of these multiple connections between the cults of Venus, Magna Mater, and the Trojan legend, Perret's contention that the cult of Venus and the Aeneas legend existed separately is not very compelling. On the other hand, there is no indication in our sources that the dedication of the Erycina temple on the Capitol in 215 B.C.

[110] Made by Koch, *RE* 8A (1955) 855.

was an act of *primordia consecrare*—consecrating the origins of Rome.[111]

Nor are Mars and Venus Erycina likely to have already been considered the ancestors of the Roman people at the *lectisternium* in 217 B.C.[112] Rather, because the goddess had led them to victory over Carthage, the Romans added to the already composite character of the Sicilian goddess a new trait and successfully Romanized her by placing the emphasis on this new aspect of victory. This is evident from the first Roman coins with her picture (Figs. 54b and 129), issued by the Considii in the 60's and 40's B.C. She there appears with a laurel wreath and diadem, while Victoria with her quadriga often is represented on the reverse.[113] The typological inspiration stems from some coins of Eryx which show the quadriga of Victory on the obverse (Fig. 130a) and the Erycina, with her dove and Eros, on the reverse (Fig. 130b).[114] Even in imperial times, when the Eryx Venus was hailed as the Genetrix of the Julians and then of the entire Roman people, she still was known as *Venus Victrix in Capitolio*.[115] Since Venus had to become "martial" first before being associated with Mars, the concept of Victrix preceded that of Genetrix;[116] the victorious aspect of the goddess was stressed earlier than the genealogical one.

The transfer of Venus Erycina to the Capitol and of Magna Mater, and the establishment of the companion temples of Mens and Pietas were the work of Roman nobles. None of

[111] That it was such an act is assumed by G. Rohde, *Studien und Interpretationen* (Berlin 1962) 204; similarly, Schilling, *Vénus* 265-266.

[112] Livy 22.9.7—10.10. I follow Koch, *RE* 8A (1955) 853-854, and, with more detail, *Religio* 81-86; *contra*, Schilling 206-209.

[113] *BMC Rep.* 1.473 nos. 3830-3832, with pl. 47.21=Sydenham 886-889a with pl. 24; *BMC Rep.* 1.532 nos. 4087-4090, with pl. 52.16 (Paetus)= Sydenham nos. 992-993.

[114] Rizzo, *Monete* pl. 64.12.

[115] *CIL* 1².331 with Mommsen's commentary.

[116] Cf. Koch, *Religio* 82-85, and for the association of Venus and Mars in Rome, Chapter V, pp. 233-234.

these cults enjoyed any popularity until Augustus revived interest in them and, with the exception of Mens, their Aeneadic associations. The reason is that they owed their inception to political motives and reasons of state. In the case of the Magna Mater, the Roman nobility in fact was appalled by the cult as such, demonstratively ignored it, and treated the appeals of Asian cities in the name of Cybele and her priests with an attitude of reserve bordering on rejection.[117]

In sum, these cults were merely manifestations of the political use of Rome's Trojan legend in the field of religion. They exemplify, to use the historical categories of Jacob Burckhardt, the primacy of the state over religion which existed in Rome and other ancient states. Rome's claim to be a Trojan foundation became an important instrument in her eastern policy especially in the second half of the third century B.C. In some instances Rome used the legend of her origins to demonstrate that she was well disposed toward her "blood relations." For example, in the mid-240's the Romans asked the Syrian ruler Seleukos Kallinikos to free the inhabitants of the Troad from all taxation (Suet., *Claud.* 25.3), and in 238 they heeded an appeal of the Acarnanians for help against the Aetolians because Acarnania had been the only part of Greece that had not participated in the Trojan War (Justin. 28.1). In other instances, her Trojan ancestry served to cast an appearance of legitimacy on Rome's threats to interfere in the affairs of the Hellenistic east.[118] Once her great eastern opponents had been overcome, the usefulness of the legend

---

[117] Livy 37.9.9, 18.9-10; cf. D.S. 36.13; Val. Max. 7.7.6; D.H. 2.19.4-5; this evidence led F. Bömer, *MDAI(R)* 71 (1964) 130-151, esp. 134, to conclude that there was no connection between the Trojan legend and the transfer of the cult. For the senatorial reaction see also F. Cumont, *The Oriental Religions in Roman Paganism* (New York 1956) 51-53. Ovid, *Fasti* 4.247ff., reflects the Augustan revival by modeling the transfer of the goddess on the wanderings of Aeneas.

[118] See Holleaux (note 83, above) 53ff., and the works by Colin and Norden cited in the same note; also, Alföldi, *Urahnen* 33-34.

for the political and cultural objectives of the state was exhausted.

The deliberate use of the legend for these purposes shows that it was adopted not by the people, but by the few who were responsible for Rome's policy. It is therefore not surprising that from the early second century on, some of Rome's noble families, the *familiae Troianae*, appropriated the claim to Trojan descent for their own private purposes and that it became their genealogical prerogative. More than one hundred years ago, A. Schwegler had already observed that the legend did not have the characteristics of a living popular tradition and[119] more recently, an authority on the Etruscans remarked that "in Rome, the Aeneas legend was brought to the people from above, and never took firm roots."[120] This is certainly true of Republican Rome. Because the Erycina cult at the Porta Collina was free from any Trojan considerations, it enjoyed the popular favor that was denied to the others.

The Punic Wars, in which Romans and Sicilian Greeks were united in their common cause against Carthage, left their imprint on Rome's Trojan tradition. The Sicilian Venus became Aeneas' goddess: *est et Erucina quam Aeneas secum advexit.*[121] Because it was so closely associated with Sicily, the Trojan legend of Rome took on anti-Carthaginian overtones. This is confirmed by Alföldi's ingenious observation that the Roman state had the head of its Trojan ancestress, Rhome, put on the coins struck during the First Punic War (Fig. 131a).[122] This action constituted merely a reply to the

[119] *Römische Geschichte* 1².309.

[120] Enking (Chapter III, n. 92) 95.

[121] Serv. auct., *Aen.* 1.720; cf. Chapter III, p. 116. The name Aegestus of the chief Alban priest of the Penates cult at Lavinium (D.H. 1.67.2) also reflects the rise of the importance of the Sicilian Venus.

[122] *Urahnen* 30-33; *Early Rome* 158-159, elaborating the suggestion of E. Haeberlin, "Der Roma Typus der Münzen der römischen Republik," *Corolla Numismatica B.V. Head* (London 1906) 135-155. The head is commonly identified as that of Bellona, but H. Mattingly, *NC* 6th ser. 17 (1957) 287-288, rightly maintains that it was an intentionally composite type susceptible to various interpretations; cf. our argument about Venus/Tellus/Italia in Chapter V.

enemy; Rhome was chosen as the political antithesis to the representation of "Dido" on the coins of Magna Graecia under Carthaginian rule, which had been issued one or two generations before. We saw earlier that Rhome had been the invention of Greek historiographers and the acceptance of this tradition by the Romans once more was designed as an appeal and a reminder to the Greeks of the common Graeco-Roman cause against Carthage. As in the case of Aeneas, the Romans again endeavored to stress the Greek aspects of her appearance. The iconography of Rhome/Bellona thus underwent a change, and a classical helmet type (Fig. 131c) came to replace the Phrygian one with the griffin's crest (Fig. 131b).

The importance of Sicily and the Punic Wars for Rome's Aeneas legend also is reflected in Roman literature. In Naevius' *Bellum Punicum*, the first Roman epic, the Aeneas legend may have been introduced into the narrative on the occasion of the Segestan defection to Rome or of the campaigns near Segesta in 260 B.C., and perhaps even was told by a Segestan.[123] Aeneas' encounter with Dido, whatever its nature may have been, doubtless served as a poetic *aition* for the conflict between Carthage and Rome. Naevius was a veteran of the First Punic War, and an account of the legendary beginning of the conflict between Carthage and Rome seems very fitting indeed in connection with the city where this conflict manifested itself first in all its brutality. In two comedies of Naevius' contemporary Plautus, the character delineation of the heroines mirrors the controversy between traditionalists and innovators about the Erycina cult before her second temple was built in 184 B.C.[124] One of the plays is the *Poenulus*, whose hero is a Carthaginian.

[123] So Scevola Mariotti, *Il Bellum Poenicum e l'arte di Nevio* (Rome 1955) 27; cf. A. Klotz, *RhM* 87 (1938) 190-192; L. Strzelecki, *Cn. Naevii Belli Punici quae supersunt* (Wroclaw 1959) 62. The opinions about the epic's structure are summarized by H. T. Rowell in *AJP* 87 (1966) 210-217.

[124] See A. G. Amatucci, "L'amicizia di Palestra e il culto di Venere nel *Rudens* di Plauto," *GIF* 3 (1950) 206-210, with the remarks by Koch, *RE* 8A (1955) 853, and my article, "The Cult of Venus Erycina and Plautus' *Poenulus*," *Hommages à Marcel Renard* 1 (Brussels 1969) 358-364.

Finally, this Roman national experience of the second century found its most perfect reflection in the importance accorded to Sicily in the *Aeneid* within the story of Rome's Aeneas legend.[125] As the Sicilian episode epitomized and was inseparably connected with the development of this legend, which it brought to full bloom, so the Sicilian Book of the *Aeneid, Aeneid* 5, epitomizes the epic as a whole and is linked to its every phase. It was in Sicily that the Romans became fully aware of their claim to Trojan descent; it is in Sicily that Aeneas begins to understand the implications of his mission. In spite of the Italic roots of Aeneas, the adoption of the legend by Rome had had something artificial about it. Vergil therefore deliberately stressed that aspect of the Trojan legend which was most realistic for the Romans: its mobilization against the Carthaginians during the Punic Wars. This accounts for the importance of Sicily in the epic, which many scholars have considered excessive or, at least, unprecedented.

The revival of the claim to Trojan descent had been the result of political calculation and cultural ambition. After these objectives had been fulfilled, Aeneas belonged to the *familiae Troianae* until the time of Augustus. It was due only to the impact of the *Aeneid* that he became the truly popular property of the whole Roman people. Attention has already been called to the deluge of artifacts with the Aeneas theme in the first two centuries A.D.[126] And it is on an artistic monument of the Augustan age, which was in large part inspired by the *Aeneid*, that Rome's Trojan legend and its Sicilian overtones found a most felicitous and lasting expression.

---

[125] This paragraph is a capsule summary of my article, "*Aeneid* V and the *Aeneid*," *AJP* 89 (1968) 157-185; cf. Chapter III, pp. 110-111.

[126] See Chapter I, p. 4 with note 4.

CHAPTER V

VENUS IN A RELIEF OF

THE ARA PACIS

AUGUSTAE[1]

E VER SINCE the discovery of the marble slabs composing the outer frieze on the enclosure of the Ara Pacis Augustae, the interpretation of the scenes represented on them has been the subject of continuous discussion. This is not surprising. No other artistic monument of the Augustan era expresses with comparable elaborateness and symbolic intensity the aspirations of the young Principate and, primarily, of the emperor himself. This point deserves to be stressed from the outset. The recent controversy between S. Weinstock and J. Toynbee, while proving little else except that not much in connection with the Ara Pacis can be "proved,"[2] has at

[1] A preliminary version of this chapter appeared in *AJA* 70 (1966) 223-244 (see Preface, p. viii). Additional bibliographical details may be found there, although much new material has been added.

It was not until the summer of 1967 that I came upon Erika Simon's *Die Geburt der Aphrodite* (Berlin 1959) 102-103, where she briefly suggested the interpretation that is set forth here in more detail; cf. her discussion in W. Helbig, *Führer durch die öffentlichen Sammlungen klassischer Altertümer in Rom* 2⁴ (Tübingen 1966) 692. To Miss Anne Booth of Brown University the same idea had occurred independently of my work, and I am grateful to her for letting me see a draft of her article "Venus on the Ara Pacis," *Latomus* 25 (1966) 873-879. Ultimately our interpretation may be said to have originated with Benndorf, *Vasenbilder* 77-78, who saw the relief in Florence without realizing that it was part of the Ara Pacis.

[2] S. Weinstock, "Pax and the Ara Pacis," *JRS* 50 (1960) 44-58; J. Toynbee, "The 'Ara Pacis Augustae,'" *JRS* 57 (1961) 153-156. Miss Toynbee concludes: "Dr. Weinstock has most forcibly and usefully reminded us that we have no ineluctable, explicit proof that the Campus Martius Augustan altar is the Ara Pacis Augustae. But he has not, to my mind, succeeded in proving to us that 'it is certainly not the Ara Pacis Augustae.'" The very

least pointed up very clearly that the altar was not built merely for the cult of Peace. It also had a very personal connection with Augustus, for it was decreed, as he himself tells us, *pro reditu meo* (*Mon. Anc.* 2.39), in thanksgiving for his home-coming from abroad. Initially the Senate had planned to build an altar in honor of Augustus in the Senate-chamber itself and further had decreed that "those who supplicated him while he was inside the pomerium would be granted immunity" (τοῖς ἱκετεύσασιν αὐτὸν ἐντὸς τοῦ πωμηρίου ὄντα ἄδειαν εἶναι: Dio 54.25.3). In place of this altar for suppliants, the Ara Pacis, approved by the emperor, was built *ad Campum Martium*. But the fact that the Altar of Peace was modeled on the Altar of Pity, the traditional sanctuary of suppliants at Athens,[3] seems to indicate once more that an "Augustan" altar was foremost in the builders' minds. The Altar is not merely Ara Pacis, but Ara Pacis Augustae.

Another principle that one has to take into account in any discussion of the Altar is its close dependence on or reflection of Augustan poetry. It is the artistic counterpart of what Horace and Vergil did in poetry; it is, to use Moretti's felicitous phrase, "un poema artistico."[4] As in Horace's *Odes* or the *Aeneid*, the unity of the frieze is achieved primarily not by the action that is represented or described, but by a complex

---

starting point of Weinstock's argument is amiss; Pax need not be represented on the altar, but is the sum total of the scenes represented on it;
cf. pp. 237-238, below, and Booth 873 n. 1.

[3] See H. Thompson, *Hesperia* 21 (1952) 47-82. The literary references to the Athenian altar may be found in J. G. Frazer, *Pausanias' Description of Greece* 2 (London 1889) 143-144, and W. Judeich, *Topographie von Athen* (Munich 1931) 356-357.

[4] See Moretti, *APA* 307-310 and 216 (whence the quotation is taken); D. Norberg, *Emerita* 20 (1952) 105-106; G. E. Duckworth, *TAPA* 87 (1956) 314-315; Hanell, *Opusc. Rom.* 2 (1960) 119, sums this up best by stating: "On the Ara Pacis poetry is joined with pictorial art. It is only with the help of Augustan poetry that the reliefs receive their full meaning and the entire decoration of the outer walls is united in harmonious unity." H. Malmström, *Ara Pacis and Vergil's Aeneid: A Comparative Study* (Malmo 1963), postulates too one-sided a dependence of the altar on *Aeneid* 6, and his rearrangement of the frieze slabs on this basis is rather arbitrary.

interweaving of motifs. There are several levels of meaning, and symbolism rather than allegory is the outstanding characteristic of the Ara as well as of Augustan poetry.[5] The relationship between the individual frieze groups is determined by a complex system of balances and contrasts: "Everything in this work of art is determined down to the last detail. It is full of relationships and allusions which we today cannot grasp in their entirety."[6]

Although we may never be able fully to explore the wealth of associations of the relief decoration, one relief in particular deserves to be carefully studied again. This is the so-called Tellus, or Italia, relief (Fig. 134), which flanks the south side of the east entrance gate of the Altar. Its character fully justifies such investigation. One scholar has aptly observed that "among all the other reliefs of the Ara Pacis, this relief is richest in thought and religion."[7] To a greater extent than any other relief of the Altar, the representation on this particular slab draws on a multiplicity of inspirations and fuses a variety of traditions into a new homogeneous unity. Petersen, who was the first to recognize the "central" importance of the relief, placed it initially in the center of the east wall.[8] After the discovery of the entrance he reluctantly agreed to assign the relief the place it had held since, although he maintained that its "centrality" pointed to a borrowing from another monument where the slab had been flanked by two other reliefs.[9] For the movement of the figures to the right and left of the

---

[5] Cf. V. Pöschl, *Die Dichtkunst Virgils*[2] (Vienna 1964) 36-37. By symbol I mean that several significances are intended, whereas an allegory establishes just one equation. The complex character of Augustan coin types which, for good reasons, have always been called symbolic rather than allegorical, is discussed by J. Liegle, *JDAI* 46 (1941) 91-119, and by M. Grant, *NC* 6th ser. 9 (1949) 22-35.

[6] W. Lübke-Pernice, *Die Kunst der Römer* (Vienna 1958) 245.

[7] G. E. Rizzo, *BCAR* 57 (1939) 159: ". . . fra tutti gli altri rilievi dell' Ara Pacis quella maggiormente piena di pensiero e di religione."

[8] *APA* 48-54.

[9] *JOAI* 9 (1906) 303-304; *contra*, J. Sieveking, *JOAI* 10 (1907) 186.

central figure is clearly directed toward the adjacent slabs. This, however, in no way impairs the inner unity of the composition.[10] The significance of the slab is further underscored by its place on the east side of the enclosure, where it is part of the front of the Ara Pacis. Besides, the interrelation between form and content is realized in this relief to a remarkably high degree. The background of the relief is not its termination, but is penetrated by the physical forms of the figures represented and thus helps to create the "atmosphere" which is peculiar to this relief.[11] The expressiveness of the artistic form is matched by the intellectual conception behind the representation. By general concensus, it has truly universal significance; it comes close to being "il punto centrale" of the great frieze.[12]

The relief so far has received two primary interpretations. Some scholars regard the female figure seated in its center as Italia while others consider her as Tellus or Terra Mater. Since their arguments are important for the interpretation to be proposed here, their validity may be examined as briefly as clarity permits.

Italia

The main piece of evidence A. W. Van Buren has adduced to identify the matronly figure in the center of the relief with Italia is the similarity of motifs between this relief and the famous *laudes Italiae* passage in Vergil's *Georgics* (2.136-176).[13] But only some of the motifs of this passage recur in the relief while others, which are equally important, are miss-

---

[10] Petersen, *APA* 54, followed by Moretti, *APA* 234, did not see any inner connection between the figures as Tellus and Aurae (see pp. 202-203, below). But formally the figures are closely integrated with each other; see F. Matz, *Gnomon* 32 (1959) 294-295, and this has to be taken into account when one tries to interpret their meaning.

[11] F. Matz, *Welt als Geschichte* 4 (1938) 196-197; cf. Riemann, *RE* 18 (1942) 2106.

[12] Moretti, *APA* 236.

[13] *JRS* 3 (1913) 137-138.

ing from it.[14] For instance, besides being hailed as *magna parens frugum* (2.173), Italy also is the *magna parens virum* (2.174). There are several *viri* represented on the friezes, especially the Julian family, a group of Roman senators, the emperor Augustus and, closely identified with him, his ancestor Aeneas.[15] Is Italia truly the *magna parens* of all these men? The repeated *magna . . . magna* also is reminiscent of the Magna Mater, Cybele,[16] and this association of Italia and Cybele should have its counterpart and perhaps even find its explanation in the relief. Furthermore, the parallels Van Buren sees for the *ver assiduum* ("flowers in full bloom"), and the *mare quod adluit infra* ("the sea is indicated to the right")— but the sea alluded to can be only the *mare inferum*, the Tyrrhenian sea—are labored, as is the parallel to *portus*: "The position of the main figure, facing the sea, indicates interest in maritime affairs." A more natural explanation is that the figure is turned to the right primarily to balance the Roma figure which faces left on the north side of the east entrance.[17] Besides, "Italia" does not look at the sea, but her attention belongs to the child which sits on her left knee and offers her an apple (Fig. 135). The figure's being seated on a rock should not be construed as a parallel to the *saxis* on which Italian men built their cities (*Georgics* 2.156), but, given the position of the figure between marsh and sea, it was the only way the sculptor could save her from drowning in the water.[18] Nor does the rivulet in the relief glide beneath any *antiquos muros*. Finally, whereas Vergil explicitly emphasizes that Italia is free from the Theban dragonseed (2.141) and the

[14] Cf. M. Schäfer, *Gymnasium* 66 (1959) 295.

[15] Augustus and Aeneas are identified in that Augustus' sacrifice is merely a repetition of Aeneas'; see Hanell, *Opusc. Rom.* 2 (1960) 72-74; Sieveking, *JOAI* 10 (1907) 187-188; and Chapter I, p. 10.

[16] This was noticed by Simon, *MDAI(R)* 64 (1957) 58 n. 94. She thus identifies Magna Mater directly with Italia, but it seems that at least one intermediate step should be taken before this identification is made.

[17] Cf. Wagenvoort, *MNIR* 1 (1921) 110.

[18] Wagenvoort, *loc.cit.*

threatening, scaly *anguis* (2.154), the sculptor included in the relief a rather graphic representation of a hissing, coiling, scaly sea-dragon to serve as a faint reminder of the perils which might always threaten the *Pax Augusta*.[19] The valid parallels that Van Buren cites in support of his theory thus are too few in number and too little specific to support the identification of this figure with Italia on the basis of the Vergilian text.

There are also iconographic objections to the Italia interpretation. The type of Italia nursing her children is unknown at so early a date.[20] Eugenie Strong argued that this "Italia" differed from the Tellus type in none of her characteristics, whereas whenever the Tellus type was taken over to represent a province, the transformation was indicated by some detail, such as a rabbit and an olive branch for Hispania, an elephant head-dress for Africa, and so on.[21] The most relevant representation of this kind escaped Strong's notice: in the right corner of the upper half of the Gemma Augustea (Fig. 136), the figure which is often considered as Terra because she holds a cornucopia and has two children beside her is in reality Italia. For she wears around the neck a *bulla*, an amulet typical of Italy and, especially, Etruria.[22] On a conceptual level, Strong rightly asserts that "compared with the Earth-Mother, august embodiment of an ecumenical concept, which was deep-rooted in philosophical and religious speculations, any provincial impersonation—be it Italia or other—cuts but a sorry figure."[23] This assertion is not invalidated by the argument that the provincials would recognize in this Italia the homeland or motherland of the whole Empire and thus a symbol

[19] So Riemann, *RE* 18 (1942) 2092.

[20] See G. Lugli, *Capitolium* 11 (1935) 379-380, and E. Strong, *JRS* 27 (1937) 122; cf. Riemann 2092.

[21] For details see Strong 122-123; cf. L. Curtius, *SHAW* 14 (1923) 11 n. 3.

[22] See Mau, *RE* 5 (1897) 1048.

[23] *JRS* 21 (1937) 125.

of their own homes. No expression of such a feeling on the part of the provincials is known in art or literature.[24] But since this Italia conception resembles Moretti's argument that this figure as "Tellus" reflects the import of the Ara Pacis for "tutte le regioni, tutte le provincie, tutto l'impero,"[25] it is evident even at this early point that the line between Tellus and Italia cannot be drawn very rigidly.

Another attempt to identify the figure almost exclusively with Italia ultimately depends on the assumption that the reliefs of the Ara are so arranged as to represent two parallel but separate processions. As Van Buren puts it: "The two parallel processions leave the rear portal to the care of their divine guardians, and on reaching the front at the west, they will find their respective ancestral representatives of the heroic age."[26]

This almost conventional interpretation has been most cogently rejected in Krister Hanell's study of the Ara Pacis, after Loewy and Petersen much earlier had already recognized the basic unity of the friezes.[27] The several correspondences between the two "processional" friezes indicate that they form a whole rather than two rigidly divided parallel groups. The two long friezes, then, do not represent a procession which is still moving forward. Rather, the figures which are represented on them stand in a circle around the sacred act performed by Augustus.[28] The inner circle of Augustus and his lictors is flanked on the left by the participants from

[24] Toynbee, *PBA* 39 (1953) 81, suggested that the provincials in this way identified with Italy. But see J. Palm, *Rom, Römertum und Imperium in der griechischen Literatur der Kaiserzeit* (Lund 1959) passim, and J. H. Oliver, *Gnomon* 32 (1960) 501.

[25] *APA* 237.

[26] A. W. Van Buren, *AJP* 70 (1949) 421. The front of the Altar, however, is the east side; see Kähler, *Festschrift Schweitzer* 322-330.

[27] Hanell, *Opusc. Rom.* 2 (1960) passim; Petersen, *APA* 78; E. Loewy, *JOAI* 23 (1926) 53.

[28] Hanell 60; cf., earlier, A. Gardthausen, *Der Altar des Kaiserfriedens* (Leipzig 1908) 19, and A. von Domaszewski, *JOAI* 6 (1903) 61.

the north frieze and on the right by those of the south frieze.

One consequence of this basic unity of the frieze groups is that the "Italia" relief corresponds not merely to the Roma slab and is related not solely to the sacrifice of Augustus and Aeneas, but within this new integrated whole it is also connected with the Mars-Lupercal slab, which is diagonally across from it on the north part of the west side. This connection will be explored more fully later.

A few other arguments in favor of the Italia interpretation may be considered briefly. One is the restoration which Kähler has suggested for the frieze that covers the altar itself.[29] The central band of this frieze, which is approximately sixty centimeters high, probably consisted of a series of Amazons, which Kähler, on the analogy of similar representations on the armor of the Prima Porta Augustus and in the Hadrianeum, reconstructed as personifications of Roman provinces.[30] As the concept of the *orbis terrarum* is already expressed by them, Kähler argues, the figure to the left of the entrance cannot be Tellus, but has to be Italia. But as Kähler himself seems to realize, the evidence on which he bases his reconstruction is too slight to allow any definite conclusions as to the nature of the figures represented. Of the nine fragments published by Moretti, only one can definitely be assigned to a standing figure,[31] the posture which Kähler assumes to have

[29] Kähler, *JDAI* 69 (1954) 84-86, and *Festschrift Schweitzer* 327-328.

[30] For Moretti's attempt to reconstruct the very fragmentary material as representing Minerva and the Amazons see *APA* 83-89. Moretti is not very explicit about the connection between the figures, especially since there is no mythological precedent. His interpretation, however, is not so Greek that it could not apply to the Ara Pacis as Kähler (*Festschrift Schweitzer* 328) objects. For the Altar combines Greek artistic traditions and Roman concepts and is likely to have been the work of Greek sculptors; see J. M. C. Toynbee, *The Art of the Romans* (London 1965) 52. The identity of the figures on the Augustus armor is also not above question; see A. Alföldi, *MDAI(R)* 52 (1937) 60-62, who rightly points out that they more generally represent peoples rather than specific provinces.

[31] Fig. 70 on p. 84=Kähler, *JDAI* 69 (1954) 98 fig. 25. Fig. 72 (= Kähler, *ibid.*, fig. 24) could also come from a standing Amazon leaning on

been characteristic of most of the "provinces." None of the twenty-nine Hadrianeum or the two Prima Porta figures is represented with a shield, whereas the shields of two of the Ara Pacis figures are conspicuous. Lastly, as Moretti rightly observed, the significance of the altar frieze bands is proportionate to their height. The bottommost frieze, therefore, which is considerably higher than the one with the "Amazons" or "provinces," and on which the virtues of *pietas, clementia, iustitia,* and *aequitas* or the blessings of *copia, securitas,* and *faustitas* may have been represented, is of greater importance for the interpretation of frieze decorations on the outside.

The slab which one must consider in any interpretation of the "Italia" relief is the latter's counterpart on the west side, depicting, according to the generally accepted interpretation, a sacrifice of Aeneas at Lavinium (Fig. 8). The iconographic details which suggest this location of the sacrifice are the sow and the Penates, shown in their temple on the upper left side.[32] The question whether the sacrifice is that for the Penates or that which Aeneas offered at his very arrival in Italy (*Aen.* 7.135-143) has been the subject of endless discussion. If the second interpretation is accepted we cannot conclude that "the goddess with whom the sacrifice must be associated is a specialized form of the earth goddess, Italia."[33] For Aeneas does not sacrifice solely to the Tellus of Italy, but also to several other deities, among them *Idaeus Iuppiter* and *Phrygiam ex ordine matrem* (*Aen.* 7.139). Moreover, the sow is shown on the relief and Vergil writes that Aeneas sacrificed her to *maxima Iuno* (*Aen.* 8.84). The very

---

a spear, although Kähler 99 believes that a seated figure is represented. The posture of the two figures (Kähler figs. 27 and 29), whose fragments Kähler adds to Moretti's nine fragments, cannot be determined. Moretti's reasons for assigning his fig. 78 on p. 86 to the taller frieze seem to me to be more cogent than Kähler's reasons for assigning her to the Amazon frieze (fig. 26 on p. 99).

[32] Cf. Chapter IV, p. 155.

[33] Taylor, *Divinity* 198.

lack of sufficient evidence to name conclusively the deity of the sacrifice suggests that the sculptor did not intend to represent one particular sacrifice, but instead chose deliberately to combine the characteristics of various sacrifices so as to achieve that very multiplicity of associations which is typical of the "Italia" relief. While no clear-cut inferences for the identity of the goddess on the east frieze can thus be drawn from the nature of the sacrifice, any identification of her must do justice to the close association between the Aeneas and the "Italia" relief on its various levels.

All this is not to say that the goddess, which, in our opinion, is a composite type, is not *reminiscent* of Italia.[34] Her juxtaposition with Roma certainly points in that direction. Italia and Roma appear as pendants in Horace, *Odes* 4.14.43-44, where the poet praises Augustus as

> o tutela praesens
> Italiae dominaeque Romae.

It has rightly been observed, however, that in the context of this Ode the close connection between Italy and Rome is explained by the fact that the Gerauni, Breuni, and Raeti, who were defeated by Drusus and Tiberius in 15 B.C., were enemies who indeed controlled the Alpine access to Rome and Italy.[35] The Horatian passage therefore is not very relevant to the interpretation of the Ara Pacis relief.

More important is an iconographic and conceptual precedent which so far has been completely overlooked. This is a coin that was issued to allude to the pacification of Italy after the end of the Social War (Fig. 137).[36] On its reverse

[34] Here Simon, *Ara Pacis Augusta* 31, has misunderstood me: I am not arguing that the goddess represents exclusively Venus. Nor is she exclusively Tellus or Italia. She combines traits of all three, although those of Venus to me seem to predominate.

[35] See Schäfer, *Gymnasium* 66 (1959) 296.

[36] *BMC Coins Rep.* 1.415-416 nos. 3358-3363, with pl. 43.5; Sydenham no. 797. The probable date of the coin is between 71 and 67 B.C.

it shows Roma with her right foot on the globe and with her right hand extended to Italia, who is holding a cornucopia. Behind Italia, there is a winged *caduceus*, a herald's staff and token of a peaceable embassy. On the obverse are shown the conjoined heads of *Honos*, crowned with a laurel wreath, and of the helmeted *Virtus*. The coin commemorates the *pax* established between Rome and Italy. In the hymn he wrote for the secular games, the consecration of the *Pax Augusta*, Horace linked all these virtues with the cornucopia, the symbol of plenty (*C.S.* 57-60):

> iam Fides et Pax et Honos Pudorque
> priscus et neglecta redire Virtus
> audet, apparetque beata pleno
>   Copia cornu.

Tellus

The iconographic type which the female figure seems to resemble most strongly is that of the Tellus or Terra Mater of Augustan and later Roman art.[37] Often, though not always, Tellus has a child at either side, and in every representation she is distinguished by the cornucopia or even a pair of cornucopiae. This absence of the official emblem of the *saeculum frugiferum*, immensely popular since the second Triumvirate, is unique indeed in the Ara relief, and cannot convincingly be explained away. Strong has suggested that this symbol was represented on the Roma slab since a cornucopia appears in the Roma relief of the altar of the Gens Augusta at Carthage, but it seems better to work with the extant fragments of the Ara Pacis, especially in view of the

---

[37] For a list of representations see Strong, *JRS* 27 (1937) 116-121, with pls. 3-20. The most comprehensive discussion of the Tellus type is D. Levi, *Antioch Mosaic Pavements* (Princeton 1947) 263-269. Cf. G. Downey, in R. Stillwell, *Antioch on the Orontes* 2. *The Excavations in 1933-1936* (Princeton 1938) 205-212.

numerous restorations proposed for the Roma relief.[38] Since there is also no agreement on the interpretation of a similar "Tellus" relief from Carthage in the Louvre (Fig. 162), no valid inferences can be drawn from the latter for the subject of the Ara Pacis relief, especially as we have no full knowledge about the monument of which the Carthage relief was a part.[39] What was Terra in one artistic context may have been "Africa" in another. Labored also is the suggestion[40] that the cornucopia in the Ara Pacis relief may be hidden behind the rock and thus account for the growth of flowers and the ears of corn visible behind "Italia's" child.

Those who favor Tellus/Terra Mater quote the eighth stanza of the *Carmen Saeculare* (29-32) in support of their argument:

> fertilis frugum pecorisque Tellus
> spicea donet Cererem corona;
> nutriant fetus et aquae salubres
> et Iovis aurae.

It is evident, however, that the poet's words have to be some-what twisted to apply to the scene that is actually represented on the relief.[41] For instance, where on the slab does Mother Earth give Ceres a crown of corn? Furthermore, the association of the two *aurae velificantes sua veste* with Terra is unique and neither Horace's *Iovis aurae* nor any iconographic precedents can account for it. The only literary evidence for this connection is the obscure verse of Pacuvius: *terra exhalat auram ad auroram humidam* (Varro *L.L.* 5.24). But, as we shall see, it may be significant that Pacuvius, whom Quin-

---

[38] For a comprehensive discussion of earlier views see Moretti, *APA* 248-251, and Riemann, *RE* 18 (1942) 2092-2093; cf. Toynbee, *PBA* 39 (1953) 80.

[39] For the relationship between the two reliefs see pp. 229-233, below.

[40] Made by Schäfer, *Gymnasium* 66 (1959) 295.

[41] See the detailed discussion by E. Loewy, *Atti Primo Congr. Naz. di Studi Romani* 1 (Rome 1929) 104-109.

tilian (10.1.97) characterizes as *doctiorem*, speaks of Aurora and *aura* in one breath. At any rate, if the Tellus/Aurae interpretation is accepted, indeed "the entire representation seems to be somewhat superficially connected."[42]

Besides, what is the relationship between Aeneas and Terra Mater? The sacrifice, as we have seen, may or may not be made to her. But is Tellus really the goddess suitable for the Trojan half of the altar, the goddess with whom Augustus tries to associate himself? Also problematic is the interpretation of the figure as *Saturnia tellus*. In the *Aeneid*—and it is the *Aeneid* we must consult on Aeneas' landing in Italy— "Saturnian" has lost the "golden" connotations it had had in the *Georgics*.[43] For instance, *Saturnia tellus* in *Aen.* 7.202-204 is the land notable for its absence of law, while later, in 8.321-322, Saturn, a prototype of Aeneas, is said to have brought law and order to Latium. *Saturnia* as an epithet of Juno thus connotes both sympathy for the old Italy and extreme hatred of the new Italy as represented by Aeneas' destiny. It is not plausible to assume that such overtones should appear in the reliefs of the Ara Pacis.

The Tellus theory, however, in one important point is preferable to the Italia interpretation: Italia hardly has sufficient religious significance to balance Roma. We know of no cult or temple of Italia, whereas Tellus or Terra Mater had a temple and ancient ritual. The goddess which is primarily represented in the relief therefore must be equal to Tellus and Roma in this respect.

Venus

Earlier writers have tended to consider the Aurae as mere space fillers that have little intrinsic connection with the cen-

---

[42] Loewy 109. This interpretation, of course, does no justice to the formal coherence of the relief; see note 10, above.

[43] See L. A. McKay, "Saturnia Juno," *Greece and Rome* 3 (1956) 59-60, and W. S. Anderson, "Juno and Saturn in the Aeneid," *Stud. in Phil.* 55 (1958) 519-532.

tral figure. But they almost emanate from the main figure and strive to link the adjacent relief slabs more closely to her. They give the scene its basic and important "Roman" symmetry in that they flank the central figure and thereby underscore her importance. An understanding of the iconography of the Aurae is thus basic for the interpretation of the female figure between them. Or, to go one step further: because of their close connection with the central figure, they may simply be considered as different manifestations of this goddess. We thus have to look for a deity who often appears with a *velificatio* and is represented on a swan or a sea monster. All three motifs can be found in Hellenistic art, to which the Ara Pacis was heavily indebted, but it seems better to search first for parallels drawn from the art of the late Republic and the early Empire.

The Nereids on the so-called Altar of Ahenobarbus and the Aurae on the Tazza Farnese have often been considered the most likely analogues to the Ara Pacis Aurae.[44] The similarity, however, is purely formal and not in any way related to the content. Nereids on Tritons are fitting for the Ahenobarbus base because the subject of the frieze is the marriage of Poseidon and Amphitrite, while the "Aurae" on the Tazza Farnese are male and personify the Etesian winds. A much closer parallel occurs on the armor of the Prima Porta Augustus whose "program" in many ways resembles that of the Ara Pacis frieze. Until recently the *velificans* (Fig. 138) of the armor generally was considered as Phosphoros. A more convincing interpretation has shown that she is Venus, who serves the double purpose of announcing dawn as well as protecting

---

[44] E.g. by Wagenvoort, *MNIR* 1 (1921) 107-108; Strong, *La scultura romana* (Florence 1923) 21; Curtius, *SHAW* 14 (1923) 11 n. 3. An illustration of the Nereid frieze is found in Brunn-Bruckmann, *Denkmäler griechischer und römischer Skulptur* 3, pl. 12.2. A recent discussion of the Tazza Farnese is J. Charbonneaux, *MMAI* 50 (1958) 85-103 with fig. 1.

Augustus as Venus Genetrix of the Julian house.[45] This Venus *velificans* recurs on a coin struck in Spain (Fig. 139) and is combined with the representation of a capricorn, the symbol of the month in which Augustus was born.[46] A Pompeian mural from the Casa del Naviglio shows Venus being carried on the wings of Cupid (Fig. 140).[47] In his hands he holds a cornucopia whereas Venus carries a scepter. These two symbols suggest that she is the great patroness of the Pompeians, *Venus Pompeiana*. The best known representation from Pompeii is perhaps the goddess' majestic ride in a shell over the waves (Fig. 141).[48] Her yellow mantle billows over her in the wind almost like a sail, giving the impression that the goddess is propelled by it. She is represented under the aspect of Venus Marina, the goddess of the sea.

The development of the *velificatio* motif has been thoroughly studied by Friedrich Matz, according to whom *velificatio* is typical of the deities of the atmosphere "over whom vaults the firmament."[49] In the early fifth century B.C. the motif of Aphrodite carried through the air was already well-known in Greek art. A particularly well-preserved example is the painting on the inside of a cup from Kameiros on which

[45] Simon, *MDAI(R)* 64 (1957) 54. This identification has been rejected by M. R. Rebuffat, *MEFR* 73 (1961) 161-228. Rebuffat agrees that the billowing mantle is characteristic of Venus but points out that there are no known representations of a torch-bearing Venus. His interpretation of the figure as Nyx, which is based primarily on parallels from Byzantine manuscripts of the eleventh and twelfth centuries, cannot be considered preferable to Simon's. The torch-bearing Venus may well be a conflation of the torch-bearing Cupid with the traditional Venus type. Besides, A. Momigliano has reminded us "the symbolism of the Ara Pacis did not set a pattern" (*JWI* 5 [1942] 230), and this accounts for the uniqueness of the entire composition as well as some details; cf. p. 240 below.

[46] *BMC Coins Emp.* 1.62 nos. 349-350, with pl. 7.4. See the discussions of J. Gagé, *Apollon romain* (Paris 1955) 605 n. 1, and Simon 55 n. 72.

[47] Published by L. Curtius, *Die Wandmalerei Pompejis* (Leipzig 1929) 410 and fig. 223; cf. P. Herrmann, *Denkmäler der Malerei des Altertums* 2.35 fig. 9.

[48] See Herrmann 256-259 with pl. 189.

[49] *Abh. Mainz* (1952) no. 10, 726-773.

the identity of the goddess is made certain by the inscription ΑΦΡΟΔΙΤΕΣ (Fig. 142).[50] Also important is the representation of Aphrodite on an Attic lekythos where the billowing mantle of the goddess is studded with stars, thus making manifest her function as the goddess of the heavens, as Urania (Fig. 143). The motif of Aphrodite *velificans* continued in vase painting into the fourth century B.C.[51]

The motif was equally popular on mirrors and in terracotta statuary. The oldest example of Aphrodite on a mirror dates from the last quarter of the fifth century (Fig. 144), while the bulk of these representations appear a quarter of a century later.[52] On a terracotta altar from Tarentum of the second half of the fifth century, Aphrodite *velificans* rises from the sea in a chariot which is drawn by Iris and Zephyros (Fig. 145).[53] An example of east Greek art of the Hellenistic age is a female terracotta protome in the Metropolitan Museum in New York (Fig. 146).[54] A billowing veil rises behind her head; at her right breast she holds a flower with her right hand, and a small bird is perched on her left hand below her left breast. These iconographic details are not inconsistent with an interpretation of the figure as Aphrodite. A further example of the

[50] British Museum D 2, attributed to the Pistoxenos Painter. Beazley, *ARV²* 862 no. 22. The most recent discussion is E. G. Suhr, "The Spinning Aphrodite in the Minor Arts," *AJA* 67 (1963) 66-67, who points out the emphasis the painter put on Aphrodite's function as the goddess of creation. The same holds good of the Ara Pacis relief, although it is accomplished there by iconographic details other than a spindle.

[51] Aphrodite Urania: Benndorf, *Vasenbilder* 75-82 with pl. 37.3; A. Furtwängler, *Beschreibung der Vasensammlung im Antiquarium* (Berlin 1885), no. 2688. Suhr 63-64 with pl. 13.2, considers the billowing mantle as the full disc of the moon, but the presence of stars on the surface of the veil militates against this interpretation.—A collection of the vases with Aphrodite *velificans* in the fourth century is given by H. Metzger, *Les représentations dans la céramique attique du 4e siècle* (Paris 1951) 59-64.

[52] See Züchner, *Klappspiegel* 5-11, KS 1, 2, 4, 5, 9; cf. *AE* (1893) pl. 15.1.

[53] Heidelberg Universität, Sammlung des Archäologischen Instituts, inv. 27/25; cf. Simon, *Geburt der Aphrodite* 28-30.

[54] New York Metropolitan Museum of Art, inv. 26.164.6. Gift of the American Society for the Exploration of Sardis, 1926. I am grateful to Mr. Mark I. Davies for bringing the statuette to my attention.

art of Magna Graecia is a bronze mirror stand from Locri with Aphrodite and Adonis (Fig. 147).[55] She seizes him with her right hand, and her drapery, which she holds over herself with her left hand, is blown out behind by the wind. In Greek art, then, the goddess who is represented with a *velificatio* is almost exclusively Aphrodite.

The Aura on the Ara Pacis rides a bird which is either a goose or, more probably a swan. The iconographic line between the two cannot be clearly drawn, as so often happens, and thus Rizzo's resorting to an orthopedic correction of the bird's neck changes matters little, by however elaborate an argument it may be supported.[56] If the bird is indeed a goose, the figure represented can only be Aphrodite, who appears riding on the back of a goose in terracotta statuary since the period of the severe style. A good example now is in the Boston Museum of Fine Arts (Fig. 148).[57] The veil of this Aphrodite is very similar to the one worn by the central figure of the Ara Pacis relief. Far more frequent and beginning also with the first quarter of the fifth century is her representation, in vase painting and terracottas, on a swan which, according to some scholars, is reminiscent of her birth from the sea, while others have considered it the personification of Venus, the morning star.[58] The latter interpretation would give us, of course, an

[55] H. B. Walters, *Catalogue of the Bronzes in the British Museum* (London 1889) 45 no. 303.

[56] Rizzo, *BCAR* 67 (1939) 145-150 with pls. 1-3; answered by Moretti, *APA* 235-236. G. Bianchi, *Ragguaglio delle antichità che si conservano nella galleria Mediceo-Imperiale in Firenze* (Florence 1759) 13, had his doubts: "Un volatile cui difficile sarebbe il suo vero nome assegnare." *Contra*, O. Jahn, *Arch. Zeitung* 119 (1858) 230-244, esp. 243-244 with pls. 118-120. Jahn, followed by virtually all later scholars, was sure the bird had to be a swan.

[57] L. D. Caskey, *A Catalogue of Greek and Roman Sculpture in the Museum of Fine Arts* (Boston 1925) 83-86 no. 36. For further examples see e.g. A. Furtwängler in Brunn-Bruckmann, *Denkmäler griechischer und römischer Skulptur*, discussing pl. 577; *BMC Terracottas* pl. 15 no. A424; *AA* (1894) 31 fig. 20.

[58] For details see Jahn (note 56, above) passim; A. Kalkmann, *JDAI* 1 (1886) 231-260; Benndorf, *Vasenbilder* 75-76. H. A. R. Munro, *JHS* 12

additional connection between the scenes of the Prima Porta armor and the Ara Pacis since Aurora on the armor is represented carrying off the *Veneris astrum*. On a red-figure lekythos from Cyprus, which is ascribed to the Achilles Painter, a majestic Aphrodite adorned with a diadem and a scepter is shown riding on a swan (Fig. 149).[59] Another good example of Venus on a swan is found on an Etruscan mirror where the inscription *Turan* leaves no doubt about the identity of the figure (Fig. 150).[60] The composition is pleasantly surrounded by a wreath of myrtle leaves. Literary testimonia which associate the swan with Aphrodite are not lacking. Only two passages from the literature of the Empire need to be quoted:[61]

> illa quidam monuit, iunctisque per aëra cycnis
> carpit iter.
>
> (Ovid, M. 10.708-709)

The same applies to the Trojan Venus from Mount Eryx:

> dicitur Idalios Erycis de vertice lucos
> dum petit et molles agitat Venus aurea cycnos
> Pergameas intrasse domos.
>
> (Statius, Silvae 3.4.21-23)

One scholar therefore categorically declared all representations of women on swans to be Aphrodite.[62] The methodological fallacy of this assumption has rightly been criticized by G. E. Rizzo. There is no evidence, for instance, of an Aphrodite cult at Camarina, where tetradrachms of the middle of

---

(1891) 318, suggests that the swan might be connected with Aphrodite because she has her home on the *plaga lactea caeli* (Statius, *Silvae* 1.2.51) of which Cycnus is the brightest constellation. Simon (in Helbig, *Führer* 2.⁴692) relates the swan to the legendary King Cycnus of the Po Valley.

[59] Oxford 324, attributed to the Achilles Painter; Beazley, *ARV*² 993 no. 82: *CVA* Great Britain III pl. 131.2.

[60] Gerhard, *Etruskische Spiegel* 4.321.

[61] Cf. Ovid, *A.A.* 3.809; Horace, *C.* 4.1.10; Statius, *Silvae* 1.2.140-144.

[62] Benndorf, *Vasenbilder* 75.

the fifth century B.C. show an Aura which is perhaps the closest iconographic analogue to the Aura on the Ara Pacis relief (Fig. 151).[63] In both cases, the position of the swan, its wings, and of the female figure are virtually the same. The Italian scholar, for good reasons, rejected Jahn's interpretation of the figure as the nymph Camarina. Rather, Rizzo hypothesizes, the Aura is the *aura* of a lake near Camarina symbolizing the purificatory powers that emanated from the lake. Rizzo thus considered the swan to be primarily a symbol of Apollo. In his opinion an allusion to Apollo could not be missing from the Ara Pacis and would be very much in keeping with the invocation of the *Carmen Saeculare*, the "Apolline" passage in Aeschylus' *Eumenides* (903-915), and the Augustan program in general. The Italia/Tellus relief, then, was viewed by Rizzo primarily as alluding to the religious reforms of Augustus and the cult of Apollo.

While the association of the Camarina coin with the Apolline spirit is purely conjectural, a narrow identification of the swan of the Ara Pacis relief does little justice to the richness of associations that is characteristic of the reliefs of the Altar. Above all, we have to take into account that two swans are represented on top of the floral scroll directly beneath the relief (Fig. 135). One of them is so placed under the swan of the relief that the two could not fail to be associated with each other. The swan of the floral decoration has for good reasons been considered as that of Apollo,[64] and this observation is corroborated by the presence of the laurel branches that are grafted on the acanthus shoots. It would be altogether fitting if the scroll swan of Apollo were complemented by the swan of Venus on the relief slab, but no such clear-cut distinction can be made. In the frieze of the Apollo altar at Arles,

[63] Rizzo, *BCAR* 67 (1939) 150-168 with figs. 7 and 8; cf. Booth, *Latomus* 25 (1966) 876.

[64] By H. P. L'Orange, "Ara Pacis Augustae—la zona floreale," *Acta Inst. Roman. Norveg.* 1 (1962) 12-13.

which perhaps served as the base for a statue of Augustus, the swans suggest the emperor's descent from Venus as well as alluding to the Augustan Apollo.[65] The significance of this Gallic parallel should not be underestimated, since the floral frieze of the Arles theater is the most immediate known fore-runner of the Ara Pacis scroll.[66] It can also be considered more than a purely formal coincidence that the central figure in the Ara Pacis relief so strongly resembles the Actium Apollo in her posture, while the modeling of her companion figures is very similar to that of the upper part of the body of this Apollo.[67] This strong interrelation between Apollo and Venus by means of common symbols not only is relevant to the Augustan context, but has its roots in Greek art and myth. Aphrodite on a swan appears on a bell krater of the early fourth century in close association with Apollo at Delphi (Fig. 153).[68] It is she, and not Apollo, who hovers over the Delphic omphalos, while the seated Apollo watches her. On the far right a Thyiad, who had partaken in the winter-long Dionysiac revel on Mt. Parnassus, prepares to leave. The arrival of Aphrodite on the swan heralds the coming of spring because swans accompanied Apollo to Delphi in the spring.

On the Ara Pacis the figure on the swan thus is too full of associations to be interpreted merely as a generic Aura. Con-sidering that she appears in a frieze which connects Augustus with divine beings, we must look for a goddess who is closely related to Aurae, but who, at the same time, is placed over them. Again this goddess turns out to be Venus. In Euripides' *Medea* 835-840 the chorus chants that "Poets sing how Cypris drawing water from the streams of fair-flowing Cephis-

[65] Details in J. Formigé, *RA* 6th ser. 21 (1944) 28-34; cf., for the chro-nology, C. Picard, *REL* 28 (1950) 327.

[66] So P. Kraus, *Die Ranken der Ara Pacis* (Berlin 1953) 48-49.

[67] See the remarks of V. M. Strocka, *AA* (1964) 830 and fig. 1.

[68] Vienna, Kunsthistorisches Museum inv. IV 935; discussed by Kalk-mann (note 58, above) 258-260; Metzger (note 51, above) 176 no. 31, with pl. 22.4; Simon, *Geburt der Aphrodite* 34.

sus breathes over the land a gentle breeze of balmy winds"[69]
(τὰν Κύπριν κλῄζουσιν ἀφυσσαμέναν / χώραν καταπνεῦσαι
μετρίας ἀνέμων / ἡδυπνόους αὔρας). In Augustan literature,
Ovid also describes Venus as the mistress of the Aurae (Her.
16.23-24):

> illa dedit faciles auras ventosque secundos:
> in mare nimirum ius habet orta mari.

On the Altar, therefore, the Aura on the swan is merely a different manifestation of Venus.

We must now turn to the Aura riding the sea monster. If
she were merely a sea nymph, her iconography would be
unique; no other sea nymph appears with an inflated mantle.[70]
Nor is she likely to have been made *velificans* for the sole
purpose of balancing the figure on the swan for purely formal
reasons. It can be assumed, therefore, that there is a similarity
of content as well. The counterpart of Venus on the swan thus
is Venus on the sea dragon. The inflated mantle again characterizes her as an elemental goddess: she is Venus Pelagia
or Marina. The motif of Venus/Aphrodite sitting on the back
of a sea monster was popular in ancient art; it is found, for
instance, on an askos whose reliefs may have been copied from
metal prototypes in Athens.[71] As in the Ara Pacis relief, the
creature which she is riding is hybrid; its head is that of a
horse while its body tapers off into the coils of a serpent. An
equally close parallel is the representation of Aphrodite *velificans* astride a hugh sea dragon on a gem in the Hermitage

[69] Cf. Aeschylus, *Danaids* frg. 44 (Nauck).
[70] At least not until considerably later; see Levi (note 37, above) 100-
104, 195-196, 269-271, and pl. 60, panel A (with copious bibliography);
Stillwell (note 37, above) 180-181 with pl. 23, panels C, F, G, H (catalogue
of mosaics, no. 33); Reinach, *Répertoire de peintures* 36-43; C. Robert,
Die antiken Sarcophagreliefs 5 (Berlin 1939) 42-75 nos. 101-205.
[71] See W. Züchner, *JDAI* 65 (1950) 178-180 and fig. 7, and Suhr, *AJA*
67 (1963) 67 with pl. 13.5, where the correct interpretation of the figure
as Aphrodite is given.

Museum in Leningrad (Fig. 152).[72] On another gem Aphrodite, accompanied by a dolphin and two Erotes, rides on one sea horse and guides another.[73] The posture of the Ara Pacis Aura on the sea monster is identical to the posture of the newly born Venus in a mural from the Casa di Trittolemo in Pompeii.[74] Venus there is carried to the shore sitting on the coils of a bearded Triton. Also in Pompeii is a painting with Venus *velificans*, riding on a sea centaur and holding a scepter (Fig. 154).[75] Another example is a mosaic from Aquileia of about the beginning of the second century A.D., which shows Venus riding over the sea on the back of a bull whose body tapers off into the coils of a serpent.[76]

There are further iconographic details that round out the picture. The figure on the left cannot be considered merely an Aura of the land; she seems to rise from a reedy marsh, and a rivulet gushing forth from an urn is an additional indication of the figure's relation to fresh water. This is quite in keeping with the worship of Aphrodite "in the gardens, reeds, and marshes" (ἐν κήποις, ἐν καλάμοις, ἐν ἔλει). On a more general level, Aphrodite was the goddess of the humid soil, and of the humid air and seasons.[77] Furthermore, the crane standing on the urn, rather than suggesting a possible African provenience of the relief, is another bird with whom Aphrodite is frequently represented as, for instance, on an Athenian mirror (Fig. 155) and on a lekythos

[72] Published by Furtwängler, *Die antiken Gemmen* 2.197, with pl. 41.42.

[73] Furtwängler, *ibid.*, with pl. 41.43; cf. A. F. Gori, *Gemmae antiquae* 2 (Florence 1732) 97, with pls. 48.1 and 4.

[74] Schefold, *Wände* 193; Herrmann (note 47, above) pl. 191.

[75] Casa dei Capitelli Colorati; Schefold, *Wände* 183; Helbig, *Wandgemälde* no. 308.

[76] O. Jahn, *Die Entführung der Europa auf antiken Kunstwerken* (Vienna 1870) 52-54 with pl. 10.

[77] See e.g., Strabo 8.343; 14.683; Athen. 13.572F; cf. Preller-Robert, *Griechische Mythologie* 1⁴ (Berlin 1894) 358, and E. Langlotz, "Aphrodite in den Gärten," *SHAW* (1954), fasc. 2. The seated Venus on the Ara Pacis conforms in all respects to the iconography of Ἀφροδίτη ἐν κήποις.

of the Kertsch style.[78] Her representation with poppy and apples has a precedent in the statue of Aphrodite by Kanachos (Paus. 2.10.4). For Venus was generally regarded as the goddess of spring, of blossoming nature, of fertility, and of exuberant vegetation. Thus Horace hails Augustus, as bringing the light of Apollo and the spring of Venus to Rome and her people (*C.* 4.5.5-8):

> lucem redde tuae, dux bone, patriae:
> instar veris enim vultus ubi tuus
> adfulsit populo, gratior it dies
> et soles melius nitent.

The swan of Venus, especially, is symbolic of the coming of spring.[79] Thus the swan in the relief, associated as he is with the copious fruits and flowers, evokes, as does his counterpart amid the abundance of the floral scroll, Augustus' associations with Apollo and Venus. This is the context in which we should view the *ver adsiduum* of the *laudes Italiae* (Vergil, *Geo.* 2.149).

Far from being linked artificially, then, the Aurae of the Altar form a real unity. Like the *aurae velificantes sua veste*, which Pliny saw in the schola of the Portico of Octavia (*N.H.* 36.29), they form a contrast, but also complement each other. The pleasant, naturalistic details of the relief cannot conceal its hieratic and strictly symmetric organization: the Aurae flank and give prominence to the most important and venerable figure of the relief which is seated in its center.[80]

Given the close connection between the Aurae and the cen-

---

[78] For the mirror see Züchner, *Klappspiegel* KS 12; for the vase, K. Rhomaios, *AE* (1906) 106 and fig. 7. Moretti, *APA* 236 associated the crane with Africa.

[79] See especially *Pervigil. Ven.* 84-85; further passages and discussion in A. Furtwängler, *SBAW* (1899) 604-607. Cf. pp. 209-210, above.

[80] Petersen, *APA* 53, considered the aurae in the Porticus of Octavia to form "eine doch wohl gegensätzliche Zweiheit." The importance of the Aurae for the composition of the Ara relief has been stressed, for instance, by Simon, *Geburt der Aphrodite* 102, and Booth, *Latomus* 25 (1966) 876.

tral figure, the identity of the latter can also be defined more clearly. Her very posture cautions against an identification with Terra or *Saturnia* Tellus/Italy. For Terra is uniformly represented as lying prostrate or semi-erect on the ground, and she usually props the upper half of her body on her left forearm.[81] Her children always surround her but never sit on her lap. In posture, the closest parallel to our figure is the Italia in the Gemma Augustea (Fig. 136), but the difference between the two figures is even more important. Italia leans with her right arm on the *subsellium* of Augustus; her face is turned away from the children beside her. On the Ara Pacis, the communication of the figure with her children is very intimate: she embraces the two children, one of whom offers her an apple, the symbol of Venus. The child on the left is tugging at her breast, and perhaps he is trying to be fed. The latter motif is typical of Venus representations in which the Amores frequently play with her drapery. Sometimes she offers them her breast and thus is called *kourotrophos* (*Ant. Pal.* 6.318). This is exemplified by a scaraboid of the fifth century on which Aphrodite is shown sitting on a rock and facing in the same direction as in the Ara relief.[82] A veil covers her head and falls down over her shoulders. These details are also repeated on the Ara Pacis. Another forerunner of the Ara Pacis figure is the representation of Aphrodite and Eros on a cast from a bronze cheek piece in Bonn (Fig. 156).[83] A veiled Aphrodite has bared her right breast and tenderly offers it to an imploring Eros. The veil that covers the head of this Aphrodite and the one on the Ara Pacis can be traced back to the cult statue of Aphrodite in Elis, which was made by Phidias. A late

[81] See the works listed in note 37 above, and J. M. C. Toynbee, *The Hadrianic School* (Cambridge 1934) 140-143 with pls. 6.22-25.

[82] Published by Furtwängler, *Die antiken Gemmen* 2.62, with pl. 13.4; *AJA* 70 (1966) pl. 53 fig. 13.

[83] See *Enciclopedia dell'arte antica* 3 (Rome 1960) 431 and fig. 525; E. Langlotz, *Phidiasprobleme* (Frankfurt 1947) 85-87 with pl. 30; Booth, *Latomus* 25 (1966) 875-876 with pl. 40.3.

copy in Naples reflects the Phidian sculpture in this respect.[84] This is consistent with the observation that the Ara was modeled on the Altar of Suppliants in Athens and that its sculptors were Greeks.[85] Venus wears the same kind of veil in the main mural of the Casa di Adone Ferito (Fig. 157).[86] Finally, the splendidly modeled breasts of the Ara Pacis figure have no counterpart in the known representations of Terra or Italia. They are doubtless an attribute of Venus/Aphrodite (Homer, *Iliad* 3.397) and are rendered in the same draped and expressive manner in many Venus Genetrix statues and reliefs (Fig. 17).

There can be no doubt that the figure represents a composite type. Certain iconographic details, such as the heifer and the sheep, may have little connection with Venus and be associated more fittingly with Terra Mater. The animals, however, should not be related too narrowly to the identification of the goddess because they are the very sacrificial animals which appear on the small frieze beneath the volutes of the altar itself (Fig. 158). This frieze represents the annual sacrifice to Pax at the Ara Pacis. White heifers were sacrificed to Pax (Ovid, *Fasti* 1.720) and the sheep may be intended for a sacrifice to Janus whose shrine in the Roman Forum, the Ianus Geminus, seems to have inspired the architectural design of the Ara Pacis with its two entrance gates.[87] Moreover, the garlands on the inside of the enclosure walls are suspended from the skulls of heifers sacrificed to Pax (Fig. 159). The animals on our relief, therefore, allude to Pax rather than Venus, Italia, or Terra.

The remaining iconographic clues justify the assumption that the relief, on its first and primary level, represents Venus.

---

[84] See Langlotz 87-88, and Brunn-Bruckmann, *Denkmäler griechischer und römischer Skulptur*, text to pl. 673; cf. Stuart-Jones, *Catalogue Capitoline Museum* pl. 21.

[85] See p. 192, and note 30, above.

[86] Schefold, *Wände* 101; Helbig, *Wandgemälde* no. 340.

[87] See Simon, *Ara Pacis Augustae* 9 and 15, for details.

The goddess is represented in the triple aspect under which she was worshiped on Cnidos (Paus. 1.1.3): as Douritis, the goddess of the giving earth (the central figure); as Acraia, the goddess of the air and the fresh water (primarily the figure on the left, although the figure on the right, because of her *velificatio*, also symbolizes the air); and as Euploia, the goddess of the sea (the figure on the right). This triple element of her cult was well remembered by the Roman poets, who used it as an almost stereotyped formula to characterize the goddess:[88]

> illa quidem totum dignissima temperat orbem;
> illa tenet nullo regna minora deo,
> iuraque dat caelo, terrae, natalibus undis.
>
> (Ovid, *Fasti* 4.91-93)

> Perque caelum perque terras perque pontem subditum
> pervium sui tenorem seminali tramite
> inbuit iussitque mundum nosse nascendi vias.
>
> (*Perv. Veneris* 65-67)

> en verum naturae prisca parens, en elementorum
> origo initialis, en orbis totius alma Venus.
>
> (Apul., *Metam.* 4.30.1)

As Benndorf has already pointed out, the representation of Venus here should not be taken as a mere allegory.[89] Rather, the three types that symbolize her are united in the frieze on the basis of the parallelism recurrent in literature.

The closest artistic parallels are the cult images of Aphro-

---

[88] Cf. *Orphic Hymn* 55.5-7: καὶ κρατέεις τρισσῶν μοιρῶν, γεννᾷς δὲ τὰ πάντα, / ὅσσα τ' ἐν οὐρανῷ ἐστι καὶ ἐν γαίῃ πολυκάρπῳ / ἐν πόντου τε βυθῷ ... Eur. frg. 898 (Nauck): τὴν 'Αφροδίτην οὐχ' ὁρᾷς ὅση θεός; ... ἐρᾷ μὲν ὄμβρου γαῖ' ... / ἐρᾷ δ' ὁ σεμνὸς οὐρανὸς πληρούμενος / ὄμβρου πεσεῖν εἰς γαῖαν 'Αφροδίτης ὑπὸ. Artemidorus, *Oneirocr.* 2.37, p. 142 (Pack); Cornutus, *De nat. deorum* 24, p. 137 (Osann).

[89] *Vasenbilder* 78.

dite, the patron goddess of Aphrodisias in Caria. Several of these statues have been found with a distribution that ranges from Asia Minor to Portugal, but they all can be assumed to go back to one common model in the goddess' temple at Aphrodisias. A recently found example comes from Aphrodisias itself (Fig. 160)[90] and is typical in that the garment of the goddess, aside from its topmost part, is divided into four segments. On the lowest, which sometimes was omitted, three Erotes are engaged in a sacrifice of incense, a theme which is frequently found on funerary reliefs. The scene above it shows Aphrodite *velificans*. She is riding over the waves on a sea goat and accompanied by a dolphin. The next zone is subdivided, with representations of Selene and Helios, while the center of the final scene is held by the Three Graces. These mythological representations proclaim, respectively, Aphrodite's power over the underworld, sea, sky, and earth. Especially her representation as sea goddess corresponds closely to the relief on the Ara Pacis. It is likely that the date of this cult image is Hadrianic, although the statue type goes back to late Hellenistic times.

Several fragments of statuettes of the Carian Aphrodite have been found in Rome, which suggests that the artists of the Ara Pacis must have been familiar with the representation of Venus under her various aspects. What is more, the Carian Aphrodite was assimilated to the Roman Venus beginning with Sulla. The Delphic oracle bade him to seek her favor because he belonged to the race of Aeneas (Appian, *B.C.*

[90] For the picture and the pertinent information I am indebted to Professor Kenan Erim; cf. the *National Geographic Magazine* 132 (1967) 285. For discussions of the statues see e.g. C. Fredrich, *MDAI(A)* 22 (1897) 361-380; H. Thiersch, *Ependytes und Ephod* (Stuttgart 1936); F. Magi, *RPAA* 12 (1936) 221-231; F. Eichler, *JOAI Beiblatt* 42 (1955) 1-22, who gives a complete list of the known statues. Most of the Roman fragments have been published by Maria F. Squarciapiano in *BA* n.s. 2 (1959) 97-106; *ArchClass* 12 (1960) 208-210; *RPAA* 38 (1965) 143ff.; she will also publish the statue shown here.

1.97),[91] and Sulla sent her a gold crown and a double axe. The latter had been the traditional symbol of the Aphrodite at Aphrodisias, who was a goddess of victory; and this facilitated her syncretism with the Roman Venus, who had become Victrix because of the Erycina. Sulla's initiative, as Schilling has pointed out, "led to the extension of the Roman Venus religion into the east. Far from borrowing his religion of Venus Felix from Caria, Sulla imposed the Trojan mystique on the oriental sanctuary. It is in effect in the name of the Trojan mystique that the goddess of Aphrodisias entered into the Roman orbit."[92] As in the transfer of the Erycina, the Trojan legend was used to present yet another Venus as the "parent" of the Roman one. This process, and its subsequent repetitions, are reflected in the *Aeneid* where Aeneas founds sanctuaries of Venus all over the Mediterranean, and it may well be reflected by Dionysius' mention of the sanctuaries of Aphrodite Aineias.[93] Sulla's action speeded up the syncretistic development of the Roman Venus cult, and the assimilation of the Carian and the Roman Venus continued, for obvious reasons, under Caesar, Augustus, and the other Trojan-descended Julio-Claudians. This syncretism explains the composite representation of Venus on the Ara Pacis; on the coins of Aphrodisias we in fact find the same conjunction of Augustus and the composite Aphrodite as on the Augustan Altar.[94]

The poetic inspiration for the Ara Pacis Venus, who is represented simultaneously as the goddess of land, sea, and air,

[91] πείθεό μοι, 'Ρωμαῖε. κράτος μέγα Κύπρις ἔδωκεν
Αἰνείου γενεῇ μεμελημένη. ἀλλὰ σὺ πᾶσιν
ἀθανάτοις ἐπέτεια τίθει, μὴ λήθεο τῶνδε
Δελφοῖς δῶρα κόμιζε. καὶ ἔστι τις ἀμβαίνουσι
Ταύρου ὑπὸ νιφόεντος, ὅπου περιμήκετον ἄστυ
Καρῶν, οἳ ναίουσιν ἐπώνυμον ἐξ 'Αφροδίτης.
ᾗ πέλεκυν θέμενος λήψῃ κράτος ἀμφιλαφές σοι.

[92] Schilling, *Vénus* 293; I owe much in this paragraph to his discussion on pp. 289-295.

[93] See Chapter II, p. 65.

[94] *BMC Coins Caria* 39 nos. 85-89, pl. 7.1, with the legend: ΑΠΟΛΛΩΝΙΟΣ ΑΦΡΟΔΙΣΙΕΩΝ ΥΙΟΣ.

and who makes the earth in all its abundance produce fruits
and flowers, comes from the opening lines of Lucretius' *De
Rerum Natura*. Twice Venus is called upon as the goddess of
the sky and the air (*tibi . . . placatumque nitet diffuso lumine
caelum* [line 9]; *caeli subter labentia signa* [line 2] = the
velificantes "over whom towers the vault of heaven"), twice
as the goddess of the sea (*mare navigerum* [line 3]; *aequora
ponti* [line 8]), and twice as goddess of the earth that brings
forth (*terras frugiferentis* [line 3], and even more fittingly:

> tibi suavis daedala tellus
> summittit flores.)
> (lines 7-8)

These lines find a further artistic reflection in the floral frieze
of the Altar.[95] This combination of cosmic and Trojan aspects
in Lucretius' proem was anticipated by Sulla's assimilation of
the Carian to the Roman Venus. As in the proem, the Venus
of the Ara Pacis is the *Aeneadum genetrix*, the ancestress of
all Romans as well as the divine mother of the Julians. Associated with Aeneas and the family of Augustus, she is the
Trojan goddess of the "Trojan half" of the Altar. Her identity
can therefore be established somewhat more specifically: she
has many of the characteristics of the Trojan Venus from Mt.
Eryx in Sicily. While the conceptual influence of the Carian
Aphrodite should not be denied, the "adoption" of the latter
would have been impossible without the precedent of the assimilation of the Erycina, and it was the Erycina who became
the Venus Genetrix of the Julii. Let us see how this conclusion
fits the picture.

We saw earlier that the Eryx goddess was introduced into

---

[95] L'Orange (note 64, above) 14: "Sembra essere concetto universalmente
diffuso che la natura al tocco divino o all' apparire della divinità fruttifichi
al massimo grado . . . all' apparire di Venere la natura sorride e la terra
maestra di arte fa sbocciare ai suoi piedi i fiori più belli." Simon in Helbig,
Führer 2⁴.692, and Booth, *Latomus* 25 (1966) 876-877, also stress the
importance of the entire Lucretius proem for the interpretation of the relief.

Rome in 215 B.C. She originally seems to have been a goddess of seafaring—Aphrodite Pelagia or Euploia—and perhaps she was connected with the Aphrodite Urania, whose name is preserved by a dedicatory inscription from Segesta.[96] The ground had been prepared soon after the First Punic War by the association of Aeneas' landing in Sicily with Eryx and Segesta. While the foundation of the Eryx sanctuary by Aeneas was a Roman-inspired later addition to the Aeneas legend, the Romans, at any rate, skilfully exploited the Trojan milieu of the land of the Elymians to convert the goddess, who had traditionally been connected with Carthage, into a truly Roman deity.

This explains why an allusion to Juno in Aeneas' sacrifice on the Ara Pacis would be very appropriate.[97] *Pius* Aeneas, upon his arrival in Italy, sacrifices to Juno (*Aen.* 8.84), the patroness of Carthage, who insists on the obliteration of Troy and the Trojan name (*Aen.* 12.828). But Aeneas' sacrifice takes place under the benevolent eye and protection of Venus, his divine mother. Juno's demands have been met long before she makes them. Resplendent in the armor given to him by Venus, Aeneas is the *Romanae*—and not *Troianae*—*stirpis origo* (*Aen.* 12.166). For good reasons, therefore, he is juxtaposed with Romulus on the Altar. Once Juno has ceased interfering with Venus' domain—land, sea, and air—she reverts from the *aspera Iuno/quae mare nunc terrasque metu caelumque fatigat* (*Aen.* 1.279-280) to being the *Saturnia coniunx* (12.178) who lets order and *fatum*, on whose side Venus has been throughout the epic, take their course. Venus has not yielded a point and, as in the Ara Pacis frieze, it is made explicit in the *Aeneid* that the Emperor will be *pulchra Troianus origine* (1.286).

This emphasis on genealogy is consistent with what we know about the cult of Venus Erycina. She was not associated

[96] *IG* 14.287; cf. Chapter II, p. 74.
[97] See p. 199, above. Cf. J. Garstang, *Vergilius* 8 (1962) 18-26.

with the *Aeneadum genetrix* from the outset, but, beginning
with the second century B.C., Rome's Trojan families capitalized on her cult. Among them were the Memmii, who claimed
Aeneas' companion Mnestheus (*Aen.* 5.117) as their ancestor
and placed Venus Erycina on their coins.[98] This adds to the importance of the Lucretius proem as a prototype for the representation of Venus on the Ara Pacis. It was not until the
early Empire that Venus Erycina emerged from her narrowly
genealogical stage, and it was then that she began to be identified with the *Aeneadum genetrix*. The concept of Venus
Genetrix was probably not formed in complete independence
from the Venus Erycina cult, although there is no direct
evidence for such a connection.[99] The place of Venus on the
Altar frieze best expresses this delicate balance: flanking the
relief with the Augustan family, she is associated somewhat
more markedly with the *clarus Veneris sanguis* (Hor., *C.S.*
50) than with the Roman people in general, whose *Aeneadum
alma parens* she had become by the time of Tiberius.[100]

As we have seen, Venus and Apollo are closely associated
in the Venus relief and in the scroll beneath it. The artistic
precedents for this association are pre-Augustan, but the link
between Venus and Apollo in the Augustan context is made

---

[98] Venus Erycina on the coins of the Gens Memmia: *BMC Coins Rep.*
1.204-206 nos. 1328-1356, with pl. 31.5-7, and nos. 2421-2439, with pl.
37.18-19; Sydenham nos. 574, 574a, and 712; on the coins of the Gens
Iulia: *BMC Coins Rep.* 1.174 nos. 1140-1142, with pl. 27.19; Sydenham
no. 476; cf. Rizzo, *Monete* pl. 64.14. For Venus Erycina as Julius Caesar's
ancestress see also Malten, *ARW* 29 (1931) 46.

[99] An independent development is claimed by Koch, *Religio* 83-84, but
the close connection between Rome's Trojan legend and the Erycina cult
must be taken into account; cf. Chapter IV, p. 186. Venus Erycina and
Venus Genetrix eventually merged, just as the genealogical emphasis on
the Trojan descent of the Julian house gave way to the broader conception
of the Trojan descent of all Romans.

[100] *CIL* 10.7257 (=Dessau 939) on the base of a statue of Tiberius.
There were, therefore, still some genealogical overtones; cf. Tac., *Ann.*
4.43.5: Tiberius promises to restore the temple of Venus Erycina in Sicily
libens ut consanguineus.

most explicit by Horace's *Ode* 1.2,[101] which takes on a certain importance from its position immediately after the dedicatory Ode. The theme is civil strife and the fall of the state. Augustus is finally represented as the deliverer from these evils, but not until the poet has called on three divinities—Apollo, Venus Erycina, and Mars (lines 29-36):

> cui dabit partis scelus expiandi
> Iuppiter? tandem venias precamur
> nube candentis umeros amictus,
>   augur Apollo;
> sive tu mavis, Erycina ridens,
> quam Iocus circum volat et Cupido;
> sive neglectum genus et nepotes
>   respicis auctor.

The Ode probably was written around 28 B.C. at the beginning of Augustus' program. Could it not be expected, then, that a reference to the same gods should occur on the Ara Pacis, the monument symbolizing the successful completion of this program? The goddess thus is linked to Augustus as a partner in expiating the Trojan *scelus*, for *scelus* and *nefas* in the political Odes of the first three Books of Odes squarely refer to Troy. And since the Venus on the Ara Pacis is Trojan, a synthesis of incongruous Trojan elements is achieved which is even bolder than that created by Vergil. Vergil sought to eliminate the dichotomy between the *Troianus barbarus* and the *Troianus nobilis atque divinus* by making Aeneas' ancestor Dardanus a native of Italy, and thus rid the concept of Trojan descent of the *odium* with which it had been connected, especially since Antony's activities in the East.[102] Unlike Dardanus, the goddess is Italianized only faintly. Primarily, as we have seen, she is the Trojan goddess of the Trojan half of the Altar,

---

[101] Especially since Apollo is asked for *venia*, a quality or noun traditionally associated with Venus: see Schilling, *Vénus* 39-42, and for the connection between Venus Erycina and *venia*, *ibid.* 265.

[102] So, with good documentation, Buchheit, *Sendung* 151-172.

but far from being identified with the Trojan *culpa*, she participates in the sacrifice to Pax, which marks the end of all the disturbances and wars that had plagued Rome as a consequence of the *periuria Troiae* (Vergil, *Geo.* 1.502).

The connection between the Venus slab and the relief with the return of the native son Aeneas to Italy therefore takes on a more profound meaning. There is an additional element of correspondence which enhances it. One of the motifs of the Aeneas relief is that of landing; there is a καταγωγή. It is contrasted with the departure, the ἀναγωγή of the Aurae. The rites of καταγώγια and ἀναγώγια were typical of the Carthaginian Ashtoreth Erech.[103] It is not unreasonable to assume that, although the celebration of the rites was abolished by the Romans, a memory of them was preserved in art. Considering that all other elements of the cult were transformed *ad maiorem Romae gloriam*, it is not surprising that this motif should appear on the altar glorifying the achievement of the Roman emperor.

In view of the representation of the Aura on the swan, which is reminiscent of the coins of Camarina (Fig. 151), the coins of Eryx, well known to Roman *monetarii*, may have served as prototypes for the central Venus figure. The Eryx coinage shows some of the rare representations of an Aphrodite seated on a throne (Figs. 55b, 161 a and b).[104] On the coins, as in the Altar relief, the goddess is fully dressed and her breasts are modeled expressively. On the Eryx coin, the relationship between Aphrodite and the Eros boy is very similar to the relation between Venus and the child on her left knee in the Ara relief. Eros offers Erycina a garland of flowers (Fig. 161a) while the child on the Ara offers Venus an apple. The drapery on the lap of the Eryx Aphrodite is arranged in a loop not unlike the one on the lap of the Venus on the Ara. Furthermore, on several coins Aphrodite appears with a crane,

[103] See Chapter II, p. 71 with note 26.
[104] Rizzo, *Monete* 296 with pl. 94.10-14, and fig. 93a.

which has been interpreted as an allusion to the oriental character of Eryx.[105]

The question why a composite Venus/Terra Mater type was chosen for the Altar again leads us back to the Eryx Venus. There was a close connection between her cult on the Capitol and the introduction of the Phrygian Cybele of Pergamum/Pessinus into Rome.[106] The Delphic oracle and Apollo also had a part in the transfer of the latter.[107] The connection between the Trojan Venus and Apollo on the Ara Pacis may be reminiscent of that event. A further link between Venus and Cybele is the family of Aeneas in the *Aeneid*. Creusa, for instance, while attempting to flee from Troy is detained there by Magna Mater (2.788). Pausanias is even more explicit about the connection between Venus and Cybele: "About Creusa the story is told that the mother of the gods *and* Aphrodite rescued her from slavery among the Greeks, as she was, of course, the wife of Aeneas" (10.26.1). Aeneas himself is associated with Cybele continuously, especially when he builds his fleet. This development culminates in his invocation to her in *Aeneid* 10.252, where he addresses her with Venus' epithet *alma* (cf. 10.220), and especially in his prayer of thanksgiving *pro reditu suo* after the happy fulfillment of the tables prophecy, a scene that is implicit in the Aeneas relief of the Ara Pacis (*Aen.* 7.137-140):[108]

> Tellurem Nymphasque et adhuc ignota precatur
> flumina, tum Noctem Noctisque orientia signa

---

[105] Details in G. de Ciccio, *Num. Circ.* 39 (1931) 331-332 and figs. 11-13. For the association of Aphrodite and a crane see *Roscher's Lexicon* 1.402, and O. Keller, *Die antike Tierwelt* 2 (Leipzig 1913) 185; cf. p. 212 and note 78, above, with Fig. 155.

[106] See Chapter IV, pp. 176-177.

[107] Livy 29.10.6: . . . *legati, qui donum Delphos portaverant, referebant et sacrificantibus ipsis Pythio Apollini omnia laeta fuisse et responsum oraculo editum maiorem multo victoriam quam cuius ex spoliis dona portarent adesse populo Romano.*

[108] Cf. pp. 199-200, above. For the association of Aeneas and Cybele see, e.g., *Aeneid* 2.801; 3.5-6; 9.80-89; 10.230-235, 252-255.

Idaeumque Iovem Phrygiamque ex ordine matrem
invocat.

The relationship between Aeneas and Cybele therefore is comparable only to his connection with Venus, a development "without precedent in previous legend."[109]

The passage which most clearly conveys the importance of Cybele for the *Aeneid* and for the Ara Pacis occurs in the center of the epic, in Anchises' exhortation to Aeneas. Since the Ara Pacis expresses in art what Vergil had expressed in poetry, the remarkable structural similarity between the work of sculpture and this speech of Anchises is not surprising (text fig. 5).[110] In both cases, we have a basic division into a Roman and an Augustan half. Each half is composed of three parts, and the halves are interrelated with each other. In the *Aeneid*, this interrelation is primarily one of theme: the mention of Romulus in the center of the Augustan half anticipates the Roman half and the program Anchises outlines in 6.847-853 (*tu regere imperio* . . .) is that of both Augustus and Rome, the *tu Romane* addressed here probably being the Emperor himself. Romulus and Augustus are somewhat more closely connected by Vergil than they are on the more public Ara Pacis, perhaps because Augustus deliberately avoided association with Romulus and preferred to consider Aeneas as his true ancestor. But the juxtaposition of Cybele and Roma is the same in both cases, although in keeping with the artistry of the Altar, the presence of the Asian Mother goddess there is suggested on a symbolic level rather than made allegorically obvious. What is the significance of this connection so familiar to us from the Gemma Augustea?

The imperial cult suggests the answer. In 29 B.C., Octavian had authorized the cult, first of Dea Roma and Divus Iulius among the Romans of Bithynia and Asia, and then of himself and Dea Roma among the Greeks of Pergamum and Nico-

[109] C. Bailey, *Religion in Vergil* (Oxford 1935) 176-177.
[110] For details see Duckworth, *TAPA* 87 (1956) 314-315.

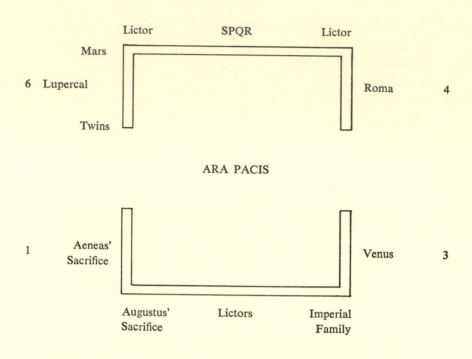

Roman Half

Lictor   SPQR   Lictor

Mars

6   Lupercal   Roma   4

Twins

ARA PACIS

1   Aeneas'   Venus   3
     Sacrifice

Augustus'   Lictors   Imperial
Sacrifice   Family

Augustan-Trojan Half

2

Horace, *Carmina* III   Vergil, *Aeneid* VI

1. Simplicity of living ⎫ ROMAN   760-776 Alban kings   ⎫
2. Virtus   ⎬ HALF   777-787 Romulus (Roma 781,   ⎬ AUGUSTAN
3. Greatness of Rome   ⎭   Cybele 784-787)   ⎭ HALF
                                         788-807 Augustus
4. Augustus   ⎫
5. Military policy   ⎬ AUGUSTAN   808-818 Roman kings   ⎫
6. Religious and   ⎭ HALF   819-846 Republican heroes   ⎬ ROMAN
   social policy   847-853 ROMAN-AUGUSTAN   ⎭ HALF
   AUGUSTAN PROGRAM   PROGRAM

5. The Ara Pacis and Augustan Poetry

media.[111] What has been said of Vergil therefore applies also to the artist of the Ara Pacis: "When Vergil was writing *Aeneid* 6, the union of the worship of Augustus and Roma was an accomplished fact in the East, and the Emperor's opposition to its celebration in Rome itself did not prevent the poet from hinting at it indirectly. Vergil's mention of Cybele was highly appropriate and, indeed, a touch of genius. Originally an eastern goddess, she reminded his readers that in her former home Augustus and Rome were already deities."[112] In the frieze, therefore, the representation of Venus Erycina/ Cybele on its various levels adds to the emphasis on the divinity of Augustus, which is one of the main themes of the Altar.

The clearest expression yet of the godlike Augustus' association with the abundance of the earth and, at the same time, with Venus, is found in the proem to the first two *Georgics*, which sets the tone for the *laudes Italiae* and the *laudes Romae*. After invoking a whole canon of gods, the poet at last calls upon the deity which thus implicitly is recognized as the greatest: Augustus, the *auctor frugum* (*Geo.* 1.27). The phrase is echoed later by the *magna parens frugum, Saturnia Tellus* (2.173); the second passage has to be read in the light of the first. Like Venus, Augustus rules over land (*terrarum*: line 26), air (*tempestatum*: line 27), and sea (*maris*: line 29), and this is why his temples are crowned with the myrtle of Venus:

> Caesar,
> terrarum velis curam, et te maximus orbis
> auctoremque frugum tempestatumque potentem
> accipiat cingens materna tempora myrto,
> an deus immensi venias maris . . .
>
> (*Geo.* 1.25-29)

---

[111] Dio. 51.20.7-8; Tac., *Ann.* 4.37; cf. A. D. Nock, *HSCP* 51 (1930) 27-29, and *CAH* 10 (1934) 485-486.

[112] R. J. Getty, *CP* 45 (1950) 9. Cf. Bömer, *MDAI(R)* 71 (1964) 138-

Already in the *Eclogues* the appearance of Caesar, the son of Venus, was hailed as bestowing the very bounty and blessing on the earth which finds its visual expression on the Ara Pacis relief (*Ecl.* 9.47-49):

> ecce Dionaei processit Caesaris astrum,
> astrum quo segetes gauderent frugibus et quo
> duceret apricis in collibus uva colorem.

Theocritus already had called the Erycina Dione (*Id.* 15.106), and Aeneas sacrifices to his *Dionaeae matri* (*Aen.* 3.19) whose star guided him on his wanderings (Varro in Serv., *Aen.* 1.382). Behind the Tellus/Venus relief, therefore, stands

> Augustus Caesar, divi genus, aurea condet
> saecula qui rursus Latio regnata per arva
> Saturno quondam.
>
> (*Aen.* 6.792-794)

Augustus will reestablish the Golden Age, "but with the important difference that, as the new ruler and Jupiter's representative, he is to replace Saturn, its king in former times."[113] This adds to the ambiguity of Saturnia Tellus, a phrase that was so unhesitatingly seized upon by earlier scholars. The implication of the Ara Pacis, however, is that Tellus evokes the old Saturnia Tellus, but primarily she is Tellus *Augusta*.

The support found in Horace's poetry is no less convincing. It has long been noted that Book 4 of the *Odes* reflects to a considerable extent the themes and motifs alluded to in the Ara Pacis reliefs.[114] There are a few references to Terra and Italia, but the Venus theme is set in relief much more sig-

---

145, who stresses the Augustan revival of Cybele's cult and considers Venus, Cybele, and Dea Roma as manifestations of the same deity (140).

[113] Getty 12. The same idea appears in Ovid, *M.* 15.857-860; cf. Horace *C.* 1.12.49-52.

[114] See Benario, *TAPA* 91 (1960) 339-352; Duckworth, *TAPA* 87 (1956) 314-315, and Norberg, *Emerita* 20 (1952) 105-106.

nificantly. It strikes the note on which the book begins (4.1.1-2).

> intermissa, Venus, diu
> rursus bella moves?

and on which it ends (4.15.31-32):

> Troiam et Anchisen et almae
> progeniem Veneris canemus.

As in the Altar relief, the Venus of the First Ode rides a swan (line 10), and she is entertained by the flutes of the *Berecyntia mater*, Cybele (lines 22-23). She makes Horace pursue Ligurinus, who is *volucer* like the figure on the left in the relief, and Horace follows him through the Campus Martius (lines 38-40), the site of the Ara Pacis. After the Venus theme has recurred prominently throughout the Book, it is powerfully summed up by the mention of the Venus who is *alma* like the Erycina on the Ara Pacis[115] and who, like the one on the Altar, is the Trojan *genetrix* of Augustus and then of the Romans.

One of the most important archaeological and iconographic problems[116] connected with the Venus relief is its relation to a

---

[115] For a discussion of the Venus theme in Book 4, see E. Fraenkel, *Horace* (Oxford 1957) 413, and with more detail, D. H. Porter, *Book IV of Horace's Odes: An Interpretive Study* (Diss. Princeton 1962) 32-37. The Lucretius proem was the model of the invocation to Venus Erycina in *Odes* 1.2; see S. Commager, *AJP* 80 (1959) 48, and the *alma* Venus Horace invokes in 4.15 was in turn to recall the Venus of *C.* 1.2 (Porter 36 n. 36). The significance of these parallels for the interpretation of the Ara relief is evident. For *alma* Venus cf. Ovid, *Fasti* 4.1: *alma, fave, dixi, geminorum mater Amorum*, which is reflected in the representation of Venus on the Altar.

[116] Its principal stages: Kalkmann, *JDAI* 1 (1886) 255-258 (both reliefs have the same symbolic content, but the Roman relief is inferior and therefore later); T. Schreiber, *JDAI* 11 (1896) 89-96 (the Carthage relief is earlier because it reproduces an Alexandrian model more faithfully); Petersen, *APA* 173-175 (basically follows Schreiber); Studniczka, *Abh. Leipzig* 27 (1909) 930 (the Carthage relief is a later one; it dissolves the unity of the Ara Pacis relief); Van Buren, *JRS* 3 (1913) 138-140 (follows Stud-

relief from Carthage in the Louvre (Fig. 162). The latter has often been used as a reference point for the interpretation of the former. There is considerable disagreement, however, on the subject of the Louvre relief and on the question of priority. A brief summary of the main points of the controversy may serve to point up the limitations of any such comparison, before any further conclusions can be suggested.

1. Of all the arguments that have been advanced in favor of such subjects as Africa between Selene and the Syrtes (Van Buren), Terra Mater between Sun and Moon (Méautis), or a local goddess, Dea Caelestis (Petersen and Kalkmann), none has been accepted as particularly cogent or convincing.[117] No definitive interpretation can be expected until we know more about the monument of which it was a part, but it is important to note that it was connected with a relief representing Venus Genetrix and Mars at the side of Divus Augustus or Iulius (Fig. 163).[118]

2. There is no need to introduce another unknown quantity into the discussion by postulating a Hellenistic prototype from which both the Carthage and the Ara Pacis reliefs were de-

niczka); G. Méautis, *Bronzes antiques du canton de Neuchâtel* (Neuchâtel 1928) 17-28 (the Carthage relief is a lesser copy of an Alexandrian original; its content reflects Stoic conceptions of nature; this was not understood by the Ara Pacis artists, who used the Carthage relief as a model); A. Grenier, *Le génie romain* (Paris 1925) 424 (the Carthage relief adorned an Ara Pacis at Carthage modeled on the Roman Ara Pacis); Moretti, *APA* 232-237 (the whole priority question is unimportant, but the Carthage relief supports the Tellus identification); Toynbee, *The Hadrianic School* 141 n. 1, and *PBA* 39 (1953) 81 (the Carthage relief may have been inspired directly by the Ara Pacis, or both reliefs may have stemmed independently from a common parent); Sieveking, *Festschrift Arndt* 22 (the stronger formal coherence of the Roman relief indicates its priority); A. Adriani, *Divagazioni intorno ad una coppa paesistica del Museo di Alessandria* (Rome 1959) 31-32, with detailed bibliography on 72 n. 161 (back to Schreiber); Matz, *Gnomon* 32 (1960) 294-296 (elaborates Sieveking's arguments further).

[117] Cf. Momigliano, *JWI* 5 (1942) 228.

[118] See S. Gsell, *RA* 3rd ser. 24 (1899) 37-43 with pl. 2 and *Histoire ancienne de l'Afrique du nord* 8 (Paris 1928) 177; cf. M. Rostovtzeff, *MDAI(R)* 38-39 (1923-1924) 294.

rived. The Venus relief is a genuine Augustan creation.[119] Nor can the Carthage relief be proved to be of Alexandrian provenance, and there is nothing in either relief that would suggest an acquaintance with Alexandrian or Egyptian surroundings. Generally, it can be said that "not until the late Roman Republic or early imperial period was any thorough attempt made to represent landscape in relief, and it was on Italian soil that this attempt was made."[120]

3. To settle the question of priority, two considerations are most relevant. First, considering the relief with which it is connected, the Carthage relief most probably was part of one of a series of altars that were erected throughout the empire after Augustus' death.[121] If this is the case, the Ara Pacis relief would be the earlier of the two. Secondly, the Roman relief has the tighter arrangement, which, as we have seen, corresponds to its content. Its symmetry is conspicuous without being monotonous. Yet almost every proponent of an early date of the Carthage relief bases his conclusion on the thoroughly subjective argument that the Ara Pacis slab, because of its "dull," "vulgar," and "unimaginative" symmetry, must be the epigonal work, stifling, as it were, the freshness and liveliness of the genuinely Greek relief from Carthage.[122] It is clear that only an objective analysis of style and not a prejudicial statement of taste is meaningful for the solution of the problem. All attempts of the latter kind, however, have resulted in the same conclusion, i.e. the priority of the Ara Pacis relief. For the spatial conception of the Carthage relief, and consequently, the heterogeneous representation of the three figures (the main

---

[119] So Sieveking, *Festschrift Arndt* 21.

[120] C. M. Dawson, *Romano-Campanian Mythological Landscape Painting.* YCS 13 (1940) 41; cf. P. H. von Blanckenhagen, *MDAI(R)* 70 (1963) 135-146.

[121] So, for instance, Van Buren, *JRS* 3 (1913) 138-139; Gsell, *RA* 3rd ser. 24 (1899) 37; Grenier (note 116, above) 424-425.

[122] So, e.g., Schreiber, *JDAI* 11 (1896) 91; Méautis (note 116, above) 23-28; E. Lippold, *Antike Gemäldekopien* (Munich 1951) 154; C. Picard, *Mélanges Maspéro* 2 (Paris 1937) 329-333.

figure is shown in profile, the *velificans*, in front view, while the torso of the rising figure on the right is rather twisted) represent a compromise which would be incomprehensible without the Ara Pacis relief as its forerunner.[123] Generally speaking, the Carthage relief is split up into segments, which contrasts with the unity of the Ara Pacis relief. This purely formal compromise and segmentation has its counterpart in content also. The Ara Pacis Venus is Genetrix and cosmic symbol at the same time. On the Carthage reliefs, however, Venus Genetrix is represented separately, and, in the manner of the Sorrento Base and the Belvedere Altar, she is more manifestly associated with the Emperor. The central figure on the other Carthage relief thus probably symbolizes Venus under her cosmic aspect.

This impression is confirmed by her companion figures, which, as on the Ara Pacis, are of considerable significance for the interpretation of the main figure. On her right is a torch-bearing *velificans*, analogous to the one on the armor of the Prima Porta Augustus. Rather than being Selene, whose iconographic representation, however, often resembles that of Venus, she is the morning star, *stella Veneris genitalis et roscida et prospera et salutaris.*[124] It is no coincidence, therefore, that the vegetation below her grows somewhat more copiously than the reeds under the corresponding figure on the Ara Pacis. The often suggested interpretation of the figure on the right as Sol is probably correct: Hellenistic speculation connected Sol with Apollo and Augustus. Although such overtones may be present in the Carthage relief, Sol is primarily the cosmic nature deity, and as such he is represented also on the garment of the Carian Aphrodite (Fig. 160). After the morning star has announced the new day, Sol will arise and contribute to the bounteousness of the earth: *cum sole*

[123] Matz, *Gnomon* 32 (1960) 295.
[124] Censorinus frg. 3.5; cf. Gundel, *RE* 8A (1955) 889-890, and Simon, *MDAI(R)* 64 (1957) 55-56.

novo terras inrorat Eous (Vergil, *Geo.* 1.288). Sol is rising from the sea, which was a common conception in ancient philosophy as we know from Plutarch and others.[125] As in the Ara Pacis relief, Venus fructifies the land, but the introduction of Sol as well as the star of Venus intensifies the cosmic aspect of her representation.

On the Ara Pacis, the relationship between the Venus relief and the reliefs of Augustus, Aeneas, and the Roman people is clear enough. What needs to be briefly explored, however, is the connection between Venus and Mars, Venus and Roma, and lastly, between Venus and Pax.

The connection of Mars and Venus Erycina in Horace's *Carmen* 1.2 goes back to the *lectisternium* in 217 B.C. when the two deities were associated in Rome for the first time (Liv. 22.9.10; 10.9).[126] In 138 B.C. the deities were associated again, when two colossal statues of Mars and Venus by Scopas were set up on the cella of the Mars temple of Brutus Callaecus (Pliny, *N.H.* 36.26). Genealogical implications are evident in the honorific title Caesar received from the cities of Asia: "The god-son of Ares and Aphrodite" (τὸν ἀπὸ Ἄρεως καὶ Ἀφροδίτης θεὸν ἐπιφανῆ; *SIG*³ 760) and by that time, Venus Victrix had begun to appear with the attributes of Mars. This is evident especially from the dedication accompanying the double axe which Sulla gave the Aphrodite of Aphrodisias:[127] "The imperator Sulla consecrated that one to you, Aphrodite, because I saw you in a dream exhorting my army and fighting with the arms of Ares." Venus and Mars were constantly represented together in the monuments: in the pediment of the temple of Mars Ultor and inside the temple (Ovid, *Trist.* 2.295-296), inside the Pantheon (Dio 53.27.2), in the pediment of the temple of Divus Augustus, on the Sorrento Base

[125] *De Iside et Osir.* 367E; cf. Cicero, *N.D.* 3.14.37.

[126] See Chapter IV, p. 186 and note 112.

[127] Appian, *B.C.* 1.97; for further evidence see Schilling, *Vénus* 331-338; Koch, *RE* 8A (1955) 860-863; Wissowa in *Roscher's Lexicon* 6 (1924-1937) 862-863.

and the Belvedere Altar, and on numerous coins.[128] But it was not until Augustus' time that the association of the two deities, so familiar from Greek mythology, was given a meaning significant for the Romans: Venus was proclaimed the ancestress of the Julian family as well as of the Roman people, and Mars was honored as the divine father of the founders of the city (Macrob., *Sat.* 1.12.8) and as the avenger of Caesar's murder. Their increasingly close association is reflected by the interchangeable use of the characteristic epithets: two Umbrian inscriptions, for instance, refer respectively to Mars *Cyprius* and Venus *Martialis* (*CIL* 11.5805 and 5165). Linked as she is to Mars and the victorious Roma on the Altar, the Venus in the Ara relief has the overtones not only of the Genetrix, but also of the more inclusive concept, Venus Victrix. The fact that the Victrix on coins sometimes carries a cornucopia[129] connects her even more closely with this Venus relief.

The interrelation between the reliefs with Mars and Venus is further underscored by the structural and thematic parallelism between Horace's Roman *Odes* and the Ara Pacis frieze (see text fig. 5). Like the speech of Anchises, the Roman *Odes* can be divided into an Augustan and a Roman half, yet two different arrangements of both the *Odes* and the Ara Pacis are possible and appear equally valid.[130] They may be illustrated as shown in text fig. 6.

Since there is a structural and thematic link between the Lupercal (6) and Venus (3) reliefs, it may be suggested that the representation of Venus/Tellus with two children instead of

---

[128] Liegle, *JDAI* 56 (1941) 91-119, with figs. 3 and 10.

[129] Babelon, *Monnaies de la république romaine* 2.43 no. 86; cf. p. 205, above, and Fig. 140.

[130] See Duckworth, *TAPA* 87 (1956) 304-305. The first arrangement has been proposed, for instance, by W. Port, *Philologus* 81 (1925-1926) 300, and F. Klingner, *Varia Variorum. Festschrift Reinhardt* (Münster 1952) 128; the second, by A. C. Landi, *Raccolta Ramorino* (Milan 1927) 187-196, and H. B. Jaffee, *Horace: an Essay in Poetic Therapy* (Chicago 1944) 92-94; cf. W. Wili, *Horaz und die augusteische Kultur* (Basel 1948) 156.

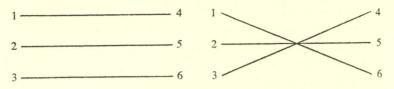

6. Two arrangements of Horace's *Odes* and the Ara Pacis

cornucopiae was chosen to parallel the representation of the twins Romulus and Remus in the former relief. The two children may thus be considered a happy compromise between the cornucopiae of Terra Mater and the two Amores, or *Iocus* and *Amor*, who fly around Venus Erycina (Horace, *C.* 1.2.34). A possible forerunner is the Venus Genetrix statue ascribed by Bieber to Arkesilaos (Fig. 17).[131] On the shoulders of this standing Venus sits a little Amor, while she leads Iulus with her left hand.

The juxtaposition of Venus and Roma is not accidental either. It reached its culmination in the Hadrianic temple of Venus and Roma, but is found first on the reverse of the coins of E. Egnatius Maxumus in ca. 73 B.C.,[132] Roma symbolizing the Romulean tradition as she stands on the head of the wolf-nurse, while Venus alludes to the Trojan heritage. But before being thus clearly associated with Venus, the iconography of Roma had been deliberately de-Trojanized,[133] and this makes for one of the several contrasts between the two reliefs on the Altar.

The subtle network of contrasting interrelations stretching on various levels across the individual frieze groups of the Altar may be illustrated by two more examples. The western frieze group, turned in the direction of the evening, represents the mythical past of Rome.[134] Aeneas lands in Italy and

---

[131] *MDAI(R)* 48 (1933) 261-276 with pl. 46.

[132] *BMC Coins Rep.* 1.401 nos. 3285-3292; Sydenham nos. 787-787a, with pl. 22.

[133] See Chapter IV, pp. 188-189 with figs. 131a-c.

[134] Cf. Hanell, *Opusc. Rom.* 2 (1960) 119-120.

the twins are saved from death by the wolf-nurse. That was the birth of Rome. The east frieze group of Venus and Roma symbolizes the new Golden Age, the future, by announcing the might of Roman world domination. This very theme is voiced in Vergil's Fourth *Eclogue* (50-52):

> aspice convexo nutantem pondere mundum,
> terrasque tractusque maris caelumque profundum:
> aspice venturo laetentur ut omnia saeclo!

Thus Venus, who also rules over land, sea, and air, and who is represented amid a κῆπος not unlike that described earlier in the *Eclogue* (lines 18-20), stands for the world to come.

However, on a different level the same contrast that exists between the east and west frieze groups recurs between Venus and Roma. Venus was always associated with the *initia gentis*, with the origins, and all *salus* was believed to come from there. The *Roma aeterna*, however points to the future.[135] Although this contrast became most evident at the time of Hadrian, it reflects a conception that goes back to Sullan times. On one level, then, the Venus on the Ara Pacis is associated with tradition, and on another, with the future which implies change and innovation. The same conflict and tension between these very tendencies as well as the resultant equilibrium were the chief characteristics of the Venus Erycina cult in Rome.[136]

Venus and Roma, therefore, complement each other. Their relationship is heightened by the fact that Venus expresses best what Anchises said of Roma: she is *felix prole virum* (*Aen.* 6.784). She is *laeta* about her offspring as is the *Berecyntia mater* (6.786-787):

[135] Details in Koch, *Religio* 90-91; cf. *id.*, "Roma Aeterna," *Gymnasium* 59 (1952) 128-143, 196-209.

[136] Cf. Chapter IV, p. 185 and Schilling, *Vénus* 266: "Elle rassurait les traditionalistes en même temps qu'elle comblait les novateurs. Cette conciliation de tendances opposées explique sans aucun doute le prestige extraordinaire de la déesse."

laeta deum partu, centum complexa nepotes,
omnis caelicolas, omnis supera alta tenentis.

Vergil thus clearly hints that Roma might be regarded as the mother of Augustus.[137] Conversely, the offspring of Cybele/Venus are not merely the Julians, but they are called *Romanos* (line 789). Because Venus and Roma share many of the same characteristics, the Venus and Roma reliefs join together the two halves of the Altar more closely than do the slabs with Aeneas and Mars. This is why Venus and Roma are represented on the front of the Ara Pacis.

Pax is not represented on the Ara Pacis.[138] This should not surprise us: the Ara frieze is suggestive rather than explicit, as is much of Augustan poetry. It is again in the Lucretius proem, which seems to have inspired the Venus relief so greatly, that Pax and Venus are associated most clearly. The proem culminates in a prayer to Venus (1.39-40):[139]

suavis ex ore loquellas
funde petens placidam Romanis, incluta, pacem.

In the *Aeneid*, Venus is portrayed as the preserver of *pax*, and to the same degree to which Juno wants to disturb it.[140] It is Venus Victrix who gives Aeneas his armor so that he can

[137] Cf. Getty, *CP* 45 (1950) 10.

[138] I hesitate to accept Hanell's theory (*Opusc. Rom.* 2 [1960] 95-98) that the three fragmentary figures at the west end of the south frieze represented the goddesses Pax, Salus, and Concordia. Another place where Pax may possibly have been represented is the largest of the friezes covering the altar itself. But Momigliano, *JWI* 5 (1942) 228-231, and Kähler, *JDAI* 69 (1954) 89, have already pointed out that Pax is inherently present in the Ara Pacis reliefs without actually being represented, and both writers single out the Tellus (Momigliano) or Italia (Kähler) relief as conveying the idea of Pax most effectively; cf. note 2, above.

[139] On the relation between Pax and the Lucretian Venus consult Schilling, *Vénus* 350-358, and C. Bailey, *T. Lucreti Cari Libri* VI, vol. 2 (Oxford 1947) 601-604; cf. the recurrence of lines 44-49 at 2.646-651, after the description of the rites of Magna Mater. Cf. note 115, above.

[140] See Buchheit, *Sendung* 70-71. The contrast between *pacem* (*Aen.* 7.285) and Juno's (*saeva Iovis coniunx*; 7.287) intervention could not be more explicit. The sacrifice made by Aeneas on the Ara Pacis to—in part, at least—Juno (see p. 199, above) thus clearly involves the notion of Pax.

wage a *bellum pium et iustum*—the means by which the first *Pax Romana* has to be achieved. Hence our Venus is connected with Aeneas, with Mars, and with Roma who is sitting on the arms of the conquered.

As Hanell has rightly pointed out,[141] Ovid is the Augustan poet who emphasizes most the relationship between the Pax Augusta and Ceres as, for instance, in *Fasti* 1.704:

> Pax Cererem nutrit, Pacis alumna Ceres.

Hanell thus favors the restoration of the goddess Pax on the south frieze to include the attributes of Ceres, i.e. especially the ears of grain:

> at nobis, Pax alma, veni spicamque teneto,
> profluat et pomis candidus ante sinus.
> (Tib. 1.10.67-68)

But Venus and Ceres share an even closer relationship: they had a joint cult.[142] From the time of the Aphrodite Aineias, Venus is represented on coins with the same symbol, the grain ear (Fig. 164a), as are Ceres and Pax. The bunch of poppies and ears of grain that appears to the right of the central Venus figure is a symbol which is recurrently associated with Pax on her coins. A particularly illuminating specimen was issued in Spain during the civil wars of 68 A.D.[143] On its reverse (Fig. 164b), between two ears of grain and two poppies, two clasped hands are shown holding a *caduceus*, the same symbol of Pax which appeared on the coin commemorating the end of the Social War (Fig. 137). Roma again is juxtaposed with

---

[141] *Opusc. Rom.* 2 (1960) 117-120.

[142] *CIL* 1².1541, 1774, 1775; 9.3089; 10.680; cf. Dessau 6371.

[143] It is significant that the composite Aphrodite Aeneias already appears with ears of grain on the coins; see Chapter II, p. 66 and *AJA* 70 (1966) pl. 54 fig. 19. Venus with ears of grain: *BMC Coins Rep.* 1 nos. 2770-2835 with pl. 40.12-14 (our Fig. 164a); Pax with ears of grain: 1) on coins from Spain: *BMC Coins Emp.* 1.290 no. 6, with pl. 49.19 (our Figs. 164 b and c); 2) on aureus: *BMC Coins Emp.* 1.305 no. 58, with pl. 51.17; 352 no. 242, with pl. 55.7.

this symbol of peace. She is represented on the obverse (Fig. 164c) sitting on her cuirass; the same juxtaposition and representation of Roma had occurred on the Ara Pacis. The apples of Pax which Tibullus mentions appear in the lap of the Venus figure of the Ara Pacis. Furthermore, as we saw earlier, the heifer and the sheep figured prominently in the animal sacrifice to Pax (Fig. 158). Thus Venus is the figure of the Ara Pacis which is most emblematic of Pax.

Finally, are Venus, Terra Mater, and Italia really incompatible with each other? Italia and Tellus certainly are not, "for each mother of a country is also earth mother as is shown especially by numismatic iconography."[144] This is also borne out by Varro's mention of an *Italia in pariete picta* in the Temple of Tellus at Rome (Varro, *R.R.* 1.2.1). Tellus therefore is simply the more inclusive concept.

The same applies, *mutatis mutandis*, to the relation of Venus and Tellus. Terra exhales moist breath towards that time of day which is most closely connected with Venus:

Terra exhalat auram ad auroram humidam.

And Tellus is subservient to Venus:

tibi suavis daedala Tellus
summittit flores . . .

They share the same symbols: cornucopiae and ears of grain, and both are connected closely with Ceres. Their iconography, as we have already noted on several occasions, overlaps repeatedly. The earliest ancient example is a Calenic relief plate (Fig. 165).[145] Aphrodite is represented in a reclining posture approximating Tellus'. A large cornucopia is in her lap and two Erotes cling to it. On a sarcophagus in Amalfi both Venus

---

[144] Kähler, *Festschrift Schweitzer* 329: ". . . denn jede Landesmutter ist zugleich, wie vor allem die Münzbilder lehren, Erdmutter."

[145] See R. Pagenstecher, *Calenische Reliefkeramik. JDAI Ergänzungsheft* 8 (1909) 54 and fig. 30, with a list of seven similar representations, and Simon, *Geburt der Aphrodite* 102-103.

and Tellus are represented in the same relief in the very same reclining posture. Venus has a Cupid on each side, whereas Tellus holds the cornucopia.[146] Finally, this association of Terra Mater with Venus must have been familiar to the Botticelli group of painters in the Renaissance. For their representation of Venus they chose the reclining posture which is more typical of Tellus than of Venus, although it is not without ancient precedent (Fig. 167).[147]

On the armor of the Prima Porta statue Tellus, Magna Mater, and Italia are symbolized by the same figure.[148] Because of the link between Magna Mater and Venus,[149] the symbolism of the Ara Pacis figure is even more extensive. By choosing what is primarily a Venus figure, the sculptor of the relief tried to realize to the fullest possible extent the complex web of associations which gives the frieze its unity. This complexity, more than anything else, explains why the symbolism of the Ara Pacis was not widely followed,[150] and why no similar representation of Venus is known.

In the Ara Pacis reliefs, the Trojan legend of Rome reaches

[146] See Robert, *Die antiken Sarcophagreliefs* 3.2 fig. 193, pl. 60.

[147] London National Gallery no. 916. See also Botticelli's "Mars and Venus" in the National Gallery (no. 915); a painting, by another Botticelli follower, of Venus and Cupids in the Louvre (no. 1299), and Titian's "Venus and the Organist," formerly in the Kaiser Friedrich Museum in Berlin (no. 1849); cf. Strong, *JRS* 27 (1937) 114-115. Strong's article was inspired by the iconographic similarity between Renaissance paintings of Venus and ancient Tellus representations. It did not occur to Strong that the motif in ancient art also was related to Venus.

[148] Simon, *MDAI(R)* 64 (1957) 58.

[149] A Venus statue probably stood in the east sacellum of the Magna Mater temple on the Capitoline; see A. Bartoli, "Il culto della Mater Deum Magna Idaea e di Venere Genitrice sul Palatino," *Mem. Pont. Acc. Arch.* 3rd ser. 6 (1947) 229-239. Ostia, at any rate, furnished a precedent: see R. Calza, "Sculture rinvenute nel santuario della Magna Mater a Ostia," *ibid.* 224-227. Cf. Graillot (Chapter IV, n. 93) 343. G. A. S. Snijder, *De forma matris cum infante sedentis apud antiquos* (Vienna 1920) 41-42, believes that Terra Mater and Aphrodite originally were one and the same, but this syncretism is no more than conjectural; cf. Chapter II, note 26. On the Patera from Parabiago Terra Mater and Cybele are associated in that the former watches the wedding of the latter.

[150] Cf. Momigliano, *JWI* 5 (1942) 230, and note 45, above.

its most mature development and interpretation. Victorious Roma, sitting on a pile of arms and paired with Mars, still hints at conquest. Some of the Augustan poets still expected the emperor to engage in new wars and extend the boundaries of the Roman Empire.[151] Even the hero of the *Aeneid*, much as he strives for *pax*, can achieve it only through a bloody war, which is the theme of the second half of the epic. But on the Ara Pacis, the Trojan reliefs, flanking the scene with the princeps' sacrifice, symbolize his peaceful aspirations. Aeneas performs a sacrifice like Augustus'. The Sicilian Venus, who ordinarily was known as Victrix,[152] is represented between the two *velificantes* rising from land and sea, and she serenely watches over the children at play: *terra marique pax*. The claim to Trojan ancestry had reflected the political and cultural aspirations of the Romans in the third century B.C.; the Sicilian Venus had been associated with war and resistance to the enemy. The Trojan legend then had been restricted to the narrow confines of genealogy. In the Augustan age an attempt was made to put it on a broader, more popular foundation. The spirit of the age was marked by a longing for *pax*, and Aeneas and the Trojan Venus from Sicily became its symbols.

[151] See, most recently, H. D. Meyer, *Die Aussenpolitik des Augustus und die augusteische Dichtung* (Cologne 1961) for a detailed analysis of this phenomenon.

[152] See Chapter IV, p. 186 with Fig. 129.

APPENDIX

SCULPTURAL FINDS FROM THE

TEMPLE OF VENUS ERYCINA

IN THE GARDENS OF SALLUST

EVEN BEFORE the identification of the round building in Panvinio's sketch with the Temple of Venus Erycina *ad Portam Collinam* could be considered certain,[1] three monuments were regarded by some scholars as belonging to the sculptural decoration of that shrine. They are the colossal head of a goddess (Fig. 166), the so-called Ludovisi Throne (Figs. 168a-c), both in the Terme Museum in Rome, and the counterpart of the Ludovisi relief, the Boston Throne (Figs. 169a-c).

The exact place of discovery of the female head is unknown. It belonged to the Ludovisi collection and may have come from the general area of the Sallustian Gardens, but this cannot be ascertained.[2] The head is a Greek original which dates from the first quarter of the fifth century and was part of an acrolithic statue. The features of the head suggest that it belonged to a cult statue of Aphrodite. A smile plays around her lips—φιλομειδής—and numerous perforations indicate that she was adorned either with bronze curls or a diadem as well as earrings and necklaces. The jewelry with which Venus Erycina appears on the coin of Considius is reminiscent of these adornments (Fig. 129).[3] Originally the head seems to have been covered by a tin-plated veil and her mantle thus seems

[1] See Chapter IV, pp. 180-183.

[2] See the discussions by E. Paribeni, *Sculture greche del quinto secolo. Museo Nazionale Romano* (Roma 1953) 11 no. 1; T. Schreiber, *Die antiken Bildwerke der Villa Ludovisi in Rom* (Leipzig 1880) 59-60 no. 23; Helbig, *Führer* 2³ (Leipzig 1913) 83-84 no. 1288.

[3] Cf. Schilling, *Vénus* 259.

243

to have been arranged like the one of the mourning Venus on the Boston Throne (Fig. 169a).

Of all scholars, Petersen went furthest in claiming that this head belonged to the cult statue of an Aphrodite seated on the Ludovisi Throne at Eryx in Sicily and that both throne and statue were transferred to Rome in 181 B.C.[4] The view that statue and throne were so closely linked has rightly found little acceptance, although the opinion that a Greek work of art—either the throne or the statue, or both—were brought from Eryx to Rome, has been repeated since.[5] In spite of the Hellenization of Segesta, however, the cult at Eryx was thoroughly dominated by the Phoenicians, especially after their disastrous defeat in 480 B.C.—the very period of the creation of both throne and statue—and their subsequent retreat to northwest Sicily. The goddess worshiped at Eryx was the Ashtoreth Erech; and Diodorus, for good reasons, omits mention of the Greeks in his enumeration of the peoples who worshiped the Eryx goddess at Eryx (4.83.4). This contrasts, for instance, with his mention of Greek temples and cults at Motya (14.53.2), a description which has been confirmed by the archaeological finds from the sixth century in that Punic city. As in the case of Segesta,[6] Greek form is likely to have been restricted to the outer shell of the shrine, and it is very improbable that the Elymian/Punic "cella" in the fifth century contained major works of Greek sculpture.

The head has often been associated with Sicilian art, but these parallels ultimately lead back to the school of Kritios

[4] E. Petersen, *MDAI(R)* 7 (1892) 32-80. If the three-sided relief was indeed used as a throne, which is doubtful, the colossal goddess was too large for it; her arms, for instance, would have protruded considerably beyond the armrests.

[5] E.g., by J. Colin, "Les trônes Ludovisi-Boston et les temples d'Aphrodite Erycine," *RA* 6th ser. 25 (1946) 23-42, and Simon, *Geburt der Aphrodite* 97-98.

[6] See Chapter II, pp. 73-74. The brief reference to the Eryx temple in Thucydides 6.46 is too inconclusive to prove that the sanctuary was thoroughly Hellenized.

and Nesiotes.[7] A technical device, which is found nowhere else in Greek sculpture, was used only for the head of this statue and the head of a kouros from Agrigento.[8] By means of a few incisions, which are more marked than the others, the sculptors divided the tops of both heads into a few preliminary segments. This method enabled them to draw the numerous incisions, which marked the hairs, with greater regularity. The Agrigento kouros most probably was a product of the Selinuntine school, which in turn closely adhered to the tradition of Kritios and Nesiotes. The provenience of the colossal archaic head therefore may well have been Attica. The statue would have been eminently suitable for the temple of Venus, but it is uncertain whether it stood there in fact.

The Ludovisi and Boston Thrones, however, were found in close proximity to the Venus temple. They evidently were used in a sacred building, and their connection with the Erycina temple cannot be dismissed lightly.[9] The two sculptures are unique in that they are obviously interrelated, architecturally as well as iconographically. The most widely accepted definition of the purpose of the two three-sided reliefs is that they were ornaments set on the narrow ends of a rectangular altar. Close architectural analogies are lacking, and the same holds true for the representations found on the re-

[7] Details in Helbig, *Führer* 2³.84.

[8] This was pointed out by W. Amelung, *JDAI* 35 (1920) 56-57 with fig. IV, showing a top view of both heads.

[9] Cf. Chapter IV, p. 185, and Nash, *MDAI(R)* 66 (1959) 136-137 with a map on p. 111 marking the places of discovery of the two sculptures. The literature on the Boston and Ludovisi reliefs is immense, and the reader may be referred to the bibliography (from 1909-1962) listed by L. Alscher, *Götter vor Gericht* (Berlin 1963) 127-129. Since then, the most important publications have been those by Jucker and Ashmole (see note 11); H. Möbius, *AA* (1964) 294-299; and F. L. Bastet, *BVAB* 38 (1963) 1-27. Summaries of the controversy about the iconographic and tectonic aspects of the two monuments are given by H. Möbius in K. Schauenburg ed., *Charites. Studien zur Altertumswissenschaft* (Bonn 1957) 47-58, and Alscher 7-24. Still basic because of its wealth of iconographic and architectural documentation is the first monumental discussion by F. Studniczka, *JDAI* 26 (1911) 50-192.

2 4 5

liefs. Like no other monument, therefore, the Boston Throne especially has been the center of controversy, at times violent. The Ludovisi Throne is generally recognized to be a genuine work of Greek art, dating from ca. 470 B.C. or shortly thereafter.[10] The authenticity of the Boston relief, which has been debated with rare subjectivity, can be considered certain after a detailed study of its "root-marks" was made in 1964 and 1965 by two scholars independently of each other.[11] No forger has been able to imitate, with anything remotely approaching success, these "root-marks," which are a sure indication of the monument's antiquity. It is impossible that the Boston Throne was manufactured in 1892, when the great importance of the Ludovisi Throne was recognized, then buried in the ground, covered with a grown patina, and shortly thereafter "discovered" in 1894.

The Boston Throne therefore is either contemporaneous with the Ludovisi Throne or was made at a later time to complement it. If both triptychs had been created simultaneously to be used on the same monument, their different dimensions would be hard to explain. As a result the Boston Throne either was newly created at a later time or is the copy of a lost original. The fact that the Ludovisi Throne was deliberately

[10] The relief is dated to 470 B.C., e.g., by G. M. A. Richter, *A Handbook of Greek Art*² (London 1960) 92; Studniczka 190; and C. Picard, *Manuel d'archéologie. La sculpture* 2 (Paris 1939) 141. It is considered a product of the late severe style of ca. 460 B.C., e.g., by Alscher 24; G. W. Elderkin, *Art in America* 5 (1916-1917) 284; Paribeni (note 2, above) 113. C. Vermeule, *Greek, Roman, and Etruscan Art* (Boston 1963) wisely dates it to the decade 470-460 B.C.

[11] See the brief summary by B. Ashmole, *Bull. Mus. of Fine Arts Boston* 63 (1965) 59, who promises a more detailed paper on the subject, and H. Jucker, *MH* 22 (1965) 117-124; cf. *MH* 24 (1967) 116-119, and 194. Earlier, D. Mustilli, who contributed the article on forgeries to the *Enciclopedia dell'arte antica* 3 (Rome 1960) 568, already came to this conclusion: "Argomenti sostanziali contro l'autenticità del monumento non si sono acquisiti; la tecnica e l'iconografia, che s'inquadra perfettamente nel repertorio figurativo greco e che trova forse pure risonanza in quella persistenza di motivi classici che si avverte nell' arte del medioevo, rendono molto esitanti a pronunziarsi in senso negativo."

mutilated to be adjusted "to a novel situation"—the creation
of the Boston Throne—[12] supports the view that no original
existed for the latter and that both sculptures were related
to each other only at a later time, i.e. when the Boston Throne
was made. For this event primarily two periods and locales
have been suggested: Magna Graecia in the fifth century and
Rome in the early Empire, especially the time of Tiberius.
Those who believe that the Boston Throne was the work of a
provincial sculptor in southern Italy stress the severity of its
style, which seems unparalleled in classicistic Roman art,[13]
and the sculptural similarity to some Locrian *pinakes*.[14] The
Locrian terracotta reliefs, however, and larger sculpture such
as the Boston Throne are different media which require different principles of execution, and the Locrian terracottas therefore do not furnish a valid formal parallel to the sculptures of
the Boston Throne.[15]

Those who favor a Roman date stress the eclecticism of the
relief, which in spite of its "severity" also shows indications
of later periods of style.[16] In this we may see again a confirmation of the assumption that the Boston Throne was a genuinely
new creation. In creating it, however, the artist could not work
as independently as, e.g., the sculptor of the Venus relief of
the Ara Pacis, which has often been used as a point of reference. For he was asked to provide a pendant to an already
existing work of art, and to strive for an optimum of formal

[12] This view is held, e.g., by R. Carpenter, *MAAR* 18 (1941) 47, who,
however, assumes that this was done still in the fifth century; W. Hahland,
JOAI 40 (1953) 31-37; F. Krauss, *JDAI* 63-64 (1950) 40-69. *Contra*, A.
van Gerkan, most recently in *MDAI(R)* 67 (1960) 156. It is strange that
van Gerkan, who for decades had disputed, on the basis of measurements
taken from a copy, the authenticity of the Boston Throne, never saw fit to
come to Boston to see the original.

[13] See Möbius (note 9, above) 57.

[14] See especially B. Ashmole, *JHS* 42 (1922) 248-253.

[15] See F. Baroni, *Osservazioni sul "Trono di Boston"* (Rome 1961)
37-38.

[16] See especially Bastet (note 9, above) 4-27; cf. Alscher (note 9, above)
79-80, who, however, considers the relief a fake.

resemblance, although there was no original that he could imitate. This unique dilemma, if one wishes to call it by that term, accounts best for the stylistic inconsistency and singularity of the Boston Throne, which one scholar has called "styleless."[17] The sculptor was not entirely able to reproduce the style of the Ludovisi relief, because the Boston relief was, after all, a new creation fusing a variety of precedents into a new unity. For these reasons, the Boston Throne is different from other neo-Attic Roman reliefs, e.g. the Nemi relief in Copenhagen, which was based on a Greek model.[18] To use this "deviation" from other Roman sculpture of the early Empire as proof that the Boston relief could not belong to that period is to miss the point entirely. Besides, the tendency to scrutinize mercilessly a work of sculpture from the standpoint of schematic and mostly presumed "laws"[19] is particularly inappropriate for the art of the Augustan age, which draws on a multiplicity of inspirations. In sum, considerations of style and form are not inconsistent with dating the Boston relief to the Roman period.

The only other objection to this date is more, and at the same time, less specific. It is a reply to the suggestion, which we will discuss shortly, that the Boston Throne was the work of the Pasitelean school. Miss Baroni considers this attribution impossible because "the relief, rather disorganized, results, as we have seen, from a total of motifs that are not harmoniously combined with each other. Pasiteles . . . cannot have executed such a disorganized work, which is devoid of style and personality."[20]

This is the same type of argument as the one that has been used in connection with the Venus relief of the Ara Pacis,

---

[17] F. P. Johnson, *AJA* 60 (1956) 61.

[18] For the Nemi relief, see, most recently, Möbius (note 9, above) 57, and Alscher 80 with fig. 55.

[19] As is done by Alscher 78-83 and 25-30 ("Reliefgesetze") with unhappy results; cf. the comments by Jucker, *MH* 22 (1965) 123-124.

[20] Baroni (note 15, above) 40.

and it has just as little validity.[21] More importantly, however, it raises the question whether there are any positive clues that the relief is Roman.

The Boston Throne is not based on the Roman foot, as Colin assumed, but on an older, Attic-Euboeic one.[22] Some scholars have seen in the centrality of the composition a typically Roman trait for which the Ara Pacis relief again furnishes the best parallel, whereas others, especially G. W. Elderkin, have stated that the composition of the central relief is "conspicuously Hellenic,"[23] and adduced various iconographic analogies from which the Ludovisi Throne was inexplicably omitted. Miss Baroni, as we have just seen, considers the composition to be so disorganized that it cannot have been the work even of a neo-Attic sculptor; another scholar regards the composition as being far less "additive" and more thoroughly integrated than the Ara Pacis relief, and thus concludes the work could have been made only by a Greek or a clever forger.[24] Again we are treading here on the slippery ground of subjective analysis of style, and such criteria cannot be used as proof for or against the "Romanity" of the relief.

Strict proof that the Boston relief was made in Rome is not possible, but the suggestion that a member of the Pasitelean school, perhaps Menelaos, who lived in the last decades of the first century B.C., was the artist of the Boston relief deserves at least some consideration.[25] Pasiteles, whose floruit was between 70 and 50 B.C., worked as a *toreutes* as well as a sculptor. Apparently he did leave his mark on the Arretine workshops. On an Arretine vase of the first century we find a rep-

[21] See Chapter V, pp. 231-232.

[22] See Möbius (note 9, above) 50, against Colin (note 5, above) 27 and 155-157.

[23] (Note 10, above) 280.

[24] Alscher (note 9, above) 79-80.

[25] See C. C. van Essen, *MNIR* 2nd ser. 7 (1937) 29-41; Colin (note 5, above) 151-153; A. N. Zadoks-Jitta, *RA* 6th ser. 36 (1950) 153-154; cf. E. A. Gardner, *JHS* 33 (1913) 81.

resentation of the birth of Dionysus.[26] A woman, partly covered by a kind of curtain, is in the center of the composition. Silenus holds the child on the left, and a female attendant is on the right. It is impossible not to think of the central panel of the Ludovisi Throne as the inspiration for this vase. If Pasiteles—or one of his disciples—was given the task of creating a pendant to the Ludovisi Throne, he may well have re-adapted the subject of the latter for the representation on the Arretine vase. This would of course be additional confirmation of the prevailing interpretation that the central panel of the Ludovisi relief represents the birth of Aphrodite.

This brings us to the interpretation of the reliefs, which, especially in the case of the Boston Throne, is admittedly hazardous, and this difficulty sometimes seems to be the ultimate reason for its being considered a fake. Some twenty-five years ago, Carpenter aptly remarked that "as in the Homeric question, where almost every possible view has had its champion, it is more important to choose and combine correctly amid the old than to advance new hypotheses,"[27] and the situation has not changed since. Instead of reviewing the various interpretations that have been proposed, it is more suitable within the scope of this study to investigate whether the interpretation of the relief and the creation of the Boston Throne can be reconciled with and even explained by its location in the Temple of Venus Erycina *extra Portam Collinam*.

If the Ludovisi relief stood there, its central panel most certainly represents the birth of Aphrodite. Iconographic parallels show that the goddess in fact was represented as dressed at her birth from the sea.[28] More importantly, the tripartite composition reflects the same principles as those on which the Venus relief on the Ara Pacis is based. The figures on the side panels represent different aspects of Aphrodite. On the left sits a nude,

[26] U. Viviani, *I vasi arretini* (Arezzo 1922) fig. 1, and van Essen, pl. 7.
[27] Carpenter (note 12, above) 61.
[28] Details in Simon, *Geburt der Aphrodite* 36-51 with figs. 22-30.

flute-playing hetaira (Fig. 168b), with her legs casually crossed. She is complemented on the right by a matron who offers her sacrifice of incense (Fig. 168c). The *thymiaterion* on which she burns the incense is also found in the hands of the winged goddess who carries Venus in a mural in the Macellum of Pompeii.[29] The two female figures represent the two kinds of women who worshiped Venus especially in Rome:[30]

> rite deam Latiae colitis matresque nurusque
> et vos, quis vittae longaque vestis abest.

The more traditional aspect of the Erycina prevailed in her temple on the Capitoline, whereas her more exotic features were given greater freedom in the cult at the Porta Collina, and "this reconciliation of opposing tendencies doubtless explains the extraordinary prestige of the goddess."[31] The more popular temple of Venus Erycina outside the *pomerium* therefore would be an eminently fitting place for the Ludovisi relief.

The iconography of the Boston Throne has been considered more problematic. Its central panel evidently uses iconographic elements of a *psychostasia*, the weighing of souls, and a precedent for Eros holding the scale is lacking. But as we have seen repeatedly, iconographic uniqueness is not an isolated phenomenon in Augustan art. The closest parallel, heretofore overlooked, to this representation is a mirror from Corinth, dated to the middle of the fourth century (Fig. 170).[32] Eros,

[29] Published by P. Herrmann, *Denkmäler der Malerei des Altertums, Text* 2 (Munich 1939) 35 with fig. 9.

[30] Ovid, *Fasti* 4.133-134, quoted, for instance, by Schilling, *Vénus* 258-259, and Simon 100.

[31] Schilling 266.

[32] Brussels, Musées Royaux d'Art et d'Histoire, Section de l'Antiquité, R 1266b; cf. Jucker, *MH* 22 (1965) 124. This disproves the rather authoritative claim of P. Cellini, *Paragone* 65 (May 1955) 46, that the Eros was "specularmente copiato" from a fourth century column base of the Artemis temple at Ephesus; see C. Robert, *Winckelmannsprogramm* 39 (1879) pl. 3. The mirror is described by K. D. Mylonas, *MDAI(A)* 3 (1878) 265-266, and Züchner, *Klappspiegel* 17-18 with fig. 5 (KS 20).

smiling like the Eros on the Boston Throne, hovers between Hermes and a woman with a mirror, perhaps Aphrodite. In his hands this winged Eros holds a fillet, and his function is to favor Hermes' advances, to give him what he desires. This is quite consistent with the very simple and persuasive interpretation Miss Richter long ago proposed for the central scene of the Boston relief.[33] Accepting as we do the premise that the Boston and Ludovisi Thrones belong to an altar or monument sacred to Aphrodite, she argued that the Boston relief could be expected to complement the important subject of Aphrodite's birth with subjects in equally direct and vital relation to the cult of the goddess. Aphrodite of course is the goddess of love, who either bestows all the gifts pertaining to happy love and marriage, or withholds them. Miss Richter's further remarks on the subject deserve to be quoted in full:[34]

> It is in this character of bestower or withholder of her bounties that the goddess, to my mind, appears on the Boston relief. To one woman, she gives her heart's desire— be it husband, or lover, or child; to the other, she denies it. Where she grants, there is rejoicing, where she refuses, there is sorrow. The symbol of the balance was a natural one to the Greek mind as we see not only in the scenes of the Psychostasia, but in the well-known representation—more closely allied in subject—of the weighing of small Erotes on an Apulian vase in the British Museum (Fig. 171).[35] Aphrodite herself does not do the actual weighing in our relief, but her representative, Eros—just as Hermes takes the place of Zeus in the scenes of the Psychostasia. Eros in this character of the executor of Aphrodite's will is of course familiar.

We may add that the close association between Hermes and

---

[33] G. M. A. Richter, *JHS* 40 (1920) 113-121.
[34] *Ibid.* 118.
[35] See H. B. Walters, *Catalogue of Greek, Roman and Etruscan Vases in the British Museum* 4 (London 1898) 109-110 (F 220).

Eros on several Greek mirrors,[36] like the one described above, may have suggested to the sculptor to equip Eros with the attribute of Hermes, the scales. Another, and perhaps better explanation is that just as the Venus on the armor of the Prima Porta Augustus was given the symbol of Amor, the torch,[37] so the attribute of Venus here is given to Amor. The woman with the scales on the Campanian vase is Venus, and she appears in the same function on a gold ring of the second half of the fifth century (Fig. 172).[38] Given the close association between Eros and Aphrodite, their symbols must have seemed interchangeable; both Aphrodite and Eros are represented, for instance, as riding on a goose.[39]

Miss Richter rightly observes that Eros is only Aphrodite's executor; it is the power of Aphrodite that is the real theme.[40] Aphrodite again is shown under a twofold aspect: as rejoicing and as mourning, as giving and withholding. Whereas two aspects of the goddess were symbolized on the side panels of the Ludovisi relief, her double representation now is combined on one panel. The closest analogue again is the Venus relief on the Ara Pacis. A Roman date for the Boston Throne therefore is not inconsistent with sculptural design and thinking in Augustan times.

The central panel of the Boston relief, therefore, conceptually corresponds to all three parts of the Ludovisi relief. The side figures of the former were chosen not so much for the purpose of integrally complementing the central panel as for being pendants to the side figures of the Ludovisi relief.[41] The nude lyre-player is the intentional counterpart of the nude

---

[36] Züchner, *Klappspiegel* 17-19 (KS 20 and 21).

[37] See Chapter V, p. 204 and Fig. 138.

[38] Boston Museum of Fine Arts 23.594; described by Vermeule (note 10, above) 124.

[39] For Aphrodite, see Chapter V, p. 207 with fig. 148, and for Eros, Züchner, *Klappspiegel* 28-29 with fig. 11 (KS 28), dated to the beginning of the third century B.C.

[40] (Note 33, above) 118.

[41] Cf. Carpenter (note 12, above) 51.

flute-playing hetaira, and the draped old woman corresponds to the draped, matronly incense-burner. Both side figures of the Boston Throne represent votaries of Aphrodite[42] and therefore are appropriate for a monument celebrating her power.

This interpretation of the Boston relief as representing Venus fulfilling and denying the wishes of her worshipers, with Amor as an intermediary, agrees well with Ovid's description of the cult practices at the Erycina temple near the Porta Collina. According to Ovid this was the favorite shrine for those who wanted to be delivered from an unfeeling heart (*R.A.* 549-554):

> est prope Collinam templum venerabile portam,
>   inposuit templo nomina celsus Eryx.
> est illic Lethaeus Amor, qui pectora sanat
>   inque suas gelidam lampadas addit aquam;
> illic et iuvenes votis oblivia poscunt
>   et si qua est duro capta puella viro.

In the speech that follows, Amor further elaborates on the various requests made to him. These requests may be granted or not, and therefore can be reason for joy as well as sorrow.

Attempts have not been lacking to relate the central relief of the Boston Throne to the Trojan tradition of Rome. Jean Colin has interpreted it as a *conclamatio* scene with Venus on the left and Juno on the right, and Aeneas and Turnus in the scale-pans.[43] But whenever warriors are weighed they appear in cuirass and helmet. The two youths here, however, are nude, and there is a playful air about them. They cannot be Aeneas and Turnus. The second objection has been that the youth in the left and sinking scale-pan is "doomed," if there is a *psychostasia*, and Venus on the left evidently is rejoicing.

She is rejoicing over the rising scale-pan on the right. This is the more important of the two scale-pans on which the atten-

---

[42] Details in Richter (note 33, above) 119-120.
[43] (Note 5, above) 159-171.

tion of both the rejoicing Venus and her counterpart is focused. It has been suggested that the figures in the scale-pans are either a double representation of Adonis[44] or represent the Dioscuri. The markedly different representation of the two youths is perhaps the strongest argument against the first suggestion, although both myths, if interpreted astronomically, have virtually the same result. B. Ashmole has pointed out that[45]

> when we remember that the Dioscuri were, according to some legends, translated to heaven as morning and evening star, it surely follows that this part of the scene directly corresponds to the scenes of simple astronomical symbolism in the Parthenon pediment, on the basis of the Parthenos and elsewhere, and shows one of the Dioscuri, who, at the hour of his setting, leaves the horse on which he has ridden the sky to plunge into the sea. Similarly, the boys in the scale of the Boston relief, recalling in form the stars of the Blacas vase, may be morning and evening star. . . .

When we remember that the morning star also was the *Veneris astrum*,[46] it is easy to explain why its rise is the focus of the attention of the two Venus figures on the Boston relief. Its rise gives reason for joy but inherent in it is also the realization that it will go down again, hence the pensive and mournful mien of the Venus figure on the right. This conception is reminiscent of the Etruscan amphora (Fig. 99) which shows Achilles at the moment of his triumph over Aeneas, but already hints at his death at the hands of Paris/Apollo. A fitting description of a mournful Venus is found in Macrobius' astronomical interpretation of the Adonis myth in which Adonis is equated with the sun:[47]

---

[44] So F. Eisler, *Münchner Jahrb. der Bild. Kunst* 7 (1912) 78-80.

[45] *JHS* 42 (1922) 250.

[46] See Chapter V, p. 232.

[47] *Sat.* 1.21.3-6: *et cum est in inferioribus et ideo dies breviores facit, lugere creditur dea, tamquam sole raptu mortis temporalis amisso . . .*

And when he is in the underworld and therefore makes the days shorter, the goddess is believed to mourn, as if the sun had been lost by the seizure of a temporary death. . . . An image of this goddess is shown on Mount Lebanon. Her head is veiled and her mien is sad. With her left hand, which is cloaked by her dress, she supports her face, and those who see her believe that tears well from her eyes. . . . But when the sun appears again . . . and passes over the boundary of the equinox of the spring and makes the day longer then Venus is joyful and beautiful: the fields grow verdant with their crops, and the meadows, with grass, and the trees, with leaves.

The interpretation of the figures as Dioscuri would of course give us a connection with Rome's Trojan legend. Perhaps the representation of the two youths was chosen to be a pendant, however small, to the two Moirae on the center panel on the Ludovisi relief. The Moirae, or Fata, helpers in birth, also can be connected with the Trojan heritage of Rome.[48] But the representation of the two youths shows above all, in what carefree, relaxed, and gay a manner the proceedings of the central panel are depicted. The little figures were not portrayed with ponderous solemnity as one might expect of such a subject, but they seem to use the weighing for gymnastic exercises of their own (Figs. 173 a and b). Statuettes of athletes,[49] of

---

simulacrum huius deae in monte Libano fingitur capite obnupto specie tristi faciem manu laeva intra amictum sustinens, lacrimae visione conspicientium manare creduntur . . . sed cum sol emersit . . . vernalisque aequinoctii transgreditur fines augendo diem, tunc est Venus laeta et pulchra: virent arva segetibus, prata herbis, arbores foliis. Cf. Eisler 78, who believes that the Ludovisi and Boston Thrones came from Eryx and argues that the latter had an oriental Punic prototype. This is unlikely, although the origins of this astronomical myth are oriental. If the myth were alluded to in the Roman relief, we would have another example of the transformation of a Punic theme *ad maiorem Romae gloriam*; cf. Chapter V, p. 223.

[48] See Chapter IV, pp. 159-160 and note 57.

[49] So Johnson (note 17, above) 61, with reference to G. Hafner, *AA* (1952) 74-86 with figs. 1-4 (in a private collection in Oberlenningen).

Marsyas, and the satyrs on the throne of the priest of Dionysus[50] have been shown to be their models. Even more evident, of course, is the gaiety of Amor and the rejoicing Venus —*Erycina ridens*—which are deliberate, although they have upset many critics. The mournful Venus on the right literally does not fully restore the balance, for the right scale-pan is rising at the moment, and cheerfulness is on the upswing. Her mien, however, is a reminder that this will not always be so. There still is nothing tragic about her; rather, her pensiveness contributes to the serenity of the composition, which Studniczka so aptly described in his monumental study of the relief.[51] The relief reflects that "relaxed tension," which an eminent interpreter of Augustan poetry has called characteristic of the classical literature at Augustus' time[52] and, we might add, of classical, Augustan art. It is this tension between the gay and the sober which characterized the Erycina cult in Rome and which, to our mind, makes her temple appear as the most fitting location for this relief.

[50] For details see Gardner (note 25, above) 81; Colin (note 5, above) 150; Bastet (note 9, above) 16 with figs. 15-18.

[51] (Note 9, above) 125-128.

[52] V. Pöschl, *Die Hirtendichtung Virgils* (Heidelberg 1964) 79-83, using Wölfflin's terminology.

SELECTED BIBLIOGRAPHY

Alföldi, A., *Early Rome and the Latins* (Ann Arbor 1965)

————, *Die trojanischen Urahnen der Römer* (Program Basel 1957)

Babelon, E., *Description historique et chronologique des monnaies de la république romaine* 1-2 (Paris 1885-1886)

Beazley, J. D., *Attic Black-Figure Vase-Painters* (Oxford 1956)

————, *Attic Red-Figure Vase-Painters*, 2nd ed. (Oxford 1963)

————, *Etruscan Vase-Painting* (Oxford 1947)

Benndorf, O., *Griechische und sicilische Vasenbilder* (Berlin 1896)

Bérard, J., *La colonisation grecque de l'Italie méridionale et de la Sicile dans l'antiquité*, 2nd ed. (Paris 1957)

Bernabò Brea, L., "Leggende e archeologia nella protostoria della Sicilia," *Atti del Primo Congresso Internazionale di studi sulla Sicilia antica. Kokalos* 10-11 (1964-1965) 1-33

————, *Sicily before the Greeks*, 2nd ed. (New York 1966)

Bickerman, E., Review of Perret, *Origines, CW* 37 (1943-1944) 91-95

Bieber, M., "Die Venus des Arkesilaos," *MDAI(R)* 48 (1933) 261-276

Bloch, R., *The Origins of Rome* (New York 1960)

Boas, H., *Aeneas' Arrival in Latium. Archaeologisch-historische Bijdragen* 6, *Allard Pierson Stichting* (Amsterdam 1938)

Bömer, F., *Rom und Troia. Untersuchungen zur Frühgeschichte Roms* (Baden-Baden 1951)

Booth, A., "Venus on the Ara Pacis," *Latomus* 25 (1966) 873-879

Bovio Marconi, I., "El problema de los Elimos en la luz de

los descubrimientos recientes," *Ampurias* 12 (1950) 79-90

Boyancé, P., "Les origines de la légende troyenne de Rome," *REA* 45 (1943) 275-290

Brommer, F., *Vasenlisten zur griechischen Heldensage*, 2nd ed. (Marburg 1960)

Brunn, H., and F. Bruckmann, *Denkmäler griechischer und römischer Sculptur* (Berlin 1888-1890)

Buchheit, V., *Vergil über die Sendung Roms. Untersuchungen zum Bellum Poenicum und zur Aeneis. Gymnasium Beihefte* 3 (Heidelberg 1963)

Caskey, L. D., and J. D. Beazley, *Attic Vase Paintings in the Museum of Fine Arts, Boston* 2-3 (Boston 1954-1963)

Castagnoli, F., "I luoghi connessi con l'arrivo di Enea nel Lazio," *ArchClass* 19 (1967) 235-247

———, "Sulla tipologia degli altari di Lavinio," *BCAR* 77 (1959-1960 [1962]) 145-172

Ciaceri, E., "Come e quando la tradizione troiana sia entrata in Roma," *Studi Storici* 4 (1895) 503-529

———, *Culti e miti nella storia della Sicilia antica* (Catania 1911)

Compernolle, R. van, "Ségeste et l'héllénisme," *Phoibos* 5 (1950-1951) 183-228

Dunbabin, T. J., *The Western Greeks* (Oxford 1948)

Förstemann, A., *Zur Geschichte des Aeneasmythus* (Magdeburg 1894)

Fondation Hardt, *Entretiens* 8. *Grecs et barbares* (Vandoeuvres-Geneva 1961)

———, *Entretiens* 13. *Les origines de la république romaine* (Vandoeuvres-Geneva 1967)

Freeman, E. A., *The History of Sicily* 1 (Oxford 1891)

Furtwängler, A., *Die antiken Gemmen* (Leipzig 1900)

Furumark, A., *The Mycenaean Pottery. Analysis and Classification* (Stockholm 1941)

Gerhard, E., *Etruskische Spiegel* (Berlin 1843-1897)

Ghali-Kahil, L., *Les enlèvements et le retour d'Hélène* (Paris 1955)

Giglioli, G. Q., "Osservazioni e monumenti relativi alla leggenda delle origini di Roma," *BMIR* 12 (1941) 3-16

Grueber, H. A., *Coins of the Roman Republic in the British Museum* (London 1910)

Hampe, R., and E. Simon, *Griechische Sagen in der frühen etruskischen Kunst* (Mainz 1964)

Hanell, K., "Das Opfer des Augustus an der Ara Pacis," *Opuscula Romana* 2 (1960) 33-123

Head, B. V., *Historia Numorum*, 2nd ed. (Oxford 1911)

Helbig, W., *Führer durch die öffentlichen Sammlungen klassischer Altertümer in Rom* 2, 3rd ed. (Leipzig 1913), and 4th ed. (Tübingen 1966)

————, *Die Wandgemälde der vom Vesuv verschütteten Städte Campaniens* (Leipzig 1868)

Herrmann, P., *Denkmäler der Malerei des Altertums* 1-2 (Munich 1904-1931)

Hoffmann, W., *Rom und die griechische Welt im vierten Jahrhundert. Philol. Suppl.* 27.1 (1934)

Holm, A., *Geschichte Siciliens im Alterthum* 1-3 (Leipzig 1870-1898)

Jacoby, F., *Die Fragmente der griechischen Historiker* (Leiden and Berlin 1923-1958)

Johansen, K. F., *The Iliad in Early Greek Art* (Copenhagen 1967)

Kähler, H., "Die Ara Pacis und die augusteische Friedensidee," *JDAI* 69 (1954) 67-100

————, "Die Front der Ara Pacis," *Beiträge zur klassischen Altertumswissenschaft. Festschrift für Bernhard Schweitzer* (Stuttgart 1954) 322-330

Kalkmann, A., "Aphrodite auf dem Schwan," *JDAI* 1 (1886) 231-260

Karageorghis, V., *Nouveaux documents pour l'étude du*

bronze récent à Chypre. Recueil critique et commenté. Ecole française d'Athènes. Etudes chypriotes 3 (Paris 1965)

Kienast, D., "Rom und die Venus vom Eryx," *Hermes* 93 (1965) 478-489

Koch, C., "Untersuchungen zur Geschichte der römischen Venusverehrung," *Religio. Erlanger Beiträge zur Sprach- und Kunstwissenschaft* (Nuremberg 1960) 39-93

————, "Venus," *RE* 8A (1955) 828-887

Latte, K., *Römische Religionsgeschichte* (Munich 1960)

Liegle, J., "Die Münzprägung Octavians nach dem Siege bei Aktium und die augusteische Kunst," *JDAI* 56 (1941) 91-119

————, "Pietas," *ZfN* 42 (1932-1935) 59-100

Malten, L., "Aineias," *ARW* 29 (1931) 33-59

Mattingly, H., *Coins of the Roman Empire in the British Museum* (London 1923-1950)

Momigliano, A. D., Review of Alföldi, *Urahnen, RSI* 70 (1958) 129-131

————, Review of Perret, *Origines, JRS* 35 (1945) 99-104

Moretti, G., *Ara Pacis Augustae* (Rome 1948)

Nash, E., "Über die Auffindung und den Erwerb des Bostoner Thrones," *MDAI(R)* 66 (1959) 102-139

Norden, E., "Vergils Aeneis im Lichte ihrer Zeit," *NJA* 7 (1901) 249-282, 313-334

Ogilvie, P. M., *A Commentary on Livy Books 1-5* (Oxford 1965)

Pace, B., *Arte e civiltà della Sicilia antica* 1, 2nd ed. (Città di Castello 1958); 2-4 (Città di Castello 1938-1949)

Pais, E., *Storia della Sicilia e della Magna Grecia* (Torino 1894)

Pallottino, M., "Il grande acroterio femminile di Veio," *Arch-Class* 2 (1950) 122-178

————, Review of Alföldi, *Urahnen*, SE 26 (1958) 336-339

Payne, H., *Necrocorinthia* (Oxford 1931)

Pease, A. S., *Publi Vergili Maronis Aeneidos Liber Quartus* (Cambridge, Mass. 1935)

Perret, J., *Les origines de la légende troyenne de Rome* (231-81) (Paris 1942)

Petersen, E., *Ara Pacis Augustae* (Vienna 1902)

Pfuhl, E., *Malerei und Zeichnung der Griechen* 1-3 (Munich 1923)

Phillips, E. D., "Odysseus in Italy," *JHS* 73 (1953) 53-67

Platner, S. B., and T. Ashby, *A Topographical Dictionary of Ancient Rome* (Oxford 1929)

Poole, S. R. (with B. V. Head and P. Gardner), *A Catalogue of the Greek Coins in the British Museum. Sicily.* Reprint (Bologna 1963)

Pugliese Carratelli, G., "Achei nell' Etruria e nel Lazio?" *PP* 17 (1962) 5-25

Rizzo, G. E., *Monete greche della Sicilia* (Rome 1946)

————, *La pittura ellenistico-romana* (Milan 1929)

Robert, C., *Die antiken Sarcophagreliefs* 1-3 (Berlin 1890-1939)

Roscher, W. H., *Ausführliches Lexicon der griechischen und römischen Mythologie* 1-6 (Leipzig 1884-1937)

Ryberg, I. S., *Rites of the State Religion in Roman Art. MAAR* 22 (1955)

Sadurska, A., *Les tables iliaques* (Warsaw 1964)

Schauenburg, K., "Aeneas und Rom," *Gymnasium* 67 (1960) 176-190

Schefold, K., *Myth and Legend in Early Greek Art* (London 1966)

————, *Die Wände Pompejis* (Berlin 1957)

Schilling, R., *La religion romaine de Vénus depuis les origines jusqu'au temps d'Auguste. Bibliothèque des Ecoles françaises d'Athènes et de Rome*, N. 178 (Paris 1954)

Schur, W., "Griechische Traditionen von der Gründung Roms," *Klio* 17 (1921) 137-152

Schwegler, A., *Römische Geschichte* 1, 2nd ed. (Tübingen 1884)

Scullard, H. H., *The Etruscan Cities and Rome* (Ithaca 1967)

Sieveking, J., "Das römische Relief," *Festschrift P. Arndt* (Munich 1925) 14-35

Simon, E., *Ara Pacis Augustae* (Tübingen 1967)

———, *Die Geburt der Aphrodite* (Berlin 1959)

———, "Zur Augustusstatue von Prima Porta," *MDAI(R)* 64 (1957) 48-64

Sjöqvist, E., "Heracles in Sicily," *Opuscula Romana* 4 (1962) 117-123

Spinazzola, V., *Pompei alla luce degli scavi nuovi di Via dell' Abbondanza* (Rome 1953)

Strong, E., "Terra Mater or Italia?" *JRS* 27 (1937) 114-126

Sydenham, E. A., *The Coinage of the Roman Republic* (London 1952)

Taylor, L. R., *The Divinity of the Roman Emperor* (Middletown 1931)

Taylour, W., *Mycenean Pottery in Italy and Adjacent Areas* (Cambridge 1958)

Tilly, B., *Vergil's Latium* (Oxford 1947)

Toynbee, J. M. C., "The Ara Pacis Reconsidered and Historical Art in Roman Italy," *PBA* 39 (1953) 67-95

Tusa, V., "La questione fenicio-punica in Sicilia," *Eretz-Israel* 8 (1967) 50-57

———, "Il santuario arcaico di Segesta," *Atti Settimo Congr. Intern. di Arch. Class.* 2 (Rome 1961) 31-40

Ussani, V., "Enea traditore," *SIFC* n.s. 22 (1947) 108-123

Van Buren, A. W., "The Ara Pacis Augustae," *JRS* 3 (1913) 134-141

Wagenvoort, H., "Ara Pacis Augustae," *MNIR* 1 (1921) 100-120

Weinstock, S., "Penates," *RE* 19 (1937) 417-457

———, "Two Archaic Inscriptions from Latium," *JRS* 50 (1960) 112-118

Wissowa, G., *Religion und Kultus der Römer. Müllers Hand-buch der klass. Altertumswissenschaft*, vol. 5, pt. 4, 2nd ed. (Munich 1912)

Züchner, W., *Griechische Klappspiegel. JDAI Ergänzungsheft* 14 (Berlin 1942)

INDEX

Only the most significant references are included for subjects to which very frequent reference is made, for example, *Aeneas, Rome, Trojans.*

PLATES

1. Sestertius of Antoninus Pius

2. Denarius of Caesar

a. Aeneas, Anchises,
and the Palladium

b. Venus

3. Denarius of Trajan

4. *Pietas Augusti*. Sestertius of Galba

5. Roman lamp with the Trojan group

6. Statuary group from Pompeii

7. Altar of the Gens Augusta from Carthage

8. Aeneas sacrificing. Ara Pacis Augustae

9. Athena, Diomedes, Aeneas, and Aphrodite. Attic cup

10. Diomedes and Athena.
Corinthian tablet

11. Diomedes fighting Aeneas.
Fragments of Attic column-krater

12. Corinthian cup with Homeric scenes

13. Homeric battle. Siphnian Treasury, Delphi. Detail of the east frieze

14. Achilles, Troilus, and Aeneas. Cup by Oltos

15. The death of Troilus. At far right, Aeneas.
Corinthian column-krater

16. Aeneas sacrifices to Mars. Cività Castellana, Cathedral

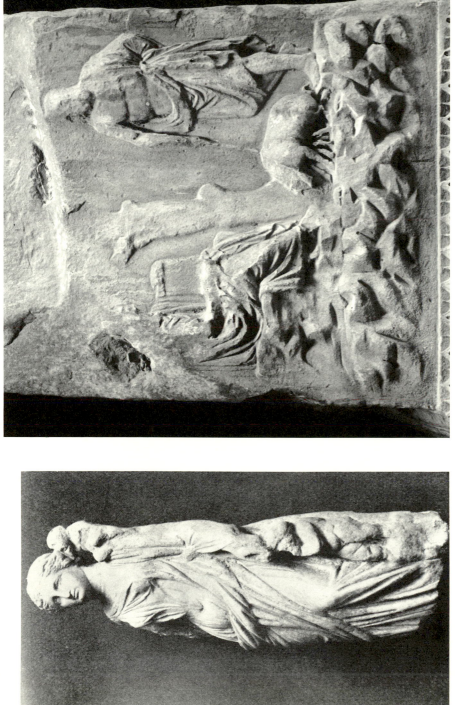

18. Aeneas receives a prophecy. Belvedere Altar, Vatican

17. Venus attributed to Arkesilaos

19. The theft of Aeneas' cattle. Relief pithos

20. Aeneas' sacrifice in Italy. Sarcophagus fragment

21. Aeneas' sacrifice in Italy. Renaissance relief

22. Poseidon, Aeneas, and Achilles. Pompeian mural

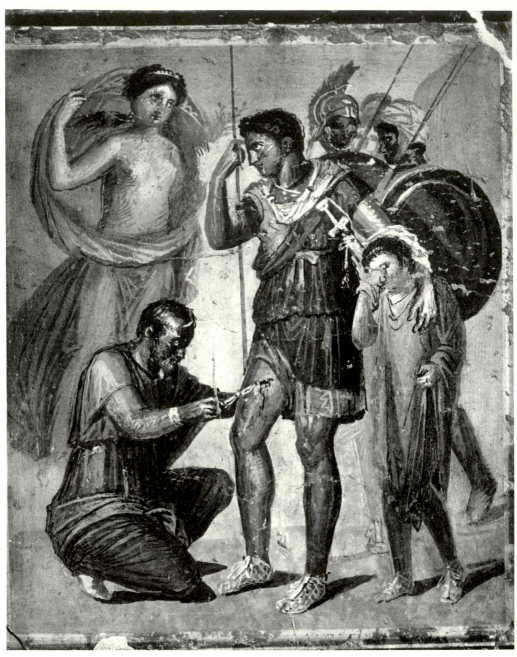

23. The wounded Aeneas. Pompeian mural

24. Aeneas and Polyphemus. Drawing after
a Pompeian mural

25. Aeneas and Dido. Fragment of a Pompeian mural

26. Aeneas and Dido. Pompeian mural

27. The Trojan group. Pompeian mural

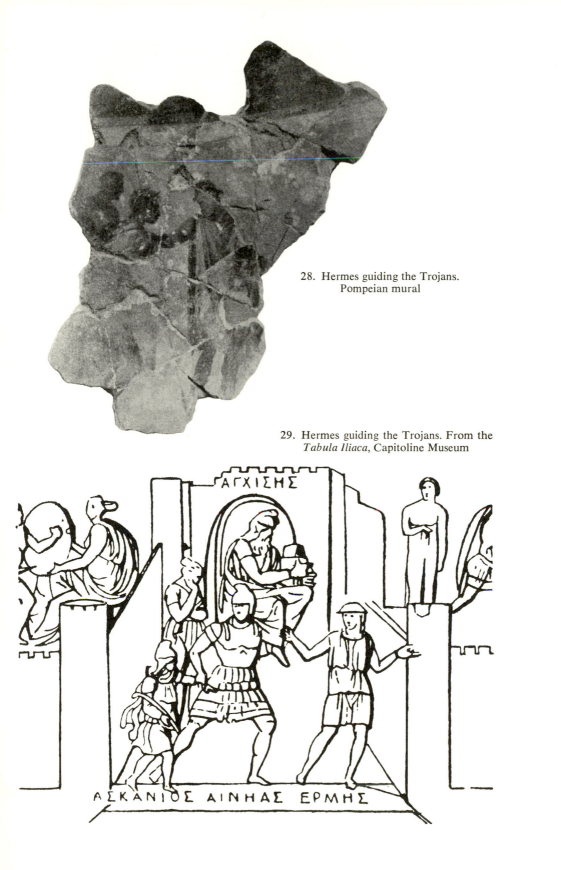

28. Hermes guiding the Trojans.
Pompeian mural

29. Hermes guiding the Trojans. From the
Tabula Iliaca, Capitoline Museum

ΑΓΧΙΣΗΣ

ΑΣΚΑΝΙΟΣ ΑΙΝΗΑΣ ΕΡΜΗΣ

30. Parody of the Trojan group. Pompeian mural

31. Poseidon defends Aeneas against Achilles.
From a *Tabula Iliaca* in New York

32. Homeric battle scene
From the *Tabula Iliaca*, Capitoline Museu

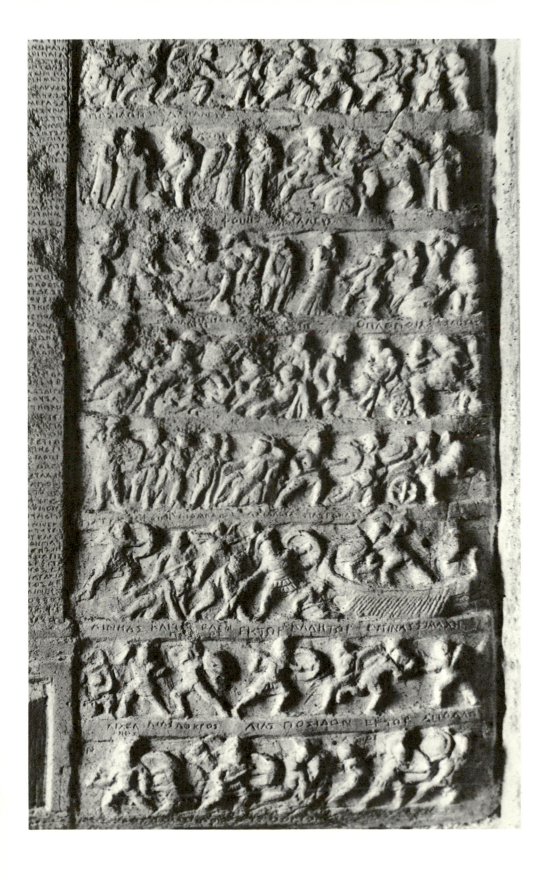

33. Aphrodite rescues Aeneas from Diomedes. From a *Tabula Iliaca* in Paris

34. Aeneas triumphant. Praenestine cista, 2nd cent. B.C.

36a. Aeneas as Paris' accomplice. Pontic oinochoe

35. Odysseus' homecoming.
Roman coin

36b. Detail of 36a

37. Aeneas guides Paris and Helen from Sparta. Attic skyphos

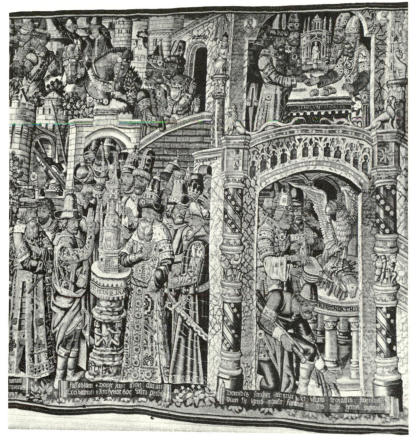

38. Aeneas betrays Troy. From a Franco-Flemish tapestry in Madrid

39. Antenor leads Aeneas from Troy. Attic kalyx-krater

40a. Pietas. Coin of
Herennius

40b. Aeneas carries Anchises.
Coin of Octavian

41a. Aeneas leads Anchises from Troy. Drawing after
a Parthenon metope

41b. Aeneas leads Anchises from Troy. Parthenon metope

41c. Aeneas leads Anchises from Troy.
Drawing from an Attic lekythos

42. Iliupersis krater in London. At right, Anchises
leads Ascanius from Troy

43. Fides crowns Roma.
Coin of Locri, 3rd cent. B.C.

44. Aeneas carries Anchises.
Etruscan scarab

45a. Aeneas and Creusa leave Troy. Etruscan amphora

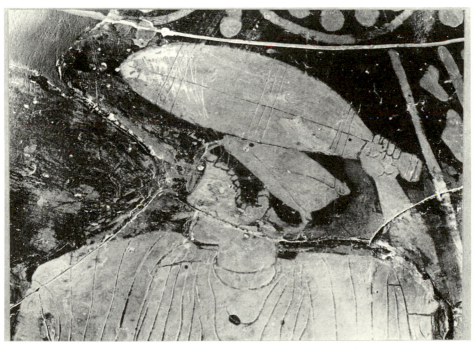

45b. Detail: Creusa carries the *doliolum* with the Trojan *sacra*

46

47

48

46. Aphrodite Aineias. Coin of Leucas

47. Coin of Leucas

48. Coin of Segesta

49. Aeneas carries Anchises.
    Coin of Segesta

50. Coin of Segesta

51. Coin of Cephallenia

52. Coin of Segesta

49

52

50

51

53. Eryx today. The Norman castle

54. Coin of Considianus   55. Coin of Eryx

a. Temple at Eryx

b. Venus Erycina

56. Punic walls at Eryx

57. Minoan birds

58. Temple at Segesta

59. Greek wall. Archaic sanctuary at Segesta

60. Statuette of a goddess. Museo Nazionale Pepoli, Trapani

61. Conca d'Oro vase from Segesta

62. Conca d'Oro cup from Isnello

63. Incised pottery, Sant'Angelo Muxaro style. From Segesta

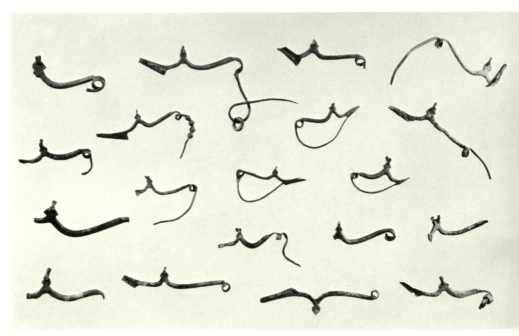

64. Fibulae from Segesta

65. Stylized vase handles from Segesta

66. "Anthropomorphic" vase from Troy

67. Red-polished idols from Lapithos, Cyprus

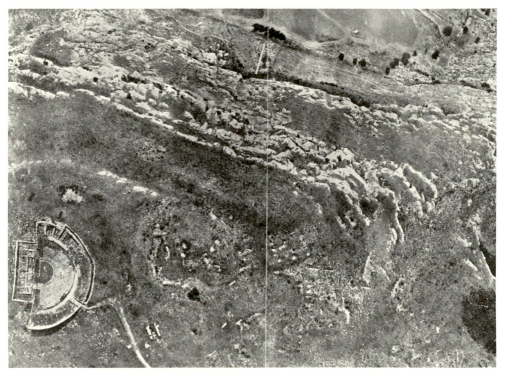

68. Aerial view of Segesta. White mark indicates site of recent
ceramic finds; the theater at left

69. Incised pottery from new deposit at Segesta

70. Painted sherds from Segesta

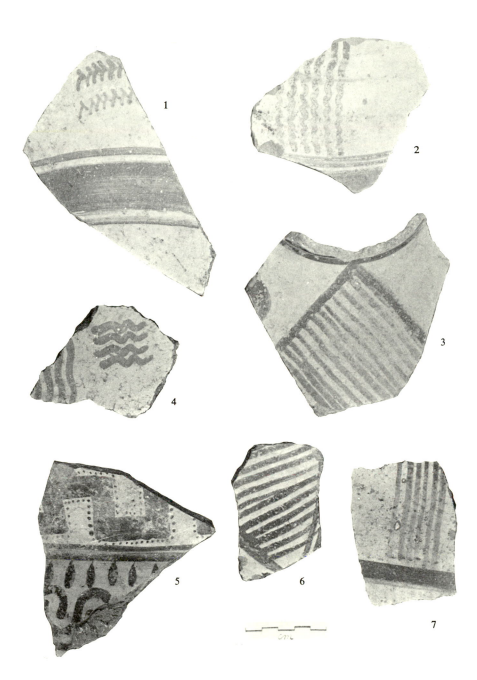

71. Painted sherds from Segesta

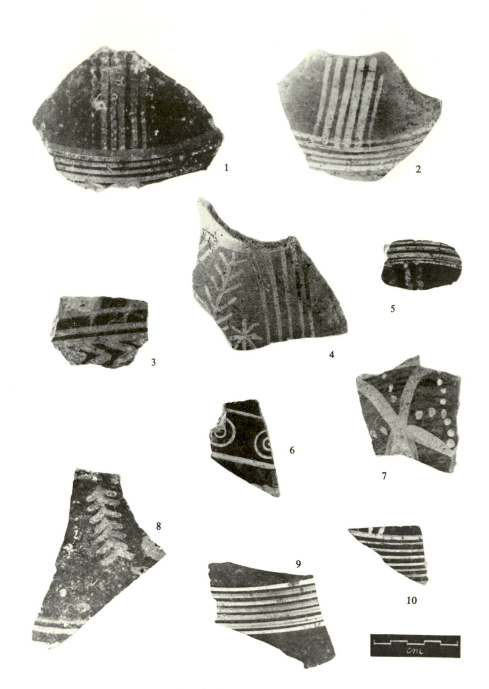

72. Painted sherds from Segesta

1

2

3

4

5

6

7

8

9

10

11

12

73. Painted sherds from Segesta

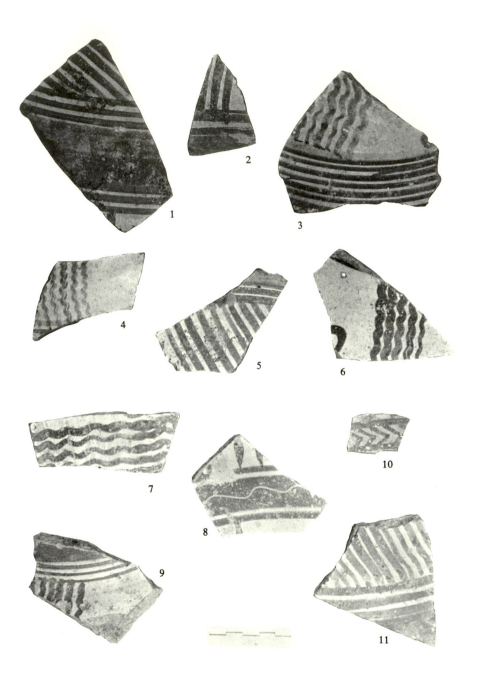

74. Painted sherds from Segesta

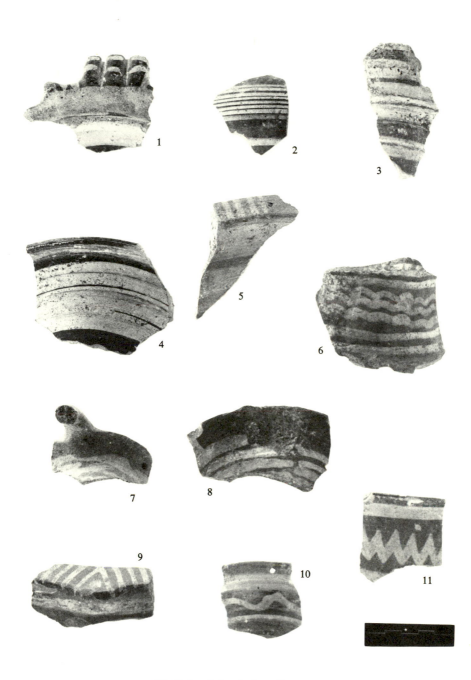

75. Painted sherds from Segesta

76. Head of a statuette. From Segesta

77. Coin of Segesta

78a and b. Gold rings from Sant'Angelo Muxaro

79. Elymian graffiti from Segesta

80. Menelaos fighting Hector. Rhodian plate (late 7th cent. B.C.)

81. Achilles fighting Hector. Attic cup

82. The judgment of Paris. Cover of an Attic pyxis

83. The Calydonian boar hunt. Detail from the François Vase

84. Odysseus blinds Polyphemus. Krater from Etruria

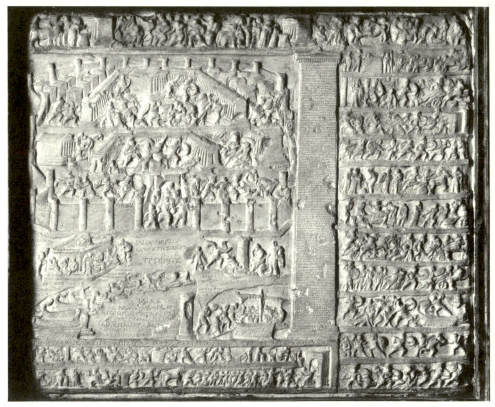

85. *Tabula Iliaca.* Capitoline Museum, Rome

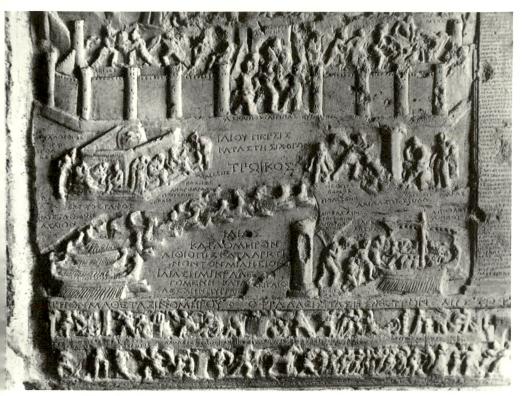

86a. The *Iliupersis* after Stesichorus. From the *Tabula Iliaca Capitolina*

86b. Aeneas boards his ship. Drawing after the *Tabula Iliaca Capitolina*

87. Aeneas and Creusa leave Troy.
Coin of Aineia

88. Etruscoid warrior from
Eryx, 7th cent. B.C.

89. Diomedes, Aeneas, and Aphrodite.
Drawing after an Etruscan mirror

90. Aeneas leaves Troy. Attic hydria

91. Aeneas leaves Troy. Attic cup

92. Aeneas leaves Troy. Attic lekythos in Syracuse

93. Aeneas leaves Troy. Attic lekythos from Camarina

94. Aeneas carries Anchises. Attic amphora in Syracuse

95. Fight over the body of Achilles. On the far left, Aeneas.
Attic amphora

96. Battle over the body of Achilles. Chalcidian amphora, detail

97. Aeneas and Hector fight with Achilles over the body of Troilus.
Attic amphora

98. Fight over the body of Troilus. Amphora in Florence

99. Aeneas fighting Achilles

100. Achilles fighting Hector

99-100. Pontic amphora

101. Homeric battle scene. Corinthian aryballos

102. Diomedes fighting Aeneas. Attic kalyx-krater

103. Fight over the body of Patroclus. Attic cup

104. Aphrodite rescues Aeneas. Attic cup

105. Aphrodite rescues Aeneas. Etruscan amphora, detail

106. Corinthian hydria

a. Hector in battle

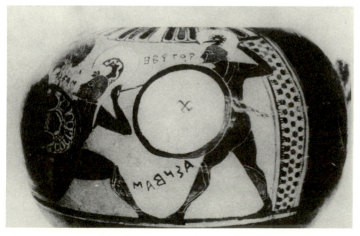

b. Aeneas comes to the rescue

107. The rape of Helen. At center, Aeneas. Attic cup

108. Paris and Aeneas at Sparta. Attic cup

109. The rape of Helen. At center, Aeneas. Etruscan urn

110. Achilles ambushes Troilus. Etruscan urn

111. Aeneas carries Anchises.
Statuette group from Veii

112. Eirene and Ploutos
by Cephisodotus

113. The Veii Apollo

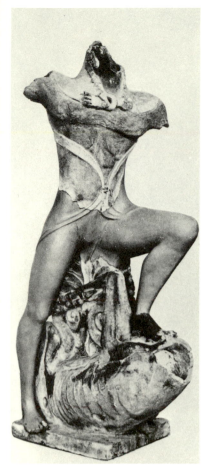

114. Heracles and the hind of Ceryneia.
Acroterion from Veii

115. So-called kourotrophos.
Female acroterion from Veii

116. Acroterial group at Veii. Reconstruction by **Silvio Ferri**

117. Row of altars at Lavinium

118. Lavinium, Altar XIII

a   a

b   b

119a and b. The Dioscuri.   120a and b. The Penates Publici.
    Coin of Fonteius   Coin of Fonteius

121. Cover of a cista with Latinus and Aeneas

122. Oath between
Latinus and Aeneas.
Roman gold coin

123. Oath between
Latinus and Aeneas.
Roman coin

124. The Great Cameo of Paris

125. Aeneas carries Anchises. Two views of Roman funerary group

a. Thetis with Achilles' armor

b. Reverse: Pyrrhus as Achilles

126. Coin of Pyrrhus

127. Athena Promachos. Coin of Pyrrhus

128. The Trojan group. Roman funerary relief

129. Venus Erycina and Victory. Coin of Considius Paetus

a. Quadriga of Victory   b. Venus Erycina

130. Coin of Eryx

a   b   c

131a. Rhome. Campanian-Roman coin

131b. Roma. Coin of C. Metellus

131c. The de-Trojanized Roma. Roman denarius

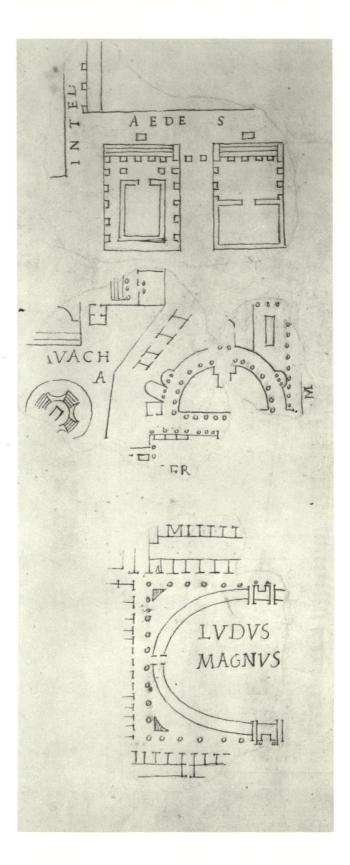

133. Marble Map of Rome. Temple of Minerva Chalcidica

134. Venus. Ara Pacis Augustae

143. Aphrodite Urania. Attic lekythos, detail

144. Aphrodite *velificans* on a swan. Athenian mirror

141. Venus on a sea shell. Pompeian mural

142. Aphrodite on a swan. Cup from Kameiros

138. Aurora carries Venus. Detail from the armor of the Prima Porta Augustus

139. Venus *velificans*. Coin from Spain

140. Cupid carries Venus. Pompeian mural

137. Italia and Roma.
Coin of Kalenus

136. Italia. Detail from the
Gemma Augustea

135. Ara Pacis Augustae. Southeastern part of enclosure

145. Aphrodite rising from the sea. Tarentine terracotta altar

146. Terracotta protome from Sardis

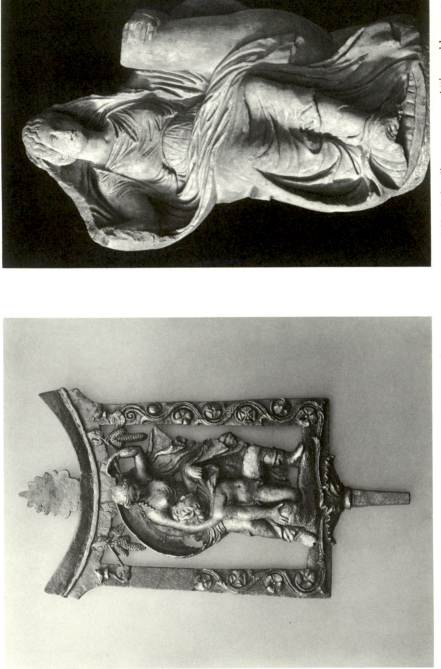

148. Aphrodite on a goose. Attic marble group

147. Aphrodite seizes Adonis. Mirror stand from Locri

150. Venus on a swan. Drawing after
an Etruscan mirror

149. Aphrodite on a swan.
Attic lekythos

151. Nymph of Camarina

152. Aphrodite on sea dragon. Greek gem

153. Apollo and Aphrodite at Delphi. Bell krater in Vienna

154. Venus *velificans* on sea-centaur. Pompeian mural

155. Aphrodite with a crane. Athenian mirror

156. Eros and Aphrodite. Cast from
a bronze cheek piece

157. Venus and Adonis. Pompeian mural

158. Procession of sacrificial animals. Ara Pacis Augustae

159. Ara Pacis Augustae. Detail of interior of enclosure

160. Colossal Aphrodite
from Aphrodisias

161a and b. Eryx goddess.
Coins of Eryx

162. Relief from Carthage

163. Venus, Mars, and Caesar or Augustus. Relief from Carthage

164a. Venus and grain ear.
Coin of Norbanus

164b and c. Coin from Spain

b. Pax and symbols

c. Roma

165. Venus and Cupids.
Calenic relief plate

166. Colossal head of a goddess

167. Venus reclining with Cupids. Painting by a Botticelli follower

a. The birth of Aphrodite, central panel

b. Flute-playing hetaira, side panel

c. Female sacrificant, side panel

168. Ludovisi relief

a. Central panel

b. Old woman, side panel

c. Lyre player, side panel

169. Three-sided relief in Boston

170. Aphrodite, Eros, and Hermes. Greek mirror

171. Weighing of Erotes. Campanian vase

172. Aphrodite
weighing Erotes.
Greek ring

a. Figure in right scale pan

b. Figure in left scale pan

173. Three-sided relief in Boston. Details